# HOW TO UNDERSTAND
# *YOUR RELATIONSHIPS*

Books in this series by the same authors

**How to Understand Your Gender**
A Practical Guide for Exploring Who You Are
*Alex Iantaffi and Meg-John Barker*
*Foreword by S. Bear Bergman*
*Illustrated by Jules Scheele*
ISBN 978 1 78592 746 1
eISBN 978 1 78450 517 2

**How to Understand Your Sexuality**
A Practical Guide for Exploring Who You Are
*Meg-John Barker and Alex Iantaffi*
*Foreword by Erika Moen*
*Illustrated by Jules Scheele*
ISBN 978 1 78775 618 2
eISBN 978 1 78775 619 9

# HOW TO UNDERSTAND
# *YOUR RELATIONSHIPS*

*A Practical Guide*

**ALEX IANTAFFI AND MEG-JOHN BARKER**

*Foreword by Sophia Graham*

*Illustrated by Jules Scheele*

**Jessica Kingsley Publishers**
London and Philadelphia

First published in Great Britain in 2025 by Jessica Kingsley Publishers
An imprint of John Murray Press

1

Content Warning: This book contains mention of abuse, sexual abuse, and transphobia.

A CIP catalogue record for this title is available from the
British Library and the Library of Congress

ISBN 978 1 78775 654 0
eISBN 978 1 78775 655 7

Printed and bound in Great Britain by TJ Books Limited

Jessica Kingsley Publishers' policy is to use papers that are natural,
renewable and recyclable products and made from wood grown in
sustainable forests. The logging and manufacturing processes are expected
to conform to the environmental regulations of the country of origin.

Jessica Kingsley Publishers
Carmelite House
50 Victoria Embankment
London EC4Y 0DZ

www.jkp.com

John Murray Press
Part of Hodder & Stoughton Limited
An Hachette UK Company

The authorised representative in the EEA is Hachette Ireland,
8 Castlecourt Centre, Dublin 15, D15 XTP3, Ireland (email: info@hbgi.ie)

This book is dedicated to all those who loved us before we could even begin to love ourselves. Thank you for showing us a way through.

# Contents

# Foreword

I'm Sophia Graham, a neuroqueer relationship geek, educator, and coach who writes and teaches about self-consent, relationships, and emotions. As you can imagine, I have a lot in common with Meg-John and Alex, so I was totally delighted when they asked me to write the foreword for this book that you're about to dive into. It was after a workshop at the contemporary non-monogamies conference in Portugal in 2015 that I spoke to MJ for the first time. We talked for a couple of hours about the concept of "self-consent" which became central to our relationship with each other. We had struggled to treat our needs, desires, and limits like they mattered, and had in various ways disowned parts that wanted to stand up for them. Moving gently towards self-consent was an antidote to some of these patterns, at least for me. That conversation profoundly impacted the work I do, pushing me to make space for myself, slow down, and ultimately leave academia to retrain as a therapist and become a full-time relationship geek and evangelist for showing up for yourself. I'm very glad to see that self-consent continues to show up in MJ and Alex's writing, too.

Alex and MJ are prolific writers and an amazing writing team. Alex's *Gender Trauma* pushed me to think harder about the ways in which my own gender has been constructed, and the context for it in my own story. Meg-John's *Rewriting the Rules* helped me enormously when I came out as queer in my late 20s, having exclusively been in monogamous and heterosexual relationships up to that point. Their writing gave me helpful questions to ask myself (and selves) about what I really wanted in my life and gave me permission to seek out my own answers rather than following the well-beaten path. Together, they wrote the trauma-informed self-care bible that is *Hell Yeah Self-Care!* which inspired me to form a mutual aid support network among the folks closest to me to explore our own histories, resources, needs, and offers. Their writings are a kind and gentle invitation to build your life and relationships with intention, so I was excited to read this, the result of their most recent collaboration.

Meg-John and Alex will tell you that they are not perfect people, because we are all flawed human beings who sometimes struggle in our relationships with each other and also with ourselves (and our selves). This is not a book about how to be perfect, or even advice on how to craft perfect relationships. It is about asking questions that will help you to co-create the relationships that work for you, internal and external. I love that it holds far more questions than answers. It invites us to look inwards, towards our internal emotional experience, to notice what is going on for each of us when we are in relationships. It also invites us to look outwards, to how we understand relationships at existential, sociocultural, and relational levels.

In my work, I see that the stories that we tell each other really matter. This book has an awful lot of stories woven throughout, from a wonderfully diverse array of perspectives. These stories give us insight into how varied our experiences are depending on our race, disability, neurotype, gender, family status, and a host of other things. I was really glad to see parts of myself reflected in some of these stories. I was also happy to see many stories about people very different from me which gave me a window into their world. I can't think of another book about relationships that includes such wide-ranging stories about so many different people. I hope you are able to find parts of yourself here, too.

One of the things I love most in my relationship with MJ, and my much more distant relationship with Alex, is how gentle they are. I hope you feel that gentleness and kindness coming through in this book. It is an invitation to look at some hard stuff, internally and externally. As I worked through some of the questions they asked with my closest people, I found surprising and interesting and relationship-changing answers. In Chapter 2, I found myself deeply affected when thinking about "[What is] the relationship *container* that might enable you to feel freer and/or safer in [a challenging] relationship?" The shame compass exercise in Chapter 4 invited me to think about what patterns from my past and ways of coping with shame I was enacting in my present relationships. These exercises, and others throughout the book, gave me new frames through which to look at my experience and new language for sharing those experiences with others.

Even when engaging with the hardest sociocultural questions, this book is gentle. As a white British woman who was raised in protectorate colonialism, who currently lives on land stolen from the Massachusett people within settler-colonialism, I appreciated the nuanced way this was discussed. It is hard to address complicity in systems of oppression and dehumanization without collapsing into shame and powerlessness. It is hard to be gentle. But this book offers some space for optimism, some possibilities for moving towards decolonizing work that can be done wherever we start out. It isn't about whether we can replace the system wholesale tomorrow (wouldn't that be nice!) but whether we can begin to move towards a 1 percent improvement, while also knowing that 1 percent is nowhere near enough.

You can choose to engage with this book in lots of ways, but really diving into this book asks a lot of you. It asks that you slow down. That you take the time to really notice where you're at. That you reflect on our wider world and on the quiet parts of yourself that you might otherwise ignore. If you do, I think working through this book will help you to get closer to having the relationships you really want. There may be hard moments; maybe you will need to put the book down for a while in order to come back to it when you are ready. But when you are, it will be waiting for you with warmth, kindness, and gentle humor.

*Sophia Graham, neuroqueer relationship geek, educator, and coach*

# Acknowledgements

We want to start by thanking our friend Hannah Darvill for hosting the writing retreat on which we wrote this book, as well as her beautiful place O Muiño da Balsiña in Galicia, the river running through it, Xoana the cat, and the new relationship energy between Xoana and Hannah that was so palpable through our trip!

Thanks to our new editors, Lisa Clark and Laura Dignum-Smith, and all at JKP, and to Dr. Anne Mauro, Hannah Darvill, Fernanda Bonini, and Dr. Sophia Graham for all their insightful feedback on early drafts of the manuscript. Thank you also to Andrew James, our first editor at JKP, for believing in us and our work. Much gratitude to Sophia Graham for providing the wonderful foreword, and to Jules Scheele for the amazing cover and illustrations.

Thank you to all the people—and other beings—who we've learned about relationships with and from, both for your support and challenges. Some of you will certainly know who you are! Others we have never even met, but your words have meant the world to us.

We could never write any of this without our main support systems and close companions. Thank you for all you do to nurture and nourish us.

Finally, we want to acknowledge those who are no longer here, but who influenced us so much along the way, particularly Trevor Butt who introduced us, and Nila Gupta who we first wrote with and had so many conversations about relationships and systems with!

# INTRODUCTION

Twenty years ago, two burgeoning activist-academics and therapists met at a conference in the North of England. After connecting over all the theories of relationships and sexualities that excited them, they quickly got together, discussing kink in a kitchen, kissing on a bridge, and retiring to one of their hall-of-residence rooms for a first night together.

This book might be a very different book had that relationship— and all the relationships around it—gone in different directions than it did. In another universe, we'd never have recovered from the break-up that happened a year or so later, and then we would never have written together at all. This book—and many others—would simply not exist. In another universe, we might've stayed together in a polyamorous relationship and be writing one of those "how to do non-monogamy" or "how to open up your relationship" books right now. Perhaps there's even a universe where we went towards monogamous marriage with each other, and this book was one of those "how to stay with the same person for the rest of your life" books. Who knows?

What actually happened was that—after a year or so of distance— we found our way back to each other as friends, and all of the ideas that had so connected us at that conference were still there. We collaborated on a few short pieces of writing together, with a third friend and colleague—Nila—and with others in our bi/polyamorous/kink community. Over time, both of us drifted away from that community, and we had our own individual journeys with gender, sexuality, relationships, mental health, disability, neurodivergence, and more. Alex moved from the UK to the US, and we both transitioned genders. We stayed in touch throughout, and kept talking about potential projects. Seven years ago, we went on our first writing retreat together and *How to Understand Your Gender* was born.

This book is our fifth book together and the third in the *How to Understand Your...* trilogy. It is the book that it is because of the journeys that our own relationship, and those around it, have taken, particularly in its emphasis on how we might do *all* kinds of relationships, not just the romantic and/or sexual kind. In a way, we have been writing this book ever since we met, and certainly since we started writing together in earnest. However, we're glad that we left it till now—20 years on—in our friend Hannah's retreat in Galicia to write it. It will be a stronger book for the different directions our relationships with ourselves and others—including each other—have taken since the start of the global pandemic. This includes our journeys of relating with ourselves, of developing understandings of our neurodivergence, of shifting relationships with our bodies and feelings during perimenopause, of disability, of moving, of traumatizing and healing relationships, of being in community, of being in solitude, of being in deeper relation with land and water, and so much more.

We do hope that you enjoy this book and find something in it of benefit to you.

## WHY THIS BOOK?

There's a phrase we love: "your mess is your message." We didn't write this book because we're excellent at relationships. In fact, neither of us had a great start when it comes to relationships, and we both had to learn how to be in relationship with ourselves, the ecosystems we're part of, and those around us, by living our lives for five decades, reading a lot about relationships, thinking about them, and by making mistakes (many, many mistakes) along the way. We even trained to be a relational (systemic) and sex therapist (Alex) and a sex and relationship therapist (MJ). You could say that relationships are one of our main, lifelong special interests, as people who finally know that we're neurodivergent.

You might be asking yourselves, "Why write a book about relationships, then, if you're not very good at them?" That is a valid question that we've also asked ourselves. One of the reasons is that we don't think we need to be perfect at something to share what we've learned on our journeys. Relationships are so complicated, and there is so much noise out there about how we're supposed to do all sorts of relationships. However, we've never found a book that covered the basics in one place. There are books about parenting, romantic relationships, sexual relationships, collegial relationships at work, friendships, and so on, but as far as we know, there isn't an accessible book for the general public that covers the whole idea of relating and relationships in general.

This book is about what relationships are, why they might be hard, and all the various issues that come up when we try to relate to one another. The aim is not to tell you how to *do* your relationships but rather how to better *understand* why you do what you do and why other people might do what they do.

Relationships are places of both connection and disconnection, healing and rupture, joy and pain. To relate with anyone or anything authentically is to risk our hearts, over and over and over again. It doesn't sound appealing, does it? Yet it's unavoidable, because humans cannot survive, let alone thrive, without relationships. Think of a baby left alone… Unless someone takes care of them, they will perish. That someone can even be an other-than-human animal, but someone is needed for us to survive from the start. We could say that we were born to be in relationship, whether we like it or not.

Those relationships are not just with other humans but also with ourselves, the ecosystems we're part of, those around us, and even those who have come before us, like ancestors, at the very least from a historical and genetic perspective. In this book, we also wanted to challenge the divisions we sometimes create between different types of relationships to give ourselves at least the illusion of control. While it's true that different types of relationships operate differently, we also feel there are some foundational principles at play that cut across different types of relationships.

Ultimately, and as is true for the other two books in the series, we wrote the book that we—two neurodivergent people with challenging family histories and a passion for understanding humans and how we relate—wanted to have in our late teens or early 20s. So we've come full circle: our mess is our message. We hope our mess resonates with yours.

## WHO ARE YOU?

It always feels helpful for us to imagine the likely readers of our books, to—hopefully—ensure that we write in a way that will be most helpful for them. As we just said, in some ways all of our books are written for the younger versions of ourselves. So this is the book that we wish we had found in the library as a teenager when we were finding our friendships and family relationships confusing and painful, or on the self-help shelf of the bookshop when we were entering our first long-term partnerships. It's the book we wish a friend had given us when we were stuck in an abusive relationship dynamic and couldn't get out, and the one we would love to have had passed around our communities when we first started exploring consensual non-monogamy. It's the book Alex would've found helpful when they started parenting, and MJ wished they had read when they first considered moving away from romantic and sexual partnerships and exploring their inner plurality. It's also a book we'd have loved to have had on the curriculum during our therapy training, and one we would have liked our own therapists—and other practitioners—to have read!

So we hope this book will be a helpful one for you, if you are in any of those situations, and more. You might like to take a moment, now, to reflect on who you are, and why you picked up this book (or perhaps why somebody else recommended it to you).

We always hope that our *How to Understand Your...* books will be helpful to a number of different kinds of readers particularly. These include:

— people who are exploring their own gender, sexuality, or relationships, perhaps for the first time

— people who have others in their lives who are identifying in certain ways or making big transitions in their way of doing gender, sex, or relationships, and who want to better understand and support them (and perhaps learn something useful for themselves)

— practitioners who want to work better with clients around gender, sex, and relationship diversity

— people who are particularly struggling, in some way, around gender, sex, or relationships.

So if you fall into any of those categories, this book is for you. Importantly, we don't write our books just for those in the minority, or marginalized, groups when it comes to gender, sex, and/or relationships. We believe that it's helpful (for ourselves and for everyone else) if *everyone* explores their gender, sexuality, and relationships, and views that exploration as an ongoing journey. So while we aim for our books to be as inclusive as possible of all ways of doing gender, sex, and relationships, we include normative and non-normative relationships with all of these things equally. We also aim—as much as possible—to make our books accessible to those who have never learned, or reflected, on these things before. And we hopefully provide useful materials for those who've already thought and read about these things quite a lot. As we know ourselves, it is always possible to find—and experience—more.

## WHO ARE WE?

We mentioned that we wrote this book because we needed it about 30 years ago. We also said we've made many mistakes along the way, so who are we really? Between us, we have over a century of experience at doing life in three different countries, two different types of training and a couple of decades of experience as therapists, about five decades combined of scholarship, and many relationships, some of which have lasted our whole life and many of which have not. We brought all of it to this book because we have found it helpful to weave the personal with the professional, as we've done in our previous books.

Throughout the book, we also uplift the work of many other people who we have learned from or who have messages that resonated with others or that we've found helpful or used as source material. We'll say more about what's in the book at the end of this introduction. For now, to give a better sense of who we are, and what our relational orientations and experiences are, we've written separate introductions from both of us below.

## ALEX WRITES:

Hello! If you've read our previous books, you might feel you already know who we are, so I'll try to keep it brief here and to focus on my relational contexts rather than try to cover all aspects of who I am. If you're new to my work, I am Italian, with a strong identity as a Sicilian in particular, in my early 50s, a new US citizen, as of a year ago at the time of writing, conditionally white, disabled, neurodivergent, trans masculine, non-binary, queer, Pagan, polyamorous parent. I'm a family therapist, also known as a systemic therapist, sex therapist, and clinical supervisor. I was a scholar, researcher, and teacher in higher education for about 20 years before transitioning out of academia.

When I think about what I want to share about relationships, I think, first of all, of my relationship to place. Maybe it's because I visited Sicily for the first time in 17 years right before writing this book, or maybe it's because being an immigrant is a strong part of my identity. Growing up in Rome with a Sicilian grandmother who was my main caregiver, I longed for all the time we spent in Sicily, which was abundant since we went to visit my great-aunts for Christmas, Easter, summer, and I Morti (the Day of the Dead). This meant that I grew up often spending four-plus months of the year in Sicily, in a small town (Francofonte) in the province of Siracusa but geographically closer to Catania. It's in Sicily that I feel the strongest sense of belonging to place, climate, culture, and ancestors. While I feel that in Italy generally, it's always strongest there. I left Italy just after I turned 22 because of work and study opportunities that weren't available to me at home and might be (and were) elsewhere. I've spent 15 years in the UK and 15 years in the US at this point in time, which means I have lived more of my life as an immigrant than not. When I moved to the US, I went somewhere—to the Dakota and Anishinaabe territories currently known as Minnesota—where I felt a strong sense of connection to land and water (both with the Mississippi and Gichigami—Lake Superior), for mysterious reasons. My relationship to place feels sacred to me, and I searched for home after leaving Italy for a long time. I feel so grateful that I found one even closer to Gichigami, in Duluth, a couple of years ago after living in South Minneapolis for 13 years. A piece of my heart belongs to Sicily, and always will, but I am so grateful that I was able to connect so deeply to where I live now and I keep thinking about what it means to be a settler and have connection to place, especially as an animist witch. Not just what it means in theory or spiritually, but what it means in practice, in relationship to the Land Back Indigenous movement on Turtle Island, and how I can try to do my best to keep showing up as an accomplice.

Writing this, I realize I could talk about so many relationships! For example, I could write about my relationship to ancestors, which is complicated because one of my ancestors is my abusive father and some of the others enabled what he did to me and to our family. Fortunately, there are beloved ancestors who, as my queer sibling Donald Engstrom-Reese would say, love me beyond all reason. Those are not just ancestors of blood but also of activism, gender-blessed and queer ancestors, transcestors, ancestors of healing lineages and community organizing. I feel gratitude for all of them because I could not be without them, and I hope that one day, in the far future, I can become a good ancestor, especially when it comes to my relational legacy. In fact, on this trip to Sicily, I realized that, in many ways, one of my roles in our family is to live shamelessly—that is, to conduct my relationships, identities, experiences out loud—in contrast to the silence and secrecy that some of my ancestors had to live in for their safety and wellbeing.

This brings me to talk a bit more about my current relational landscape. We've already written about my relationship with team MJ and how our relationship started and changed over time. I have been publicly polyamorous for nearly a quarter of a century now, which makes me feel ancient sometimes! I would say that my style of polyamory falls within the relationship anarchy umbrella but also fits well with a kitchen-table polyamory style where I like all my people knowing one another. I currently live with two nesting partners, one I have been with for 23 years right now and with whom I created my daughter, and one I have been with for six years right now and who brought our son into our lives since their child had just turned seven years old when we met. We all co-parent our children together and take care of our animal companions, currently two dogs, who live with us, and two cats who live with our daughter at college. I have also been surprised by a new relationship, just before I started this book, and just when I thought I was kind of done with new relationships, to be honest. It has been the sweetest surprise since this person and I have known and liked each other for four years, although neither of us had disclosed our crush to the other person this whole time! So here I am, writing a book about relationships just as my relational landscape is changing once more. In fact, this summer has been the time that the multiverse is telling me that maybe I don't have to be done with romantic and/or sexual relationships just because I'm in my 50s! I guess I was dealing with either some internalized ageism or relational trauma there for a few years! So here I am, heart open and ready to embrace this new relational landscape and whatever it might bring.

I am a parent, both a bio and a step one. Although I do think of our children as our children regardless, there are differences between these two experiences, and it would be disingenuous to not mention that. Any stories I share about parenting, I share with consent, which is why you'll see more stories about my daughter, who is a young adult now, than my son, who is still a young teen. I could go on, but I'll leave it here for now. Or maybe I'll mention just one more thing! I discovered that I am neurodivergent (AuDHD) recently and my physical disabilities are also becoming more impactful and visible. Both of those things are changing the relationship I have with myself significantly.

Finally, I noticed that, by the end of writing this book, I had not mentioned any experiences of intimate partner violence, even though I am a survivor and have also experienced growing up in a violent, abusive household. I have chosen to name it here because it's an important part of who I am and what shaped me as a relational being.

## MJ WRITES:

Hey there! Writing this bit of the introduction to these books is always a chance to reflect just how much has changed since the last time we wrote one. Our last book—*How to Understand Your Sexuality*—was written over Zoom during lockdown, so perhaps one of the biggest changes is that thankfully we were in a place—in the world and in our own bodies—to be safe enough to write together in person again. We're so grateful for that.

Perhaps the biggest difference, for us, is that it would no longer make sense to write this introduction using the pronoun "I." We've been using "we" throughout the introduction to this point to refer to the "we" of "MJ and Alex," but we also use "we" as MJ alone, because we experience ourselves as plural rather than singular. Plurality is something we mentioned in the last book, but it's only since writing that one that we've moved towards using "we" more publicly, and with all of our friends, except when we are talking from the position of one of us.

What does this mean? It means that we (team MJ!) have a vivid experience of being five different selves.

Several authors, activists, and therapists have suggested that people are not individuals, but rather that we all include "multitudes": that our personalities are best thought of as "self systems" composed of different parts. Plurality is a broad umbrella encompassing common experience like having an inner child or critic, spiritual experiences like inner/outer voices, and trauma-related experience like having fragmented or dissociated identities. Over the past seven years or so, we've been on a deep exploration of our own self system, and this is where we've come to in that ongoing journey. So there are a few points in this book—particularly in Chapter 4—where we've written more about how you might relate with your different parts or selves (if that understanding works for you), and also places where we've written from one of us—rather than the collective MJ.

What else to say about us? In terms of our position (see Chapter 3), we're white, British, autistic, disabled, and nearly 50 years old (although some of us feel very different ages!). The five of us have a range of different genders, so we might say our overall gender is non-binary (especially given that we've written and edited a couple of books about non-binary gender!). We also have a range of different sexualities, although, broadly speaking, we're all some kind of ace spectrum, kinky, and queer. Professionally, we're a

Figure I.1: Plurality

writer/creator (or several writer/creators!) who collaborate between us, and with others (like Alex and Jules Scheele), to make books and zines about gender, sex, relationships, mental health, and more. We also love supporting others with their creativity.

Relationship-wise (given this is a book on relationships), relationship anarchist is probably the most accurate description of our relationship style, as we endeavor to value all the different kinds of relationships in our lives. We've been on a big therapeutic/spiritual journey in recent years to understand and accept and/or shift our own relationship patterns, and address the trauma behind many of them. For us, that journey has involved choosing to live alone for a while (or rather with each other and not other beings, except a few plants and animal visitors). We've also moved away from romantic and/or sexual relationships, but that certainly hasn't stopped our relationship patterns from showing up! If those ideas are unfamiliar to you, don't worry, they'll all be explained through the rest of this book.

Finally, we'd like to say that our move towards solitude (or pluritude!) in the last few years, to focus on nurturing our inner relationships, feels—paradoxically perhaps—deeply linked to all the other kinds of relationships which Alex wrote about in their intro-duction. Plural work, for us, involves loosening traumatic relationship patterns which some of us felt very stuck in, and which hurt others and ourselves. Learning how to relate as an inner system—hope-fully—enables us to relate more wisely and compassionately with others. We're more able to recognize that others are also complex, multifaceted beings, and to understand when they act in traumatized and traumatizing ways that are now familiar to us from our plural explorations. We're also struck by the ways in which recognizing inner systems may enable more collaborative relating in groups and communities via networks of solidarity which recognize that we are systems within systems within systems. Plurality also connects us with ancestors, as we feel deeply the ways in which they—and their cultures—show up in our selves, as well as drawing upon ancestors of choice to inform how some of our holding selves show up in the world. Finally, plurality connects us with place, as we're able to foreground those of us who are more able to be present with land, water, and weather, and hold our other selves in those selves so that they can come to feel those connections more deeply too.

As we already mentioned, we feel that one of our combined strengths—in writing this book—is the fact that we have such different experiences of relationships. We've always felt that we write well together partly because—while aligned—we bring such a different range of knowledges, experiences, wisdoms, and practices together. This includes, for example, Buddhist and Pagan spiritualities; linguistic, psychological, and sociological scholarship; existential, systematic, and somatic therapeutic trainings; and experience across multiple different activist movements and anti-oppressive communities.

Relationally, while writing this book we reflected that we've gone to different extremes in recent years, with MJ living in solitude and focusing on inner relationships, and Alex living in community with multiple partners, kids, and animals. The learnings from these different experiences were super helpful in writing this book, as we feel strongly that it's important—for our relationships—to have both of these things in life (*Life Isn't Binary!*). We all need enough solitude and time to nurture our inner relationships *and* enough experience of nourishing relationships, and support from close people and communities. Not that finding the balance in this bothness is always easy.

## *HOW TO READ THIS BOOK*

There are a number of ways in which you can read this book. You might want to just go from start to finish without doing any of the activities or reflection points, or you might want to engage with all of them, or just some of them. You might want to read this book alone or alongside others, maybe people who you are in close relationship with or maybe as part of a book club with people who also want to learn more about relationships. You might even use this book more as a workbook, whether alone or with others. It truly is up to you how you choose to read it.

If you haven't yet read *How to Understand Your Gender* and *How to Understand Your Sexuality*, you might choose to read them alongside, before this book, or not at all. Once again, it's up to you. You will find mentions of both books throughout this one, and we did maintain a similar structure, albeit with different content, across this trilogy.

Now for a major **content note/warning**: we do talk about trauma throughout this book. This means that there is material that will likely be triggering. While we invite you to slow down and take care of yourselves throughout the book, we wanted to be really clear about the fact that this is not light reading. Throughout the book, you will find mentions of developmental trauma, abuse in childhood and adulthood, bullying, religious trauma, relational trauma. Please do take care of yourselves as you read this book and get the support you need as you need it. Thank you.

As we mentioned earlier, you can even use this book as a workbook. In fact, throughout the chapters you will find the following features:

— *Reflection points:* These are things to reflect on, or write some notes about, such as your own experience of a particular issue. There are usually several questions for you to reflect on in these sections.

— *Activities:* These are invitations to do a particular exercise. You can do this in the book—if it belongs to you!—or in a journal or notebook. We recommend using a journal or notebook, or a file on your computer alongside this book, since you might want to write more than there is space for within the pages of this book.

— *Multiple experiences:* These are examples of different people's experiences around relationships, to give you a sense of the diversity that is inherent in relationships, and how it actually plays out in people's lives. All of the examples given are real, in the sense that we've heard them from many people over the years, but we've fictionalized them and combined them so that no actual people are identifiable. None of them are direct quotes or a single person's experience.

— *Slow-down pages:* These are invitations to pause and tune into yourself, or notice how you're responding to what you're reading about, in order to bring in your whole bodymind—the integrated unit of your body and mind—rather than just the prefrontal cortex of your brain. They are also additional reminders to go slow and treat yourselves with care as you read this book.

You can use these features as much or as little as you like—it's (unsurprisingly, if you're used to our books) completely up to you. We hope they'll enhance your reading experience and that they'll help you apply what you might be learning to your own life. They might also give you something to discuss if you're exploring this book with others—for example, in a book club or a class.

## WHAT'S IN THIS BOOK?

When we were writing this book, we joked that we should put a warning in the introduction: *If you want answers, run away from this book now!* Our experience is that there are no easy answers when it comes to how to do relationships. What this book *does* offer is a lot of very useful questions which you might ask yourself—and the others in your life—questions that may help us to steer a more conscious and compassionate course when it comes to our relationships.

Our hope is that this focus on questions more than answers

actually sets this apart from a lot of relationship books which do profess to have "the answers" about how relationships work or how we should approach them. Such books can actually make us feel worse about ourselves and encourage us to try to shape ourselves to fit a way of doing relationships that may not suit us—or others—at all. There is no one-size-fits-all model. Different ways of relating (to ourselves, to others, and to the world) fit different people, and at different times in their lives. Understanding and accepting this can really help us in relating with ourselves—and others—more consensually and caringly.

A major emphasis throughout this book is "what we're up against" when it comes to relating with each other—particularly if we *want* to relate in ways that are conscious, consensual, caring, compassionate, and honest. There's often the sense that this is—or should be—relatively easy. Actually, it is phenomenally hard! It is the job of a lifetime to learn how to relate in those kinds of ways, and we could all probably still do with a few more lifetimes to "get there," if that is even possible. Pretty much everything in life pulls us away from being able to relate in these ways—from the human condition, through the capitalist and colonialist sociopolitical systems that dominate the world, to the traumas and complicated relationship models that most of us experience growing up, and more.

So, throughout this book, a key message is to go very gently with yourselves—and others where possible. This is tender territory indeed, for all of us.

The book is divided into six chapters, and each chapter includes four sections. Most of these sections could easily have been whole books in their own right! So please be gentle with us about the things that we haven't managed to cover—or to cover in great depth. Our hope is that the book gives you a nice overview, and signposts where you might go if you want to find out more (all of which are listed in the further resources at the end of each chapter).

As we've said, all the chapters in the book apply to all kinds of relationships, from our internal relationships (with ourselves, our feelings, our body, etc.) to our close relationships with humans and other creatures, to our group and community relationships, to our relationships with people and other beings in general, with land, water, with projects, ideas, and more.

Chapter 1 begins by setting the scene. We introduce the language of relationships, and all the different kinds of relationships we're covering in this book. We also consider how we can usefully understand relationships at multiple levels: existential, sociocultural, relational, and internal. Finally, we ask about the place of love in all of this.

As with our other *How to Understand Your...* books, Chapter 2 asks how the world around us—in dominant culture—views relationships, so that you can start to explore the impact this has on you and your relationships. We explore the cultural messages that we receive around relationships in late capitalism, and we consider the legacy of colonialism on how we conduct our relationships. Then we turn to ask what decolonizing relationships might look like, and how we might aim to do love differently, if we have question marks over the dominant cultural way of relating (spoiler alert: we very much do!).

Chapter 3 gives you an opportunity to think about your background, growing up, and how that impacted your way of doing relationships today. In this chapter, we think about relationship models, family systems, developmental and intergenerational trauma, and how we develop certain styles or patterns of relating or attaching to others. We also look at our intersections, and positioning, when we were growing up, and the influence that may have had. We briefly touch, here, on why adult–child relationships are not the same as adult–adult relationships, and need to be approached in different ways.

Chapter 4 turns to our current experiences of relationships. We invite you to map your relational landscape, and think about the foundations of your various relationships, as well as the language you use to describe them. We revisit trauma patterns and attachment styles to consider how you tend to relate in your life currently, the impact this has, and whether it is something you might want to address in any way. We revisit relationships at your current intersections and think through what getting more intentional about our relationships, and ways of relating, might look like.

Chapters 5 and 6 are longer than the other chapters in the book because here we wanted to give you as many practical resources as possible to support you in your ongoing relationship journey. We've really packed them in, and referred to lots of other materials and resources you might turn to if you'd like to explore further.

Chapter 5 focuses on living our relationships over time, including how we can get more conscious of the ways that we fit—and misfit—with others, and shape our ways of relating accordingly. We explore the concept of viewing our relationships as an ongoing practice, and consider how we might meet the inevitable changes and challenges of relationships as they shift over time, including navigating transitions and break-ups. Finally, we explore why conscious and consensual relating need to go together, and what we might aim for in terms of relating in more conscious, consensual ways with ourselves and others.

Chapter 6 broadens out to consider relationships beyond those with ourselves and our close ones. We start with a lot of practical suggestions for how we might build consciousness and consent into all of our relating. Then we explore the ways in which we might co-create relationship containers and join—or develop—communities to support us to relate in these ways. After that, we consider specific forms of support our relationships may need, and how to access that, particularly around accountability when challenges or difficulties arise. We end the book by reflecting on the legacy that we might want to leave behind in terms of interrupting intergenerational trauma and passing something on to future generations about how they relate with themselves, each other, and the wider world.

So now you have a sense of the book you're about to encounter—and hopefully develop a relationship with!—here's your first reminder to pause, and slow down, should you need it...

Welcome to your first slow-down page!

If you've read our previous books, you might be used to those.
If not, don't worry: we'll provide guidance in each one.

Since you're at the beginning of this reading journey, we
thought it might be helpful to invite you to reflect on what
kind of relationship you might like to have with this book.

What does this mean?

Take a breath, slow down, and take a few minutes
to think about why you picked this book up. Then
reflect on what is your intention for reading this book.
If you're not sure, you can always set one now.

Maybe your intention is just to learn more about
relationships, or to develop specific relational skills.

Let your intention for reading this book be what it is,
but do give yourself some time to set that intention up
clearly and explicitly, if you want to. You might even
want to write your intention here—if so, go ahead.

. . . . . . . . . . . . . . . . . . . . . . . . . . . . . . . . . . . . . . . . . . . . . . . . . . . . . . . . . . . . . . . . .

. . . . . . . . . . . . . . . . . . . . . . . . . . . . . . . . . . . . . . . . . . . . . . . . . . . . . . . . . . . . . . . . .

. . . . . . . . . . . . . . . . . . . . . . . . . . . . . . . . . . . . . . . . . . . . . . . . . . . . . . . . . . . . . . . . .

. . . . . . . . . . . . . . . . . . . . . . . . . . . . . . . . . . . . . . . . . . . . . . . . . . . . . . . . . . . . . . . . .

Then, when you're ready, let's begin our journey into
understanding our relationships... Thank you for being here.

# WHAT ARE RELATIONSHIPS?

In this chapter, we'll start by talking about language, because what people mean by "a relationship" can be very different indeed! We'll overview some of the common language around relationships, exploring what works for you. After that, we'll consider some of the different kinds of relationships we might have in our lives, including the different kinds of people—and other beings—we might relate with, and the ways in which we might relate with them.

Then we'll set out one of the main frameworks for this book, which is that we can understand relationships on multiple levels: existential, sociocultural, relational, and internal. We'll explore how relationships are challenging because we're often pulled to disconnect from others by forces at each of these levels. This can make it hard to experience ourselves as interconnected, and to relate with care and compassion with ourselves, other people, our communities, and the world. Finally, we'll ask, "What's love got to do with it?," considering different kinds of love and the various characteristics of loving relationships.

## 1.1 WHAT WORDS MEAN

It might seem obvious that we all know what we mean when we use the word "relationships," but the reality is that we have experienced different people using this word in a range of ways during our lifetimes so far. We also come from different cultural backgrounds, and our first language is not the same: Alex speaks Italian as their first language and MJ English. Even within the same language, there can be different cultural and familial connections to using this word. So, first of all, why don't we take a moment to reflect on what this word means to you, right now, at the beginning of this reading journey.

### Reflection point: Defining relationships

Take a moment to think about the word "relationship," or its plural version "relationships." Then try to write down your own definition. For example, try to complete the prompts: "A relationship is..." or "Being in relationship means..." You can also write your own reflections without using one of our prompts, of course. Please remember that every moment of reflection or activity offered in this book is an invitation that you can take, leave, or modify according to your needs, capacity, and desires in the moment. If words are not the best way for you to process, you can also make a collage, write a song, draw, or dance what a relationship is for you, at this moment in time. You may want to keep a record of your reflections to revisit later.

Things that we noticed over time is that people tend to use the word "relationship" in different ways. For example, some only use it to describe romantic and/or sexual relationships; others use it to describe any kind of relationship, including the relationship we have with ourselves, nature, animal companions, children, siblings, etc. In this book, we'll be using the word "relationship" to mean any connection, intentional or not, conscious or not, that we have within the web of life. This means that we are indeed using it as a very broad umbrella term to address our relationships with ourselves, those around us, and the ecosystems we are part of. For us, relationships also include those with our ancestors and anything around us, such as our homes, our books, spirit, and so on. If that doesn't make sense to you, feel free to take what does and leave the rest.

We'll come back to this process of discernment again and again in the book. We can only speak from our own positionalities and experiences. If what we share resonates for you, that's great! If it doesn't, please feel free to either use it as a reflection or starting point or leave it completely. We assume that not every reader will agree with us. In fact, we know we don't always agree with each other, and you might even see those moments of divergence in the pages of this book. We're also aware that meaning changes across languages, time, and space. We'll discuss these changes further in Chapter 2 when we talk about how certain ideas of relationships have changed across time and space.

## Relationships words

We've talked about the umbrella word "relationships" so far, but under that umbrella, there are many specific words that refer to specific kinds of relationships, such as partner, spouse, friend, child, sibling. There are also words we use to describe how we do certain types of relationships—that is, words like dating, parenting, caretaking, stewarding, and so on. We think it's important to notice what words we tend to use when talking about relationships because these words often portray our values and beliefs or, at the very least, the values and beliefs within whatever dominant culture we are immersed in.

Words also have the power to shape what is possible. It can be challenging to imagine that which we have no words for. This is one of the reasons why sometimes knowledge and access to language have historically been viewed as threats to power-over types of governance, such as monarchies, fascist regimes, hierarchical religious systems, and so on. Those words, of course, are also shaped by other systems, such as gender, class, colonialism, religion, culture, neurodivergence, and so on.

If it's all starting to sound a bit complicated and overwhelming, that's because it is! So let's take a moment to pause and do an activity, if you want to. Or you can just pause, at any point in this book, not just when we encourage you to. We want to invite an affirming and consensual relationship with this book, one in which you can set boundaries, take care of yourself, and go at the pace you need to right now.

## ACTIVITY: ALL MY RELATIONSHIPS WORDS

On a large piece of paper or multiple pieces of paper (whatever you have available really), take the time to write all the relationships words that apply to you. It can be easy to stop after three or four main ones, so we encourage you to set a timer for ten minutes and keep going beyond the first obvious ones. The relationships words that apply to you can be current or historical. For example, you might no longer be a dog parent, but maybe you have been at some point in time and that was an important relationship for you, or maybe not.

If you need an example, at the end of this activity's description are Alex's relationships words. However, we would love for you to find your own, so only look at the example if you need it for inspiration. You can do this as a mind map or a list, or whatever makes sense to and for you.

Once you have your relationships words mapped out, take some time to consider how you feel about these words. For example, are they all equally comfortable or not? Are some words relevant to the past but not the present? Are some of these words aspirational—that is, relationships you want to be part of in the future? Are there words that fit better than others? Are there words that feel harmful to you? Are there words you no longer want to identify with? Do certain words bring up a feeling of expansion or constriction? Which words spark joy, to paraphrase Marie Kondo, and which do not? Can you pinpoint why? It's okay if you can't, and, of course, you might not want to ask yourselves quite as many questions as we offered, but we do hope this gives you a starting point.

Below are Alex's relationships words. (Please note that some of them are in Italian because this feels important to them, but don't worry if you don't understand these words—it's not important, as it's just an example. If you speak more than one language, you might also find that some words do not translate as neatly or that you prefer some words in your own language or that you might want to list all versions of one word in all the languages you use.)

Friend, teacher, parent, mother, daughter, child, sister, sibling, therapist, family member, cousin, grandchild, brother, niece, partner, spouse, wife, husband, sweetie, sub, immigrant, emigrant, community member, healer, witch, spiritual teacher, initiator, lover, student, leader, follower, member of a congregation, celebrant, storyteller, godparent, step-parent, bonus parent, uncle, aunt, compagno/a, mamma, nipote, fratello, sorella, insegnante, home owner, cat grandparent, grandpa, assistant, facilitator, acquaintance, beloved, enemy, writing partner, sweetheart, fiancé, aspirante, professor, citizen, survivor, patient, client.

If you have chosen to do the activity, you may have noticed that some of the words in your list are gendered. If not, or you have not done the activity, you can see that some of the words in Alex's list are gendered, such as daughter, niece, sister, and so on. As we wrote earlier, language is shaped by all sorts of other systems, including gender. Feel free to take time to think about how this too shapes the way in which we think about relationships. Is being a daughter different from being a son? Try not to go with the first knee-jerk response, but really sit with those thoughts and feelings with as much compassion and non-judgment as you're able to manage at this moment.

Are there gendered expectations that some of these words place on you and/or that you place on others? This is not good or bad, right or wrong, but rather an invitation into deeper awareness of how language shapes our relationships, and how we too can shape our relationships through language. We'll talk some more about this in Chapter 2 as well.

## The language of doing relationships

Language is used to describe not only types of relationships but also how we do relationships. For example, Alex had never really come across the concept of "dating" for romantic relationships until they were 22 and had moved to the UK. They'd seen it used in Anglo movies and TV series but didn't really know what that meant in practice. Bear in mind that they're in their 50s, so the reality in Italy is likely different now than it was in the 80s and early 90s. Growing up, they'd learned that you were in a relationship or not. Of course, it could be a more or less serious or committed relationship. In Sicily, to be "fidanzati a casa"—engaged at home—would have been more serious, and they had turned down someone who wanted to do this when they were 15 years old.

Moving first to the UK and then the US, Alex had to navigate the idea of dating, which honestly is still somewhat confounding to them. As they talked with other people about relationships, especially as a family therapist, they learned that even within Anglo culture, not everyone used dating to mean the same thing. Some people expected some level of exclusivity—that is, monogamy—while dating, and others didn't. Some people felt there were "rules" for dating, such as when you can text or not after a date, how often to see each other, when to say what you are feeling, and so on.

Alex likes specificity and clarity in language as a neurodivergent person, so, recently, when entering a new romantic relationship with a friend, they had the courage to ask for what they wanted, without expectations that this would be what the other person wanted, and to express their ongoing confusion about dating. Relationships do, of course, begin and end, and change, but what *was* this dating? Was it the "try Alex for 30 days free trial" like a subscription service? Was a relationship possible? And how would entering a romantic relationship also "erase" the existing friend relationship if now, all of a sudden, they were "dating"? Thankfully, the other person was able to meet them in the relationship place but, had they wanted to date, Alex had hoped for at least some clarity of what that meant. Even though Alex is non-monogamous, and therefore did not expect exclusivity, they felt the need to know what expectations the other person had around dating, and whether these were compatible with what they wanted or not.

This is just one example of how the language to describe and do relationships can be confusing or ambiguous, especially for some of us who are neurodivergent, although we would argue that it can be challenging for everyone! Another example is people using euphemisms for what they want in a sexual relationship, whether it's a one-night hook-up or an ongoing one. If someone says they want to "make out," does this mean just kissing or do they include groping in their interpretation of the word? Are they using the word literally or as a euphemism for having sex?

Many of us have not been brought up to say exactly what we mean and want. It might even be considered rude in our culture or family to express such things so openly and directly. Some of us might even have been punished for saying exactly what we meant or wanted, so we understand that being clear when using our words is not simple. We carry all our experiences with us, and not just ours but also our cultural, social, historical, and intergenerational experiences. It's amazing that any of us find a way to relate and connect with one another at all!

The language of doing relationships can be confusing, not just in the context of romantic and/or sexual relationships, but in any relationships. When we use the word "friend," for example, are we clear on the expectations—or as my queer sibling Donald Engstrom-Reese would say, "joyful obligations"—that we have of one another when using this word? Are we able to differentiate between friends and acquaintances, between friends and family (as in logical family, family of choice, or queer family), between friends and fellow community members, between friends and colleagues, between friends and mentors? For those of us who are parents, what does it mean when we say we want to be our child's "best friend" or that they are our "best friend"? Are certain relationships words more or less compatible with specific power dynamics, such as those between children and adults, for example, especially within a family context?

These are not easy questions to ask ourselves, and they might feel even riskier to ask of one another. We believe, however, that all our relationships have the potential to be more intentional and conscious when we do the hard work of engaging with language with curiosity and a questioning attitude, and an openness to the fact that others may have different understandings to us. In the next section, we'll look at different kinds of relationships. We invite you to bring this questioning attitude and curiosity towards language in all the kinds of relationships mentioned there.

## 1.2 DIFFERENT KINDS OF RELATIONSHIPS

As we said in the introduction, our aim with this book is to cover material that will be useful for *all* kinds of relationships, while recognizing that some things might apply more—or differently—to different kinds of relationships.

There are many ways in which we might differentiate different kinds of relationships. Let's consider, here, *who* we relate with and the diverse *ways* in which people relate.

### Who we relate with

While relationships are often taken to mean our relationships with other humans, particularly those who we're close or intimate with, we can usefully expand out the concept of relationship to include our inner relationships (with our self or selves) and our relationships beyond the human world.

Consider the relationships that you engage with in the following categories, and any more that you can think of. You might find it helpful to reflect on who you engage with in the average day, week, month, or year.

— *Inner relationships:* This might include your relationship with yourself, with different aspects—or parts—of your personality, with different selves or souls who share your bodymind (if you experience yourself that way), with your body, with different parts of your body, with your feelings, with different bodily or emotional experiences...

— *Individual human relationships:* This might include your everyday relationships with friends, with family members—including across generations—with colleagues, with partners of various kinds, with neighbors, with members of your on- and offline communities, and so on. You might also think about relationships that are important where you don't actually engage in person, such as an author or influencer whom you follow. What about your relationships with people who are no longer in your life, like exes or old friends or colleagues? What about those who aren't living, such as specific people who have died, with ancestors, or past generations, or with imagined future people in your life, or future generations?

— *Groups and communities:* We also have relationships with groups of people where we may or may not engage with people individually as well. You might think about working groups, faith or spiritual communities, families (of origin or of choice), communities based on particular leisure activities...

— *Non-human relationships:* Many of us have pivotal relationships with companion and wild local animals (redbloods) and with our gardens or with the plants around our homes (greenbloods). We might feel an important relationship with land, or with particular places or landscapes...

— *Beyond:* Expanding out the concept of relationships, it can be useful also to consider our relationship with deities or spirits. Many people have important relationships with fictional characters who mean a lot to them. What about our relationship with ideas, with our projects, with home, or with things like art, sport, money, or music?

---

**Reflection point: Your relationships**

Which of these would you have automatically listed as "relationships" and which not? Who/what would you include in each category? Which feel key to you, which less so? Which ones feel like nurturing or nourishing relationships for you and which are more challenging? Did you think of other relationships we didn't include in the list?

---

## Relationship diversity

As we'll see in Chapter 2, relationships of all kinds have been done in very different ways across time and place. People have put emphasis on different kinds of relationships as being pivotal, they have engaged in different kinds of relationships for different reasons and at different times of life, and they have undertaken relationships such as friendships, marriages, working partnerships, or child rearing, in very different ways.

As we suggested in the previous section, it's important not to assume that people will want to engage in the same kinds of relationships as us, or that they will mean the same thing as we do by such relationships. Here are a few aspects of relationship diversity that have become more visible in our dominant culture in the last few years. These are worth bearing in mind, and considering yourself, in terms of their relevance to you. As with the previous list, you may well think of many more aspects. This is just a starting point.

— *Single/solo/self/selves relationships:* Whether through choice and/or circumstance, greater numbers of people are foregrounding their relationships with themselves. You might consider people who live and/or work alone, who become self-partnered, who define as solo-monogamous or solo-polyamorous (one of their partnerships being with themselves), or who experience themselves as plural or multiple in some way and the relationships within their system as key platonic, romantic, erotic, or otherwise important relationships.

- *From one to many:* Different cultures tend to have a monogamous or non-monogamous norm of how to do partner relationships, meaning that people tend to either partner with one person (at a time) or with more than one. However, there are also several relationship styles that fall somewhere between monogamy and non-monogamy (e.g. monogamish, friends with benefits, and hidden non-monogamies like long-term affairs). Non/monogamy can apply only to emotional connections, or only to erotic connections, or to both. We might also expand this concept out beyond "romantic" relationships, to consider whether we are someone who has—or prefers—one pivotal friendship, working relationships, or family relationship, or perhaps a few close ones in those categories, or many.

- *Ace, aro, and beyond:* Asexual (ace spectrum) and aromantic (aro spectrum) communities have raised awareness that many people experience romantic attraction but not sexual attraction, sexual attraction but not romantic attraction, or neither, as well as those who experience both. Feminist scientist Sari Van Anders distinguishes between "erotic" and "nurturing" connections and points out that we can experience neither, both, or one without the other, as well as finding erotic and nurturing connections in the same relationship—or relationships—or in different relationships. We might also consider what different people mean by "nurturing" and "erotic" relationships, and consider other forms of attraction, connection, or love beyond this (see section 1.4).

— *Relationship hierarchies:* Relationship anarchists, people in queerplatonic communities, and others question the relationship hierarchies that are common in dominant culture, particularly those between partnerships and friendships, and sometimes between family relationships and other kinds. We might also usefully consider here distinctions between working relationships and other forms of relationship. Increasing numbers of people engage in some form of relating as part of their work, from sex workers, therapists, healthcare professionals, and other practitioners, to wait staff, salespeople, receptionists, and all those increasing service industry jobs which require a degree of emotional and/or relational labor. Often relationships where there is some kind of work or transaction involved are denigrated compared with other forms, but it can be helpful to remember that many partnerships, friendships, family relationships, etc. include some form of (often unspoken) transaction, and many relationships that are explicitly transactional can be fulfilling in all kinds of other ways. Increasing use of the internet, particularly during the global COVID pandemic, has challenged hierarchies between in-person and online relating. Many post-human and Indigenous thinkers have challenged the hierarchies people make between relationships with humans and non-humans, particularly emphasizing the role of this in the latest global pandemic and climate crisis.

MJ's key relationships, and relationship styles, have shifted radically across their lifetime, particularly as they met different people, read different authors, engaged with different communities, and as the culture around them shifted. In their teens and 20s, they had a very culturally normative understanding of relationship, and sought "opposite-gender," monogamous, couple relationships, expecting to have most of their relational needs and desires met there. However, their close relationship with a sibling and a friend, and their sense of their capacity to love more than one person at a time, meant that they often internally questioned this model.

Meeting people in bisexual, polyamorous, and kink communities expanded out their relational possibilities, although their early "same-gender" and polyamorous relationships still had quite a monogamous couple feel to them—albeit with more than one person—and a prioritizing of romantic/sexual relationships. They noticed that their attempts to do relationships differently often still feel like tweaking normative models but retaining their foundations, rather than developing different foundations.

Over the years, they moved further towards relationship anarchy and valuing other relationships equally to romantic/sexual ones, and eventually to a more ace/aro spectrum experience, where they were prioritizing other kinds of relationships, and questioning whether they experienced romantic and/or sexual attraction to others. In recent years, their inner relationships have become pivotal, and they experience themselves as having multiple selves in different kinds of relationship with each other (nurturing, erotic, mentorship, alliances, and more). In relation to others, they've come to foreground relationships (with people, groups, animals, plants, land, projects, etc.) in which they're most able to flow between their selves.

## Multiple experiences: Different ways of relating

"The key relationships in my life are with my husband, his other wife, and our children. It is very hard to get other people to recognize these as legitimate—equally important—relationships. It frustrates me that while polyamorous relationships are recognized to some extent in my city, faith-based non-monogamy like mine is still treated with suspicion, and people assume that I must have been coerced into this relationship somehow. If we hadn't moved to this country, there would've been a lot less questioning, and more support around us."

"My work has always been my primary relationship, but no matter how much I try to explain that to friends and partners, it's very rare to come across anybody who really respects that."

"Relationship with land is just as important to me as any relationship with a human or other being. All of my life choices are informed by how connected I feel to the land in that particular location more than anything else. I mostly engage in work and relationships with others who feel similarly and who want to care for the land together."

"Friends are my family. After a number of 'failed relationships,' I realized I already actually got all my needs and desires met in the many enduring friendships I've developed over my life. Once I recognized this and stopped pursuing romantic relationships, I felt a lot better, although I have occasionally found challenges with friends who find it odd that I want to celebrate our relationship milestones, or make the kinds of agreements that people in romantic relationships make."

Having read this section, you might consider other ways of differentiating different kinds of relationships than the ones we've explored here. For example, instead of foregrounding *who* we relate with, or *what* kind of relationship style we have, we could distinguish relationships on the basis of:

- *why* we relate (differentiating relationships we engage with for different reasons)

- *where* we relate (differentiating between relationships in different contexts in our lives)

- *when* we relate (differentiating between relationships we developed at different ages or stages of life)

- *how* we relate (differentiating between relationships where we relate in more easeful or challenging ways, at different paces, with more or less of a structure to our time together, with greater or lesser intimacy, in one-to-one or group contexts, and more).

In the next section, we'll see how—in addition to recognizing multiple different kinds of relationships—it's helpful to understand how our relationship experiences play out at multiple levels simultaneously.

## 1.3 UNDERSTANDING RELATIONSHIPS AT MULTIPLE LEVELS

When it comes to understanding our relationships, it's very helpful to hold in mind multiple levels of experience. For the purposes of this book we've labeled these: existential, sociocultural, relational, and internal. You could have a sense of these as nested levels of experience, as in the diagram below.

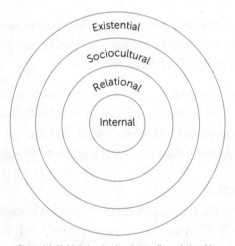

*Figure 1.1: Multiple levels of understanding relationships*

### Existential

At the outer level of experience, humans are *existential* beings. Some people might also use the word "spiritual" to refer to this level of experience. Being existential means that there are certain "givens" of our lives, which impact how we relate with ourselves and others. These include:

— the fact that we're born into a world where there are already lots of norms and assumptions about how to do relationships, what kinds of relationships we should aspire to, what kinds of feelings we should have in relationships, etc.

— the fact that we're inevitably *in* relation with other people who will all have their own ideas and expectations about relationships, and who may want similar and/or different things to us

— the fact that people generally have a pull both towards freedom and some kind of individual self-expression, as well as towards belonging and some kind of security with others, although what these things mean to us can vary a lot

— the fact that everything—including our relationships—will inevitably change over time and will eventually end, and people generally struggle with this

— the fact that people are generally motivated towards pleasurable experiences and away from painful ones, and relationally we tend to like others to affirm that we are "good," and struggle when they act as if we are "bad" in some way.

## Sociocultural

Focusing in on the norms and assumptions that already exist in the world that we're born into, at the sociocultural level of understanding we are *embedded* beings. This means that we're highly shaped by the time and place that we grow up in, and the one that we live in now. All times and places have norms of how people are expected to relate with each other, which kinds of relationships are more or less valued, how things like love and commitment work, who is allowed to relate with whom, and so on. Sometimes these things are enshrined in social systems like the legal system, medical system, and educational system, and/or in religious rituals or spiritual practices.

In some times and places, these relationships norms or rules may be quite open and flexible, in others, very closed or restricted. Also, we may find that we personally conform to some of these norms quite easily, while others feel like less of a good fit for us, and others we may strongly resist. Becoming more conscious of what these norms and ideals are, and considering how we might relate to them, is a key theme of this book.

## Relational

Focusing on the fact that we're relational beings, at this next level of understanding, we can see that we're always *entangled* in relationships with others, from the moment we're born and throughout our life. Again, this is true whether we move towards relating with others and/or whether we move away from relationships. Even someone who decided to live alone as a hermit is making a relational choice, and they are inevitably in relation with others who provide their food or otherwise enable them to make that choice!

In this book, we'll spend a lot of time considering the kinds of relationship patterns that we develop because of our early relationship experiences with caregivers and others around us growing up. We'll explore how these impact our relationships with ourselves, with others, and with the world, all the way through our lives.

## Internal

At the innermost level of experience we are *embodied* beings. This means that we all have bodyminds which operate in specific ways, because of aspects that are there from birth, and because of the experiences we have through our lives which shape how our bodyminds operate. This shaping includes the impact of things like traumatic and/or nourishing experiences of relationships growing up, as well as whether we make decisions to move towards, or away from, certain relationships or kinds of relationships.

When we think about relationships at this level, it may be the case that aspects of our neurodiversity impact how we experience touch, the pace at which we like to do relationships, how long we need to process relational experiences, etc. We also develop certain patterns in how we connect with other people due to our early experiences of relating (see Chapter 3). Also, decisions like whether we live alone, with one other person, in a family, or in community will likely have a marked impact on our bodymind over time (and, of course, such decisions are shaped by the options that are, or are not, available to us in the time and place in which we live).

All this means that—at the level of bodymind—we are likely to be similar to others in some ways and different to them in other ways, and all this will shape how easy and challenging it is for us to relate with ourselves, with specific other people, with groups, with the wider world, and more.

So what are the implications of the fact that our relationships play out at the existential, sociocultural, relational, and internal levels simultaneously? Why is it so useful to keep remembering that we are existential, embedded, entangled, and embodied beings?

One reason this multi-level understanding is helpful is that it can be very useful to hold all aspects of our experience in mind— rather than being tempted to make sense of a relationship moment at just one level of understanding.

For most of us, most of the time, our relationships are influenced by all these levels of experience, and this can help us to lighten individualized stories, for example that relationship struggles are "all our fault" or the result of us being "too much" or "not enough" in some way. If we find ourselves drawn to that way of thinking, we can usefully remind ourselves that the others involved also bring their own relationship patterns and expectations to the situation, and that the cultural context we're in—and existential pushes and pulls—also play a part.

**Reflection point: Understanding attraction on multiple levels**

Remember the last time that you found yourself very drawn to another person, group, community, or being, if that is an experience that's familiar to you. How might you understand that experience at these multiple levels?

— *Existential*—e.g. Does something about this relationship signify freedom/belonging to you? Do they perhaps affirm us in ways we'd like to be seen, or offer forms of pleasure or an escape from things we find painful, in some way?

— *Sociocultural*—e.g. Is this relationship a good fit in our wider culture or community? Or perhaps they challenge social norms in a similar way to the way we do and that's helpful for us?

— *Relational*—e.g. Do they remind us of people or relationships from our past in ways that are familiar or comforting? Or do they seem to offer something very different from painful past experiences, or give us something we lost or lacked in our early relationships?

— *Internal*—e.g. Is it that our bodyminds are a particularly good fit in some ways? Or might they be particularly good at accommodating the ways in which our bodymind works?

## Remembering what we're all up against

Perhaps this is the thing that we personally find most helpful about holding these multiple levels of understanding: the way they help us to make sense of relationship struggles. At all these levels, while there are generally deep desires to connect and relate with others, there are also very strong pulls towards *disconnection*, which can make relating with others very challenging. Reminding ourselves of this when we're struggling can really help us to not give ourselves—or others—such a hard time.

Here's an overview of how we're often pulled towards disconnection at each level of experience.

At the *existential* level, philosophers from many traditions have suggested that there is a pull to treat both other people—and ourselves—as things or objects. For example, treating other people as things might include searching for another person or group who is going to rescue us, or give our life meaning, in some way. Or it may be about projecting our past relationship experiences onto someone and expecting them to act in the same way that previous person did. Or it might be about viewing someone through the lens of their physical attractiveness to us rather than as a complex being in their own right.

Treating ourselves as objects for others might include trying to figure out what others want from us and conforming to that in the hope that it will bring us love, security, or validation. Or perhaps we give to others things that we'd like ourselves (time, energy, gifts, care, etc.) in the hope that they will give them back to us eventually.

All of these—very common!—ways of relating actually create a separation, split, or disconnection between ourselves and others, meaning that we're not fully in relation with them, and we're certainly not being all that *we* are in relation to all that *they* are.

At the *sociocultural* level, tragically, dominant culture encourages us in all kinds of ways to treat ourselves, other people, whole categories of people, and other beings in this kind of objectifying way. We'll say much more about this in Chapter 2, but for now you might consider the ways in which global capitalism relies on treating some bodies, lives, and labor as far more valuable than others, or the ways in which it attempts to convince us that we're lacking and need to buy certain products to fill that lack. Our ways of relating are strongly shaped by such things. For example, we might pursue certain kinds of relationships that are sold to us as essential for a "successful" life, or we may try to present ourselves in certain ways—on dating apps, for example—in accordance with the kinds of self we've been taught is valuable or attractive.

Again, these dominant cultural ways of relating often sever us further from ourselves and from other people. They may mean that we don't feel able to be our full selves—or to be vulnerable—with other people (which we'll see is important for intimacy). These things also may mean that we find ourselves treating others in our lives as commodities or property, in some ways, rather than as full complex beings.

At the *relational* level, many of these normative ways of relating are passed onto us intergenerationally through our families and communities, and it can be hard indeed to shift from the ways of relating that we were immersed in growing up. Also, developmental trauma can increase our likelihood of relating with ourselves and others in painful ways, such as hiding aspects of ourselves or being harshly critical of any "faults," or looking to others to give us the kinds of care we didn't get as children, or avoiding intimacy because we find it so painful.

Again, trauma of any kind increases our sense of disconnection from ourselves and others, and most of us in dominant culture experience some form of trauma growing up, whether that is more obvious kinds of abuse or neglect, and/or not having our tough experiences held carefully by other people, or not being shown that relationship ruptures can be repaired when they happen (don't worry, we'll say a lot more about all these things—and how we can address them—throughout this book!).

At the *internal* level, as we've said already, all of these ways of relating—from the existential, sociocultural, and relational levels of experience—play out through our bodyminds and impact the ways in which they work. For example, cultural and developmental trauma can mean that our bodyminds respond to tough relational moments in ways that make it very hard to be present to others and ourselves, and to relate compassionately.

Also, wider culture—and often the relationships around us growing up—teach us that the ways that some bodyminds relate are better—or more normal—than the ways others do. So, for example, if we are neurodivergent in any way, we may well have learned to mask the kinds of relating that would be a better fit for us by trying to relate in ways that were expected of us. This might include trying to make eye contact, engaging in forms of communication that don't feel comfortable to us, or consenting to things without taking enough time to process.

We may well feel more disconnected from ourselves, and from others, if we've become used to overriding our bodyminds—or the bodyminds of others—in these kinds of ways.

We say all these things here not to make you feel bad about how challenging relationships are but to reassure you that finding relationships hard makes All Kinds of Sense! We both find relationships very challenging, even after spending several decades studying relationships and working as relationship therapists! This is largely because all of us are up against so much—existentially, socioculturally, relationally, and internally—when we try to relate with ourselves, with others, and with the world.

One of the main points of this book is to explore how we can become more connected on all these levels of experience, as well as how we might move from disconnection towards connection when challenges arise or ruptures occur.

## 1.4 WHAT'S LOVE GOT TO DO WITH IT?

One thing that we haven't talked about yet but which is often associated with relationships is love. We've talked about language, different kinds of relationships, and introduced a relational framework to better understand the multiple levels on which we can experience relationships. However, we haven't talked about some of the foundational values in relationships, which is where love can come into the picture.

What do we mean by that? Some people might view love as foundational to any relationships because they might use the term "love" almost as a substitute for spirit or connection. Others might view love as only relevant to some relationships and not others, such as parent–child relationships or romantic relationships. Love can be another big, confusing, and ambiguous word, though. What do we mean when we say we love someone or something? In English, it can be particularly confusing because we might love pizza and also love our child, hopefully not meaning the exact same kind of love while using the same verb. Not all languages, though, only have one word for love. In *Life Isn't Binary*, for example, we talked about ancient Greek having seven words to describe different ways of loving, as illustrated below.

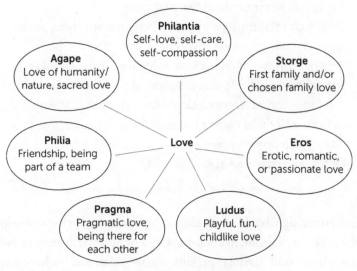

*Figure 1.2: Ancient Greek types of love*

These different types of love are not hierarchical, in our view at least, and we believe that they are all essential to the wellbeing of our bodyminds and of our relationships. Unfortunately, the dominant cultures within which we live often privilege one type of love above another, such as placing eros over ludus, for adults. We'll talk more about this in Chapter 2, while in Chapter 3 we'll explore what we learned about love and relationships while growing up. For now, let's reflect on the seven types of love in ancient Greek introduced above.

---

**Reflection point: Many ways to love**

Take a moment to review the seven different types of love in ancient Greek described above. Which types of love, out of those seven, do you have in your life right now? Which of these types do you feel more or less comfortable expressing and why? Are there types of love that you would like in your life but that are missing right now? Are there other types of love you would add to this picture? If so, which words would you use to describe these types of love?

Which relationships in your life map onto these seven types of love (or more, if you have added to the picture)? One relationship might include more than one type of love. For example, we might feel agape, storge, philia, pragma, and ludus within a relationship with one person. Make sure to remember that having more or fewer types of love in a relationship doesn't make it "better or worse"—it just helps us better understand what kind of relationships we're in.

---

Understanding what kind of relationships we're in can be very helpful because, as we said, relationships are not necessarily easy. In fact, even when—and maybe especially when—relationships have a lot of ease in them, it takes communication, vulnerability, authenticity, risk taking, and commitment to nurture them. This work doesn't need to be stressful or unpleasant; it can feel more like a labor of love, but it's labor nevertheless.

If love is such a big, all-encompassing, confusing word, what foundational values can help us to better understand whether our relationships are supportive and nurturing? We invite you to consider the following characteristics, but please note that these specifically apply to peer adult relationships. These characteristics are: differentiation, mutuality, care, and compassion.

We'll say a little more about those four characteristics later on, but first we want to highlight that not all relationships have foundations in love, and that's okay. For example, some relationships can be transactional. We might have a transactional relationship with our work. We give our time and expertise, and we receive compensation for it—that is a transactional relationship.

Transactional relationships might seem pretty straightforward, but they can also have their own level of complexity. What if our employer does not value our labor in the same way we do? What if the snow removal people we hired have a different understanding of our contract than we do? Transactional relationships also need open and direct communication to function well. A tricky situation is when we're in a relationship that we might think is founded on some type of love (e.g. eros, pragma, and philia) and the other person thinks they agreed to a transactional relationship, or is treating it as if it were a transactional relationship. We've witnessed this play out in family therapy quite a bit. Partners and/or parents are "keeping score" of who is doing what and how much value they attribute to what the person is doing. They might also have expectations of receiving back exactly what they have given in some way, shape, or form that they understand. Sometimes transactional relationships can be described as tit-for-tat or quid pro quo (which, in Latin, means "this for that") relationships.

Transactional relationships are, once again, no better or worse than other types of relationships. For example, we likely do not want deep and loving relationships with our doctor, therapist, or employer, even though these can be important relationships in our lives. We do believe it's helpful to distinguish between transactional and non-transactional relationships, though, because it can help us—and those around us—in being clear about hopes, boundaries, and expectations. This brings us back to the four characteristics of loving relationships mentioned earlier: differentiation, mutuality, care, and compassion. Let's take a moment to briefly define those, knowing that we will come back to these in a number of ways in later chapters of this book.

## Four characteristics of affirming and supportive adult peer relationships

*Differentiation* in its simplest definition means knowing that we are people with our own thoughts, feelings, identities, experiences, needs, desires, and practices, and that the people we are in relationships with are also people with their own thoughts, feelings, identities, experiences, needs, desires, and practices. It's not a sign of "success" or "failure" if we're similar or different from those around us, especially our children, parents, siblings, friends, and/or partners. For example, we, MJ and Alex, have very different needs and ways to pack for travel. Alex usually has a large suitcase (or sometimes even a large suitcase and a carry-on bag), while MJ has a fairly small backpack when traveling together. We know we have different needs and desires, and we respect those differences without feeling or thinking that one way is better than the other. Being able to do differentiation in peer adult relationships enables us to see the other people in our lives for who they are and not as clones of ourselves, as projections, or as we want them to be. We believe this to be part of a supportive and nurturing foundation for peer adult relationships of any kind.

*Mutuality* can go hand in hand with differentiation in some ways. If we are different, and both our ways of being are valid, how can we offer one another what we need? Mutuality is different from tit-for-tat or quid pro quo relationships because what we give and receive doesn't need to be equal or of "equal value," whatever that might mean under late-stage capitalism! Mutuality is about reciprocity: we exchange something for the benefit of all of us. For example, one of Alex's partners is great at dealing with filling out forms and emails, while Alex hates this but can be pretty decent at working hard and making money for their family! When we have mutuality in a relationship, we can feel understood as well as feeling that some of our needs are getting met, and that we are able to meet some of other people's needs. Mutuality does not need to be 50/50 at all times or equivalent, as that would be more trans-actional. Rather, it ebbs and flows with capacity, access, privilege, skills, knowledge, and so on.

*Care* can be expressed through mutuality, but we like giving it its own category because we believe it to be a specific characteristic of affirming and supportive relationships. Care is another big word in many ways, like love. We're using it to describe giving ourselves and those around us what we need on a physical, emotional, psy-chological, and spiritual level. What we give and receive in terms of care doesn't always cover all these aspects of ourselves (physical, emotional, psychological, and spiritual), but it needs to cover at least some of those aspects. In order for it to be authentic care, it also needs to be about what the other person needs, and not what we think they need. Maybe we need a lot of touch to feel cared for by those close to us, while another person might be touch averse. If we touch a person in our life a lot because that is what we want, but they are touch averse or just don't like touch, we aren't caring for them. We're either meeting our own needs through them or at the very least projecting ourselves onto them. Differentiation can help us to avoid using other people as blank canvases on which we project our own needs, identities, experiences, desires, and practices. Doing peer relationships in this way is not easy, and it can even be considered counter-cultural, which is where compassion comes in.

*Compassion* means "to feel together." Because of Christian supremacy and its influence, compassion is also often defined as "to suffer with." We prefer "to feel or experience with/together." Compassion helps us feel not alone, especially when we're suffering or in pain, but also when we're happy or excited, or when we're deep in shame. Compassion is often one of the things we might be looking for in relationships because it can be so hard to offer to ourselves. When we have compassion for those around us, we're showing them that they aren't alone, or they aren't separate from us or the rest of humanity. This can be particularly important when we're dealing with a lot of shame, since shame can be so isolating and alienating. Compassion within ourselves also helps us accept ourselves and others with more ease, which then helps us to recognize differentiation, offer authentic care, and express mutuality in relationships.

Open, honest, and ongoing communication is very helpful with all four of these characteristics, as well as with any type of relationships, including transactional ones. Below are some multiple experiences to illustrate what we've discussed here.

## Multiple experiences: Relating in many ways

"Before becoming a parent, I had all sorts of judgments about how other people did it. It's hard to explain how challenging this 'job' of parenting is... It's not a mutual relationship—it cannot be, not until that child is a full-grown adult. All of a sudden, you have this being who depends on you for survival, learns from you how to regulate and feel, and looks up to you initially, only to separate from you as much as possible in their teen years. It's exhausting, exhilarating, anxiety-provoking, and a way of loving that is different from anything else I've ever experienced in peer relationships."

"It can be easy to think of therapy as a transactional relationship: I pay you and you listen to me. I was surprised to eventually learn that it was still a relationship and one that I could heal some deep, relational wounds within. Before experiencing working with a therapist who shared some of my identities, such as being Black and trans, I didn't fully grasp how the mix of intimacy and boundaries could be so healing and so powerful."

"Relationships and love had always seemed confining to me. Exploring relationship anarchy enabled me to ask myself a lot more questions about what I wanted and needed, and to be curious about other people's wants and needs. I feel both freedom and mutuality in my relationships now. I also stopped putting romantic partners above friends, because it was something I never understood growing up and never made sense to me."

"As a disabled person, I have sometimes been suspicious of people's 'care.' Like everyone else, I want to give and receive care as part of loving, but I don't want to be thought of as 'needing care all the time.' Finding other disabled partners who taught me about access intimacy has changed the way I let myself be loved and the way I love others, not only in my intimate relationships, but in all my close relationships."

**REMEMBER...** We've explored a lot of different ideas of what relationships are in this chapter. It can feel really overwhelming to engage with all of this, especially if some/all of these ideas are new to you. Please remember that it's not only okay, but encouraged, to go slowly and intentionally in this book. Take what resonates, leave the rest, reflect on what seems inspiring, and, above all, tune into yourself. What do you need right now? Who might you want to discuss some of these ideas with? Just like in any other relationships, there is no rush, no "right and only way," but rather an invitation to connect and feel together into possibilities.

## Further resources

You can read more about some of the diversities of ways of doing relationships in these zines:

— Mapping Your Sexuality—by Sari Van Anders with us and Jules

Scheele—available from www.queensu.ca/psychology/van-anders-lab/sct.html#zine

- Relationship Struggles—by MJ—available from www.rewriting-the-rules.com/zines/#1652967171038-dd65bffc-16f3

For more on the implications of sex work for relationships and work, check out:

- Smith, M. and Mac, J. (2018). *Revolting Prostitutes: The Fight for Sex Workers' Rights*. London: Verso Books.

For more on love, check out:

- hooks, b. (2016). *All About Love*. New York, NY: William Morrow Paperbacks.

- Loving Beyond Gender Binaries—by Alex—available from https://docs.google.com/document/d/1kIXxiy6UIAC9nvkG6qbAU_F1MqB8GjdzZuCqyGVTxkc/edit

Check out also the resources listed at the end of Chapter 2.

Let's slow down once more.

If you've read our other books in this series, you
might be used to our slow down pages by now!

In this book, we'd like to invite you into relational slowing down.

What do we mean by this?

For this one, we encourage you to choose one of the
activities in this chapter and pick someone you want to
share it with. You might want to invite them to do the activity
with you and then share your reflections, or you might just
want to share your own reflections with them. Whatever
you do, do what feels right to you at this moment.

The person/people you share this with do not
need to be external, by the way; they can be
people and/or parts within yourself.

Then slow down some more and check in with
yourself to see how it feels to have shared this with
someone else (whether internally or externally).

What do you notice? What do you need? Can you
give yourself what you need and/or ask for what you
need? Can you let yourself be held in this process?

Whatever the answers might be, we hope you can
practice approaching yourselves with curiosity
and compassion throughout this book.

*CHAPTER 2*

# *HOW THE WORLD VIEWS RELATIONSHIPS*

In this chapter, we explore the dominant cultural messages that we receive about relationships, and the impact these have on those of us who manage to conform to these, and on those of us who don't, or who resist them. We then focus on the roots of dominant ways of relating in colonialism, asking what it might look like to decolonize love and relationships. Finally, we consider what more connected or unconditional ways of loving might look like, and how to hold our desire to move towards these, with the reality that we will inevitably often relate with ourselves and others in disconnected and conditional ways.

## *2.1 DOMINANT CULTURAL MESSAGES ABOUT RELATIONSHIPS*

As we mentioned in the last chapter, one of the main challenges in relationships is the fact that we're born into a world that already has A Lot of Ideas and Assumptions about what they are and how they should work. When we're embedded in dominant cultural messages about relationships throughout our lives, it's easy to assume that these are the "normal," "natural," or "right" ways of doing relationships, and even to find ourselves imposing these ways of relating on other people, or even on entire cultures (as we'll explore more in the next section).

It's important to say, at the outset of this chapter, that for whatever norm, rule, or expectation we have about how to do relationships, somebody somewhere will have something entirely different. That often includes people with different dominant cultures, and people in our own dominant culture who have found other ways of doing things. Relationships of all kinds have been done radically differently across time and place. You might consider, for example, the differences between cultures and communities which assume romantic relationships should start with a sudden "falling-in-love" experience versus those where love is viewed as something that builds slowly over time. You might think about places and times where it's assumed that children will be raised by one or two biological parents, versus places and times where child raising is a community endeavor.

Through the rest of this chapter, we'll say more about the foundations of dominant culture which these relationship norms stem from, and the diversity of relationship forms—and ways of relating—that exist across place and time. For now, let's consider the dominant culture of relationships, the impact this has, and why it might be worth questioning it.

Note that when we speak of "dominant culture" of relationships here, we're talking about the one that dominates in the places where we live—the US and the UK—and which has been, and still is, imposed around the world to a large extent, by everything from global capitalism to Hollywood movies. However, it's also vital to acknowledge that different cultures around the world have taken on, and resisted, this culture to different extents, and that people who live in countries like the US and UK may also have different cultural backgrounds that impact how much the dominant culture impacts them and/or provides alternatives. Traveling and accessing different faith, spiritual, political, and other communities can also give people a very different relationship with dominant culture.

As you read through this section, you can think about the extent to which you're impacted by dominant cultural messages about relationships, and what alternative relationship cultures you've been exposed to and have explored. There'll be more chance to consider this explicitly—in relation to your background and current relationships—in the next two chapters.

One of us—MJ—has written a whole book about the dominant messages about love and relationships, the impact they have on us, and how people are doing things differently. In this section, we'll cover some of the main ones, but feel free to go to that book— *Rewriting the Rules*—if you want to think more about how this applies, specifically, to topics like sex, monogamy, break-up, etc.

Perhaps the main dominant cultural message about relationships is that romantic partner relationships are all important, so let's start there. This cultural assumption is to the point that finding and building a romantic partnership is regarded as a fundamental part of the life course in most western theories of developmental psychology. Romantic and sexual relationships make up whole genres of fiction and film, and are the focus of the vast majority of pop songs. Being romantically and sexually attractive, and finding and keeping a romantic/sexual partner, is culturally viewed as part of being a successful self, and there is a stigma of failure around those who remain single and/or lose such relationships.

### Reflection point: The rules of romantic relationships

Before we explore some of the dominant cultural messages about romantic partner relationships, you might like to reflect on them yourself. What are "the rules" of how these relationships "should" work? You may find it useful to think about the classic romance story, the messages you hear in pop songs, the last romcom movie or series you watched, or the ways that people you know chat and gossip about relationships. You could consider, for example:

— what kinds of people are expected to form such relationships (and what kinds of people are not)

— how such relationships are expected to begin

— what the stages of such relationships are meant to be and when people are expected to meet those stages

— what feelings and behaviors are expected in such relationships, and what ones are seen as a problem, or even relationship-ending

— how people are viewed who do not form such relationships, or who end them.

## Gender, sexuality, and relationship normativity

The word "normativity" is used for the standards that cultures have about how they should do certain things, which are often enforced in laws, education systems, religious teachings, media representations, and so on. For example, heteronormativity refers to the default assumption that people will be straight, which is often presented as the "natural," "normal," or "morally superior" way of being, and means that anybody who is not straight has to "come out" if they want others to be aware of their sexuality.

In dominant culture, the normativities that we have around gender, sexuality, and relationships are deeply interwoven. This is one of the reasons that we have written this trilogy of *How to Understand Your...* books on these three topics. In many ways, we need to understand and explore gender, sexuality, and relationships together, because the norms around them were forged together and operate together in the way they constrain us.

What do we mean by this? Dominant culture has a binary/hierarchical model of all three of these things: gender-wise, we can either be a man or a woman; sexually, we can be attracted to the opposite or same sex (making us straight or gay); and we are expected to act out that attraction in the form of a romantic and sexual relationship. The normative monogamous couple relationship is the key place in which we're expected to play out our gendered role and manifest our sexuality.

These interwoven normativities are actually pretty recent. One of the reasons was that a cultural norm—and centering—of an "opposite gender" monogamous couple aided a certain form of capitalism, where the woman engaged in unpaid labor to care for her husband and children: the current and future workforce. A lot of our stereotypes of (strong, rugged, independent) masculinity and (nurturing, passive, caring) femininity stem from this time, as do our romantic ideals of "opposite-gender" attraction, and happily-ever-after stories around long-term relationships. This also partially explains the demonizing and stigmatizing of those who deviate from stereotypical gender roles, from heteronormativity, and from couple/nuclear family relationships, as they all pose a cultural threat to these normativities, which are viewed as essential foundations of the social system.

There are many relationship normativities that operate together, in this system. Here are a few that have been named, but you may well be able to think of more:

— *Mononormativity:* This is the norm that it is good, natural, and normal to be monogamous, and that straying outside of monogamy (overtly or covertly) is bad, unnatural, or abnormal.

— *Couple centrism:* This is the privileging of people in romantic couples or partnerships over others—for example, in everyday practices like "plus one" invitations, asking someone if they have a partner, only having commitment celebrations for this kind of relationship, legal protections for spouses, and house-sharing being set up around them and being far more difficult and expensive for solo people and people in other kinds of relationships.

— *Amatonormativity:* This is Elizabeth Brake's word for the assumption that everyone will want to pursue romantic love relationships, and that having one is a marker of a successful life.

— *Sexual normativity:* This is the assumption that everyone will experience sexual attraction and/or desire and will want sexual partners. Amatonormativity and sexual normativity come together in the assumption that a romantic couple relationship is the best—or only—place in which to experience sex, that such relationships should be sexual and remain sexual over time, and that "sex" means penis-in-vagina intercourse (see *How to Understand Your Sexuality* for more on this).

— *The relationship escalator:* This concept, explored in depth by Amy Gahran, refers to the normative idea that we should do certain things in relationships in a certain order. For example, dating, falling in love, having sex, moving in together, committing to each other, having children, etc.

— *The One:* The ideal of The One is the sense that there is somebody out there who will "complete you," be "everything" to you, and meet all of your needs forever.

## Other relationship normativities

We've spent a lot of time on romantic partner relationships here, because so many of the dominant cultural norms relate to them. Some of the main challenges with pretty much all other kinds of relationships are that they are often not recognized *as* relationships, or at least nowhere near as important as romantic partnerships. There are often no route-maps for how to do such relationships because of this. This means, for example, that workplaces often only allow compassionate leave for the death of spouses (and perhaps close nuclear family members). It can be hard indeed to get people to recognize the equivalent levels of grief we may feel over the death of a friend, work colleague, companion animal, or someone we had a long-term affair with, or to count the ending of such a relationship as a significant break-up.

However, there certainly are—often unspoken—normativities over what counts in terms of other kinds of relationships, and how we're expected to do them. Indeed, a key struggle for many neurodivergent people—including ourselves—is in navigating the expectations and assumptions that other people have around "appropriate" behavior in a friendship, collegiate relationship, family relationship, neighbor relationship, and so on.

Underpinning the romantic relationship normativities we explored above are a number of other—less spoken—relationship normativities. Here are a few that we thought of. You might well think of others.

- The people who we have certain kinds of relationships with are more valuable than other people in our lives, and other people in general.

- Relationships with humans are more important than relationships with non-humans, and humans are more valuable than non-humans.

- Friends must be in support of our romantic partnerships and never challenge or question them even if they are troubled by them. They should accept their role as lesser relationships and accept that we will prioritize our partners and/or close family members over them in times of crises, holidays, etc.

## Why question normativities?

One reason to question all cultural normativities is that, as we've seen, they are constructed—often within the context of certain social structures and systems. They are not real, universal rules about how relationships should be done, or the natural way of things, even though they are often presented in this way.

Another big reason for questioning normativities is the damage that they do, both to people who are inside of them and people outside of them.

For example, Esther Perel and others have written about how the myth of The One puts huge, impossible, pressure on people in romantic partnerships to be everything to each other. It just isn't possible to meet another person's needs for hot sex and warm companionship at the same time, and for the entire rest of your life! Let alone also trying to be each other's best friend, cheerleader, co-parent, confidant, carer, and all of the other things that become loaded on relationships. We can end up either in a never-ending painful search for somebody who *can* be all these things to us or in relationships where there is a lot of conflict and resentment because we can't.

For those outside of normativity, there can be a lot of shame about not meeting the norms of "successful" relationships. Even when we have made conscious choices away from normativity, or have pride about the ways we diverge from it, we can remain haunted by it because it is so powerful and accepted by the majority of people. Also, there are implicit and explicit punishments for not fitting normativity, which range from people looking at you oddly or not feeling able to share your life fully with work colleagues, up to hate crimes and being denied immigration or having your children taken away.

Here are a few examples of people who have challenged relationship normativities in their lives, and what this has opened up and closed down for them.

## Multiple experiences: Challenging relationship normativities

"While it's assumed that most people should be in romantic, sexual relationships, for many disabled people the assumption is the exact opposite. People in our lives, often including medical professionals and carers, assume that nobody would see us as desirable partners, and we are often infantilized to the extent that they think we shouldn't want sex, or can't possibly consent to it. Every day, my partner and I challenge this kind of relationship normativity just by existing and it is infuriating!"

"As a second-generation immigrant, the normativities around relationships in the culture around me are very different to those of my family and our culture. There can be a real pressure from both western friends and from my family to 'choose' one and reject the other, whether they realize they're doing that or not."

"There's something similar for me around class. In my working-class neighborhood, everyone was in and out of each other's houses, and I had loads of uncles and aunties who weren't biological relations. We also had pretty direct styles of communicating. When I went to college, it felt like the only way to fit in was to reject the way people did relationships and communication in my family. But when I went back home, sometimes it felt like I had to reject some of the new things I was learning that felt like a good fit for me, because they were seen as 'getting above myself.' The pressure to choose, or the energy it takes to code switch, are things that a lot of my friends just don't have to deal with."

"Realizing that I was autistic was a massive relief to me. My whole life, I've had such confusing experiences of friendships, often being told I was 'too much,' but also 'not enough.' Now I realize that I just didn't get the expectations people had—for example, that being in a friendship entails a certain type and amount of contact, but that you're not supposed to talk about that! Now I at least have a word people understand to describe myself with. I can let people know that I need expectations to be articulated clearly, and that I prefer to communicate in writing, and I can form relationships with other autistic people who work in similar ways to me."

## 2.2 THE ONGOING LEGACY OF COLONIALISM

We've discussed how dominant cultural messages impact our relationships, but where do these messages come from? For many, including ourselves, these dominant cultural messages are rooted in colonialism, anti-Blackness, white supremacy, and Christian supremacy. Let's take some time to break down what we mean here. Remember, as we go, that when we talk about white or Christian supremacy, we're talking about systems, not individual people, although individuals can certainly uphold or challenge those systems, and everything in between.

Cultures rooted in colonization, especially white supremacist ones, need to assert a more hierarchical view of relationships in order to justify their practices. Let's break that down further.

First of all, there are several types of colonialism. For example, historian Kris Manjapra lists the ones depicted in the image that follows. You might like to reflect on the ways these continue to impact our relationships with ourselves, close people, people in other cultures, the land, and more, before reading on.

In order to justify colonial approaches, people need to dehumanize Indigenous populations and they usually do so by constructing them as "primitive," which implies being less than the colonizers in a number of ways, including the ways in which they conduct relationships of all kinds.

The act of colonizing has a huge impact on both colonized and colonizer. For example, colonized groups may adapt to the

Figure 2.1: Forms of colonialism

colonizer's ways of doing relationships in order to survive, and/or they may find various creative ways of resisting this. In terms of impact on the colonizer, psychologist Ashiş Nandy suggested that, in order to justify their violent protectorate colonization—in Asia and elsewhere—British imperialists had to imagine themselves as virile adults governing childlike or less "masculine" races. This profoundly impacted the ways in which men and women, and adults and children, related in British culture. We see the ongoing legacy of this in British partner and parenting relationships today.

## Family relationships

If we grow up in colonial cultures, there are things that some of us might take for granted about relationships that are not universal values. For example, we might think that the idea of a nuclear family has been around for a long time, but it's actually a fairly recent idea. The term itself, "nuclear family," has only been around for about 100 years, and promoting the nuclear family as "the best environment" to bring children up, for example, is closely tied to capitalism. If we live in multiple, separate households, we need to buy more things—that is, we cannot have one coffee maker, vacuum, TV, or car that we share among several people. Each household needs their own set of each of these things. This framework is very compatible with, and supportive of, a capitalist economy where people need to consume more as well as more frequently.

Imposing certain norms on families around what is "best for families" is a more modern and recent idea than we might think, and the very concept of family varies across time and space—that is, throughout history and across the globe. Some people, like sociologist Brigitte Berger, have argued that nuclear families are better suited to an industrial age versus an agricultural one and that they also tend to be more child-centered. Others have highlighted the difficulties modern nuclear families have in providing enough care for children, particularly with pressures on both adults to work long hours, given the precarious financial situation most families find themselves in under capitalism. However, as always, we believe that nothing is as binary as it might seem. This is less about which type of family structure is best—nuclear or extended, for example—and more about understanding where some of these ideas come from so that we can make more intentional choices about what "family" means to us.

Part of colonialism and white supremacy is dictating what is "right," and nurturing a dichotomous mindset of right/wrong ways to do family, raise children, have relationships, and so on. In this book, we want to make sure we don't further promote this mindset. We're not trying to tell you how to do relationships "right." Rather, we want to invite you into deeper engagement with the very idea of what relationships are, so that you can find your own pathway through this maze, whatever that might be. However, we believe that to imagine where we're going, we need to understand where we've come from. On that note, let's take a moment to slow down and reflect on our own history and knowledge.

What we learned about families is probably largely dependent on a number of factors, including where we were brought up, by whom, and when. No systems or structures can step out of culture or be neutral and independent from historical, social, and political influences. This means that we might have very different ideas of family, as well as relationships in general, if we were brought up in a more individualistic culture compared to a more collectivistic one. This is a difference that we—MJ and Alex—have experienced and negotiated even between us, given that we were brought up in two very different countries and cultures. As we said in Chapter 1, we can't take for granted that when we use certain words, like "relationships" or "families," we mean the same thing. We carry not only our own stories and experiences but the legacies of our ancestors, some of whom are, at times, both colonial and colonized.

**Reflection point: What have we learned about families throughout history?**

Take a moment to think about what you've learned about families throughout history whether in school, through movies, books, or any other learning process you engaged in, especially growing up. Have families always been the same? Did you learn that certain ways of doing family were "primitive" or somehow "less evolved" or "not as good"? When you learned about families from school, books, documentaries, movies, and so on, did you see your own family structure reflected back to you? If so, was that family structure depicted in a positive, negative, or neutral light? How did what you learned about families influence the way you view the idea of family today? Take your time to reflect on some or all of these questions as well as coming up with your own questions. You can jot your reflections down in writing or through drawing, collages, mindmaps, song, or whatever process appeals to you at this moment.

## Individualist and collectivist ways of doing relationships

The way we understand our relationships is likely to be strongly influenced by where our culture of origin falls on the spectrum of individualistic to collectivist. For those of us, like Alex, who experienced emigrating as a young adult, or earlier, we might also be strongly influenced by the culture we immigrated into. Others might also have complex relationships with culture if they have multiple cultural heritages and/or are interracial adoptees, and so on. While cultural, historical, and sociopolitical influences are important to consider, they can also be complex, confusing, and hard to disentangle for many of us.

For now, let's take a moment to define what we mean by collectivist and individualistic cultures. Collectivist cultures generally tend to prioritize societal needs and norms over individual needs and desires. Within such cultures, families and communities are central, and identities might be more collective than individual. Individualistic cultures, on the other hand, tend to prioritize individual needs, desires, and wellbeing over the wellbeing of the collective. Many cultures have a mix of collectivist and individualistic values and beliefs, with some cultures being closer to one or the other end of the spectrum. One country can also include multiple cultures. For example, in Italy, the southern regions are more collectivistic culturally, whereas the north is more individualistic. Neither culture is good or bad, right or wrong; rather, they portray different ways of relating to self, others, and the ecosystems we're part of.

This influences the way we do relationships. Relationships, for example, tend to be more central in collectivistic cultures. But they might also have more social norms and rules or "joyful obligations," as mentioned in Chapter 1, than individualistic cultures where the autonomy of the individual is viewed as paramount. This is sometimes even to the detriment of relationships and social wellbeing. Most Indigenous cultures promote foundational, relational values around interdependence, for example.

Focusing in on settler-colonialism, the desire to replace Indigenous populations means not just overt, violent genocide often but also the erasure of language, culture, family structures, community values, and so on. This process is ongoing, as we can see, for example, in Turtle Island (what we currently call North America). We live, in the words of Lorenzo Veracini, "in a settler colonial global present." Many Indigenous people have also migrated for survival and often assimilated into whiteness, at least on some level, such as many Sami folks who migrated to the US and Sicilians who migrated to a number of places, including the US.

## Control and relationships

Colonial practices are usually based in control—of bodyminds, language, land, culture, economy, and so on. This control includes defining and controlling relationships as well, especially those relationships that are linked to social structures, such as familial ones, as well as relationships to land. As Alex points out in their book *Gender Trauma*, the promulgation of the "Doctrine of Discovery" by the Catholic Church, around the middle of the 15th century onwards, also justified such control. This doctrine enabled and encouraged Christian Europeans to take possession of any land not under the ruling of a Christian European monarch, since only Christian European men (and it was just men) could be considered legitimate citizens and, as such, fully human.

The impact of this doctrine is still felt by Indigenous populations globally in a number of ways. Once we start defining who counts as human and who doesn't, we've created a split that enables us not only to dehumanize people but also to own them. It's no accident that colonial ideas of marriage historically include ownership of women, for example. Even though we might think we have moved away from those ideas, they live on in our customs and practices. In English, traditional marriage vows include the following terminology:

"I, ___, take thee, ___, to be my wedded husband/wife/spouse, to have and to hold, from this day forward, for better, for worse, for richer, for poorer, in sickness and in health, to love and to cherish, till death do us part, according to God's holy ordinance; and thereto I pledge thee my faith [or] pledge myself to you."

The terms love and cherish were introduced about 100 or so years ago to replace the language of "obey," which referred to the Bible's passage in Ephesians 5:21–24 that addresses wives obeying and submitting to their husbands since they were head of the family, just like Christ is the head of the Church. While many people nowadays choose to write their own wedding vows, these vows can still be witnessed at many marriage ceremonies.

All of this can seem quite heavy, and maybe even unexpected in a book on relationships, but we believe that to understand our current experiences and imagine new ones, we need to understand where we've been and where certain beliefs and practices come from. In addition to often imposing Christianity, colonial practices also pair with white supremacy in legitimizing control over racialized groups. White supremacy is an ideological system that further enforces dehumanization and ownership through carceral logic.

## Carceral logic: Policing and punishing

The term carceral logic can be understood as the upholding of systems such as the law, policing, the judicial system, prisons, and so on. It can also be understood as the internalized ideological system that invites us to police, judge, and punish ourselves and others if we're not being "good" or if we don't follow societal rules. For example, blaming someone who has been raped because they were intoxicated and/or were wearing "provocative" clothes when the rape happened is an example of carceral logic. The victim didn't police their bodymind and behaviors "adequately," so it makes sense that they would be "punished" by this happening to them. Carceral logic is often also used when parenting, especially if that is how we were parented ourselves. If a child does not obey rules and/or expectations, they are punished either by the family, or the family is punished by the system—if a child is truant, for example.

We hope that you can begin to understand how these interconnected, colonial practices impact relationships of all kinds. When we feel the need to control how others respond to us, or feel ownership of our beloveds, or want to punish people in our lives who deviated from our expectations, we're likely playing out internalized colonial, supremacist, carceral ways of being in relationship to one another. Colonial ways of relating are controlling, contracting, limiting, and punishing, and are ultimately fear- and shame-based (see Chapter 4 for more on the impact of shame). We've illustrated some common colonial ways of relating in this image. You might like to reflect on how the forms of colonialism we described at the start of this section are present in this example, and in other common relationship dynamics.

Figure 2.2: Colonialism in intimate relationships

If you're recognizing some of these traits within yourselves, please go slowly and be gentle with yourselves. We also have our own struggles with seeing these ways of relating within ourselves, while also holding the pain and wound of colonization within and between ourselves. Go slowly, take deep breaths, and try to be as caring and compassionate towards yourself as you are able to at this moment in time. You're not alone. We're in this together, and in the next section we'll share some of what we have learned about practicing how to challenge those ideologies and patterns within and between ourselves. This is the work of a lifetime, or maybe even several ones, but we do believe it's essential work.

We don't know about you, but we definitely need a little break at this point. It's not easy to reckon with historical legacies, no matter where we fall within those histories, or whether it's something we've considered before or that is new to us.

For this slow-down moment, we would like to invite you to connect with someone who can offer you support for whatever thoughts, emotions, sensations, images, and/or behaviors that might be coming up for you. This can be a friend, therapist, healer, bodyworker, family member, colleague, or even someone who is reading this book at the same time as you because maybe you're in a class or book club together.

We understand that it's not easy to reach out to someone when we're struggling, and yet this is how we practice connecting and deepening into our relationships.

If reaching out to an external person feels like too much right now, that's okay. Could you reach out to an internal person or part instead? Could you receive support from an animal companion or a beloved greenblood, such as a tree, or maybe a body of water that is precious or even sacred to you? Is there an ancestor who loves you beyond all reason, as our friend Donald Engstrom-Reese would say, who can comfort you in this moment?

Connection is always available to us because we are interdependent and essential parts of the ecosystem of life, but we might not always feel that connection. Let's practice re-membering our connections within and around ourselves. It's okay if we don't feel very skilled in doing this at first. It's called practice for a reason. We're indeed not going to be good at this straightaway. We're here practicing with you and not being very good at it either.

When you're ready, pick this book up again and remember that you can go at your own pace, take what resonates, and leave the rest. Don't worry if you forget; we'll keep reminding you.

## 2.3 DECOLONIZING RELATIONSHIPS

The word decolonizing has been increasingly used in recent years for describing the process not only of colonizers withdrawing from colonized countries but of all of us addressing the colonizing ways in which we think and relate, and the restricted forms of knowledge that we tend to draw upon. Several scholars and activists, such as Dr. Ijeoma Nnodim Opara, Dr. Nayantara Sheoran Appleton, Dr. Eve Tuck, Dr. K. Wayne Yang, Dr. Kyle Powys Whyte, and Dr. Autumn Asher BlackDeer, to name but a few, have criticized colonizers for using the term in a more intellectual way. While we're wary of this, we've decided to keep it here since it seems the most apt word to describe what we're trying to talk about in this section, and because we do believe decolonization to be essential.

First of all, let us be clear that decolonization is not an intellectual exercise—it's an everyday practice. We also don't know who you, the readers, are. Some of you might be deep into this work, some of you might be Indigenous, some of you might have never heard the word "decolonize." We understand that we cannot possibly meet all of your needs, so we hope you bear with us as we navigate these waters together. As we said, this work is an everyday practice of critically examining what we have learned within dominant—likely colonial—culture, evaluating the impact of this learning, unpacking it, and then living by different principles in intentional ways.

Decolonizing is not about romanticizing a mythical, pre-colonial past but rather, we think, understanding where we've been, where we are, and engaging in interdependence to restore relationships on an interpersonal and global level. We cannot restore these relationships without also engaging in the reality of Indigenous folks globally often not having access to or sovereignty over their territories.

This means that we cannot talk about decolonizing relationships if we're not willing to engage with the land back movements on Turtle Island, or attempts to make reparations for enslavement and colonization, for example. We cannot decolonize anything if we're not listening to Indigenous folks where we are, and on a global level as well. We need to recognize that the current wealth of many European countries is rooted in a history of centuries of colonization of other countries around the world. In addition to stealing land, colonization also included extracting resources, and enslaving people or coercing them into unpaid or low-paid labor. There were frequently extremely violent responses to any forms of resistance. These histories are often disguised and disavowed by the countries who took part in them, especially those where the colonization happened a long way away. The ongoing impacts of these histories—for example, on debt, immigration policies, racism, health disparities between racial groups, and unequal impacts of climate crisis—are often denied or downplayed. We need to ask ourselves how we have come to be geographically where we are, if we're not Indigenous to where we live, as well as asking ourselves how the place where we live came to be as prosperous as it is. Then we need to ask ourselves how we can engage with that reality in meaningful, practical ways.

Relationships to place and land need to be part of this work. In fact, we dare say this might be the foundation of this work. Wherever we are on the globe, we're on Indigenous land, so where are you and how have you come to be where you are, and what do you want to do with that knowledge and awareness? As scholars Tuck and Yang wrote over a decade ago, "Decolonization is not a metaphor," and when we treat it as such, we only ensure the perpetuation of colonial systems under the guise of liberation.

## ACTIVITY: EXAMINING OUR RELATIONSHIP WITH LAND

Let's take a moment to put some of these ideas into practice. Please take some time not only to think about but possibly also to research and record your answers, in whichever way feels most accessible to you at this moment.

Do you know who the traditional custodians of the land where you live are? Are you Indigenous to where you live or not? If not, how have you come to be where you are? If you are, are you also within Indigenous community or have you been displaced from language, culture, and community through colonialism? If you are not Indigenous to where you live, what is your relationship to Indigenous nation(s) there and their current struggles? Is there a sense, where you live, that the land "belongs" only to certain people and that "others" should be prevented from entering it? What is your relationship to lands that have been colonized by the nation you live in?

Perhaps your family emigrated from those lands in the past, or you have visited them, or you know little about them? Are there movements to give land back or to protect the water from oil pipes and other ongoing, colonial raping of land, such as fracking? Are there movements to encourage governments and organizations to cancel debt and make reparations to people who have been colonized, enslaved, or exploited by those who lived in your nation in the past, or to recognize and address the continued legacy of these practices?

If you're not Indigenous to where you live, and/or as you learn more about the history of colonialism in your country, you might notice discomfort, numbness, disconnection, pain, shame, anger, revulsion, and any number of other feelings. We know it's hard, but if you can, and with support, please try to stay with those feelings rather than shy away from them. You might even notice trauma reactions such as fight, flight, freeze, or fawn (see section 3.2). Try to notice these feelings and/ or trauma reactions with as much curiosity and non-judgment as you can manage at this moment.

When you're ready, and after doing your research if needed, if you're not Indigenous to place, is there a locally led, Indigenous movement for land back, water protection, independence from colonial rule, or something else that you could become more involved with or that you feel able to support? In the US, in some places, as part of the land back movement, there are initiatives to pay a voluntary land tax, sometimes described as paying "rent," to Indigenous nations (https://nativegov.org/news/voluntary-land-taxes). In other countries, there might be very different, yet connected, movements. How can you commit to local Indigenous movements or to raising awareness of the ongoing legacies of colonialism where you live? What relationships do you want to nurture to heal your connections with land and sovereign nations?

While decolonizing is not a metaphor and entails concrete action and starting from relationships with land and sovereign tribal nations, we also want to talk about decolonizing relationships within the larger ecosystem we're part of and with one another. We started discussing this in section 1.4 when we distinguished not only between transactional and non-transactional relationships but also identified four characteristics of affirming and nurturing relationships: differentiation, mutuality, care, and compassion.

As we said earlier, there is no going back to a romanticized, pre-colonial past, and even imagining one is in itself a colonial practice, but we can address our foundational values and belief systems when it comes to relationships. We believe that nurturing interdependence, instead of rugged individualism, for example, can be supportive for many of us since it highlights the paradox of being autonomous human beings while also needing one another.

## The bumpy road of unlearning and re-learning

There is definitely a lot of unlearning and re-learning to do, as well as concrete actions to take, on this journey of decolonization. One of the things we've noticed is, for example, how white Anglo folks especially might separate some of their non-normative practices from those of Black and Brown folks globally.

Polyamory or ethical non-monogamies are vivid examples of this. Even though non-monogamy is actually practiced by a global majority, polyamory or the larger umbrella of "ethical non-mo-nogamy" is presented as being completely separate from polygamy, especially if the latter is happening within a religious context. Often the implication is that polygamy is not ethical, or it is exploitative, especially of women, whereas ethical non-monogamy or specifically polyamory is viewed as a "healthy" version of having multiple partners.

The reality, though, is that systems of power, privilege, and oppression can and are still at play within "ethically" non-monogamous relationships. In addition, when some people question whether women can consent to polygamy within a patriarchal, religious framework, they seem to conveniently forget that many women consent to monogamy within a patriarchal Christian supremacist framework, which is pervasive in dominant—colonial—culture. However, the latter scenario doesn't seem as "disturbing" to many people compared to various types of polygamy. Nathan Rambukkana has written about the implications of these polyamory/polygamy hierarchies, and Kevin Patterson and others have written about the ways in which white supremacy shows up in polyamorous communities.

Decolonizing relationships, then, also means challenging dichotomies that view certain relational containers, types, or processes as being more legitimate than others, or only legitimate in certain (Anglo, white) contexts. As you can hopefully start to glimpse, decolonizing can also not be separated from the struggle for Black liberation, or the struggle for body autonomy—including trans rights as human rights—or from a disability justice framework (see the image that follows). The roots of our oppressions are indeed intertwined and deeply steeped in colonial narratives. Cross-movement solidarity is not only essential but foundational.

Cross-movement solidarity is something that, for example, the Black Panther movement of the late 1960s into the very early 1980s understood and practiced. While born to counter police brutality, in Oakland, California, in what we currently know as the United States, the Black Panther movement became not only global but also focused on other struggles for liberation on occupied territories, such as Palestine. The movement didn't just focus on countering police brutality by

# DISABILITY JUSTICE PRINCIPLES

## SUSTAINABILITY

PACING OURSELVES, OUR RELATIONSHIPS, AND OUR COMMUNITIES SO THAT EVERYONE CAN CONTINUE TO TAKE PART. **E.G.** GOING AT THE PACE OF THE SLOWEST PERSON WHEN TALKING, TRAVELING, OR THROUGHOUT A RELATIONSHIP.

AND RELATIONSHIPS!

LEADERSHIP OF THE MOST IMPACTED

WE NEED TO SCHEDULE DATE NIGHTS.

ONLY IF IT'S OK TO RESCHEDULE WHEN I NEED TO!

AUTISTIC PRIDE

WHAT DO YOU DO?

I TRY NOT TO DEFINE MY WORTH BY MY CAPACITY TO PRODUCE, AND YOU?

ANTI-CAPITALIST POLITICS

## →RECOGNIZING WHOLENESS←

VALUING PEOPLE FOR WHO THEY ARE RATHER THAN FOR WHAT THEY PRODUCE, RECOGNIZING THAT WE'RE ALL COMPLEX WHOLE BEINGS. **E.G.** NOT QUESTIONING WHY SOMEONE WOULD CHOOSE A DISABLED PARTNER, OR DESEXUALIZING DISABLED PEOPLE.

## COLLECTIVE ACCESS

SHARING RESPONSIBILITY TO MAKE SURE PEOPLE CAN ARTICULATE AND MEET THEIR ACCESS NEEDS IN A COMMUNITY OR RELATIONSHIP, **E.G.** BY CULTIVATING CULTURES WHERE ALL OUR VULNERABILITIES AND STRENGTHS ARE WELCOMED AND RESPECTED.

I CAN'T DO MANUAL LABOR.

INTERDE

Figure 2.3a: Disability justice principles

# COMMITMENT TO CROSS-DISABILITY SOLIDARITY

ENSURING THAT PARTICIPATION IN A RELATIONSHIP, COMMUNITY, OR EVENT IS ACCESSIBLE TO ALL. **E.G.** INCLUDING DISABILITY RELATED TO NEURODIVERGENCE, MOBILITY, COGNITIVE CAPACITY, SENSORY SENSITIVITY, CHRONIC ILLNESS, MENTAL HEALTH, ETC.

INTERSECTIONALITY

ORGANIZING

COMMITMENT TO CROSS-MOVEMENT

RECOGNIZING THAT OPENING THINGS UP FOR SOME CAN CLOSE THINGS DOWN FOR OTHERS. DETERMINING TO WORK TOGETHER FOR ALL. **E.G.** MARRIAGE EQUALITY FOR SAME GENDER COUPLES MUST ENSURE THAT DISABLED PEOPLE DON'T LOSE BENEFITS IF THEY MARRY.

I CAN DO THAT, BUT I NEED HELP WITH ADMIN TASKS!

COLLECTIVE LIBERATION!

PENDENCE

Figure 2.3b: Disability justice principles

keeping the police in check, by openly carrying weapons and training people in self-defense; they also provided free breakfast to children within the community, created education programs, provided free community-based healthcare clinics, contributed to introducing Chinese medicine and acupuncture in the Bronx through a detox program they founded, and nurtured and strengthened solidarity across class struggles. These are, however, not the stories that most (Anglo, white) folks in North America would likely connect to the Black Panther movement. It's in the interest of capitalist, top-down regimes to separate our struggles from one another and to sabotage cross-movement solidarity and liberation strategies.

## Critical relationality

In order to be able to practice cross-movement solidarity though, we need to know how to do relationships outside of capitalist, patriarchal, colonial, and racist frameworks. This is not easy, and even the Black Panther movement struggled with this at times, as far as we are aware, which is very understandable given how counter-cultural their initiatives and beliefs were.

In our efforts to better understand how to practice new ways of doing relationships, we turn once more to Indigenous scholars, such as Sisseton-Wahpeton Oyate scholar Dr. Kim TallBear. Dr. TallBear has, among other work, addressed topics such as decolonizing sexuality and relationships, moving towards what she named as "Indigenous or critical relationality." In our understanding of her work, Dr. TallBear challenges not just settler-colonial concepts of monogamy but also those of kinship, especially with "other-than-human bodies," such as water and land.

What would it look like for us to not live in scarcity, to not hoard resources, to not try to control people or other-than-human beings, but to explore what Dr. TallBear calls "sustainable intimacies"? These are intimacies that are focused on mutuality, care, respect, and healing, among other things. We have no answers, but we know that we've found it helpful to challenge our own relationships with other-than-human kin such as land, water, greenbloods, and redbloods, as well as to question everything we thought we knew about relationships and families.

Part of questioning everything has also led us to deepen our relationship with abolitionist thinking. In this realm, we're not just talking about the abolition of the prison-industrial complex, or of geopolitical borders—although we do also think of these as essential and intertwined—but also of abolition of the family, as explored by feminist thinker Sophie Lewis.

In a way, Lewis's work is not separate or dissimilar to that of Dr. TallBear since she seems to call for larger networks of care beyond the limitation of biological family units. In fact, it just seems to us to be similar work approached from a slightly different angle—that is, that of radical feminism instead of Indigenous critical relationality.

For Lewis, the nuclear family reproduces politics that are oppressive to women who are often reduced to their ability to give birth to babies and nurture children. This is particularly dangerous for people of color, especially Black people in the US, given maternal mortality rates. This system also alienates queer children, while continuing to nurture the reproduction of existing systems of power, privilege, and oppression. Regardless of whether you agree or not with the idea of abolishing the nuclear family, we believe there is value in exploring these ideas to challenge what we've learned or have been indoctrinated to believe is "natural and good."

What becomes possible when we let go of the fixed state of what is family and what are relationships? What can love become, create, or transform into? It's to this that we turn in our next section.

## 2.4 DOING LOVE DIFFERENTLY

Many people who have written about relationships over the years have differentiated between "love" as it is often conceptualized and expressed in dominant culture and the kind of love that we might want to move towards.

We could think of such a move as shifting from the kind of disconnected individualistic, colonialist, capitalist, supremacist way of relating that we've just explored to a more interconnected, decolonized, anti-capitalist, and/or abolitionist way.

Returning to the multi-level understanding of relationships that we introduced in section 1.3, we might think beyond the sociocultural level of individualistic, colonial, capitalist, supremacist culture. We might consider the move as one from disconnection to interconnection at *all* levels. For example, this would include interconnectedness with ourselves and our bodies and feelings, with other people, with community and humanity in general, and with other beings, the world, spirit, and/or the divine—however we define that.

In this section, we'll say a bit more about how people have conceptualized these two ways of relating. Then we'll explore how it's more complex than trying to shift from the "bad" way of relating into the "good" way. Indeed, imposing a bad/good binary hierarchy, and trying to force ourselves and others to eradicate one and embrace the other, just takes us back to a colonialist, capitalist, supremacist mindset of policing and punishing ourselves! But what might the alternative be to this? That's what we'll consider here, and then draw upon during the rest of the book.

## Two ways of relating

Many writers, philosophers, therapists, and spiritual teachers have written about love and relationships in similar ways. Here, we're drawing on the ones we're familiar with, who come from traditions like existentialism, Black feminism, and Buddhist philosophy. However, you may well be familiar with other authors and teachers who say something similar, so please do add those in yourself if you are. Here's our—necessarily brief—overview of some of these ideas.

- *Having vs. being love:* In his books *The Art of Loving* and *To Have or To Be*, psychologist Erich Fromm distinguished

"having love," where we give love to get something back and/
or become enmeshed with others, and "being love," where
we can be both separate and connected, respecting ourselves
and others equally.

- *Love as a noun vs. love as a verb:* In her book *All About Love*,
included in the further resources in the previous chapter, and
several others, bell hooks distinguished between love as a
noun (or feeling) and love as a verb (or action). She suggested
that love shouldn't be defined by the feelings we associate
with falling in love, for example, but rather it's all about *how*
we interact. Particularly, it's about whether we treat others
and ourselves as equally valuable, rather than valuing one
more highly than the other.

- *Objectifying vs. mutual:* Existentialists like Simone de Beau-
voir and Martin Buber differentiated between objectifying
love, where we treat others as a thing for us, or as an "it,"
and mutual love, where we value others as equal beings, and
treat them as a "you."

- *Dependent/independent vs. interdependent:* Many Black feminist and disability justice authors, like Audre Lorde and Mia
Mingus, talk about a move from being either dependent on
others for our sense of ourselves as valid/valuable, or claiming
we could be ruggedly independent and not need others at
all, to recognizing that we're all interdependent, and building
relationships of care and solidarity in recognition of this.

- *Attachment/aversion vs. inter/connection:* Some Buddhist
authors, like Martine Batchelor and Thich Nhat Hanh, distinguish between relationships where we're relating through
attachment (trying to grasp them and pull them closer) or
aversion (trying to avoid them or push them away), and
those where we're connected with another and present to
however they—and we—actually are. When we're connected,

the whole self/other split may fall away entirely, and we may experience ourselves as one with (all) others and the world.

—  *Inauthentic vs. authentic:* Many therapists and practitioners distinguish between relationships where we present some kind of false self, perform a role, and/or hide aspects of who we are from those in which we're honest, open, and able to be vulnerable. Research links the latter with better physical and mental health.

Hopefully, you can see that all these ideas are describing something similar—a way of relating that prizes mutuality, compassion, and interdependence—albeit there are differences between them, and some of them are focused on different levels of understanding (e.g. more on the sociocultural level, the relational level, or the existential/spiritual level).

Thinking back to section 1.4, you might see the kind of relating that these authors are turning us towards as that which includes the values we set out there: differentiation, mutuality, compassion, and care. In fact, many of these authors use those very words.

## Conditional *and* unconditional

Sometimes people use the shorthand of "conditional and unconditional" to summarize these two different forms of love, or relating. Conditional would include all those kinds of relating where we're in it to get something for ourselves, or where we'll only relate well with others if they act in certain ways. Unconditional would be relating that doesn't require anything of the other, or ourselves, where we value their freedom and treat them well, no matter what.

However, there are several problems with the idea that we—and everybody else—should move from conditional to unconditional ways of relating.

The first is that, as we saw in section 1.3, on every level of human experience we are pulled strongly towards conditional modes of relating. If we expect ourselves, and others, to easily be able to move from one to the other, we are setting everyone up to fail. We really need to recognize what we're up against when it comes to relationships. Trauma of all kinds, in particular, makes it incredibly difficult—if not impossible—to relate unconditionally with others, because we develop vital survival strategies to protect ourselves from danger. These often involve treating ourselves and others in conditional ways (people pleasing or regarding others as a potential threat, for example). We can't drop such vital survival strategies until we're able—and supported—to develop alternatives to them.

Unconditional love is often misunderstood as meaning not having boundaries, sacrificing ourselves for the other, or accepting abusive behaviors. Actually, a key aspect of unconditional relating is emotional, psychological, and physical safety. This includes being clear about where we—and others—are at, and being able to move away from abusive dynamics. As bell hooks taught us, love and abuse cannot coexist.

It's easy for us to fall into searching for unconditional love in our adult relationships because we didn't receive it—or enough of it—early in life. Ironically, this is a very conditional way to treat other people! We're looking for them to be the "good parents" we never had, and to make up for what we lacked or lost as children. It often means that we find it hard to acknowledge, or bear, any of their inevitable faults or failings and then flip to seeing them as "bad" and rejecting them if they demonstrate those. We'll say more in the next chapter (section 3.4) about how caregiver–child relationships differ from adult–adult relationships. Even trained therapists cannot provide unconditional love to their clients at all times (in fact, moments of rupture and repair are vital in such relationships). However, the boundaries of the therapeutic situation enable therapists to relate more at that unconditional end of the spectrum, in order to help with what we might call "reparenting." But looking for that kind of parental—or cosmic—love from adult humans all the time is unhelpful to us and to them.

Many of the authors just mentioned recognize that we may well only experience fleeting moments of unconditional relating: precious glimpses where the self/other split falls away and reaching out to another being feels just as if we were reaching out to ourselves. When we realize that a lot of the relationships we've experienced have been conditional—perhaps in highly non-consensual ways—and when we recognize the oppressive cultures which these ways of relating developed in, it's easy to flip to insisting that others—and ourselves—immediately start relating in unconditional ways. Really, when we do that, we're demanding that everyone immediately becomes something like a fully enlightened being, or even a divine being!

One of the things MJ has been doing in recent years is working with their "inner critic" self, Morgan. Here's Morgan's reflection on this:

Morgan: "I'm the aspect of MJ who has always felt that we weren't good enough and tried to push ourselves to be better, often with violent self-attacking messages. As we worked with me, I realized that I'm also the aspect of us who carries the rage of all the assaults and other non-consensual ways in which we've been treated by others. As I came forward, I realized that I didn't trust others at all and, in some ways, was demanding that they be "all good" and rejecting them if they couldn't be, just as I was demanding that I become "all good" and attacking myself if I couldn't be. I realized that, in a way, I wanted to be like a god—all knowing, all powerful, all good, present everywhere, and immortal. I couldn't handle it when people pointed out things I didn't know, when I couldn't control things, when anyone suggested I'd behaved badly, when I couldn't do All the Things, or when I got sick. Any of those things felt entirely my fault and my responsibility. Perhaps many people—particularly in our dominant culture, and who have experienced trauma—have an aspect of them who feels—and acts—in this way. I'm still working on allowing myself—and everyone else—to be human."

So should we give up on moving towards more unconditional, connected, mutual ways of relating? Of course not! As you'd expect from the authors of *Life Isn't Binary*, it's more about moving to a place where we embrace the capacities for conditional and unconditional modes of relating.

Luke Wreford writes that many of the challenges we face—from interpersonal relationships to global injustice and ecological crises—can be understood as consequences of the *dominance* of the conditional way of viewing ourselves and others. The solution isn't to reject that way entirely and replace it with the unconditional way of viewing ourselves and others—if that was even possible. He suggests that both ways are valid and vital, and that they're actually complementary rather than contradictory. If we hold them simultaneously, or synthesize them, they can bring out the best in each of them, and minimize their weaknesses.

We might imagine it as holding the conditional view of ourselves and others *within* the unconditional view. For example, this would enable us to hold the uniqueness of our identities, and the differences between us (conditional), within the deep knowledge of our interconnectedness and the fact that we're all equally valuable (unconditional). It would enable us to pursue our needs and dreams in life (conditional), while acknowledging others' needs and dreams as just as important, and searching for mutual ways forward rather than competitive ones (unconditional).

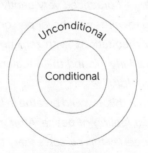

*Figure 2.4: Holding the conditional within the unconditional*

Trauma author Bonnie Badenoch expresses a similar idea when she talks about moving away from the kind of "left brain" supremacy, which is so common in dominant culture, with its emphasis on structure, analytical thinking, problem solving, making judgments, etc. She conceptualizes this move as one where the "left brain" instead becomes the *emissary* of the "right brain," with its capacity to be present, sensitive, relational, and so on.

That might still sound a bit vague, so let's think about a couple of ways it might work in practice in relationships. In these activities, MJ will give an example of how they've done these relationship practices—one solo and one in relation with others—and then you can have a go at something similar, or adapt it in ways that might work for you.

## ACTIVITY 1: HOLDING THE CONDITIONAL IN THE UNCONDITIONAL

Robin writes: *I'm the aspect of MJ who can become very frightened of other people, because of trauma! It can be hard indeed for me to recognize that, despite how much I want to relate with others in more unconditional ways, this just isn't possible when I'm in a terror—or freeze—trauma response. For example, during lockdown I became very scared of several people, to the point where I just had to avoid them, which is really not in our values. Instead of continuing to give myself a hard time—which is conditional, and which doesn't help the fear to diminish any—I practiced very gently going towards more unconditional relating towards whichever person I was currently finding triggering—in our meditations, with zero pressure to change my actual behavior. Particularly I found the Tonglen practice we learned from Pema Chödrön helpful.*

*In a simple version of this, I would breathe in the feeling of my own fear, and breathe out a feeling of peace. After a while, I'd breathe in the fear that I knew underlay this person's scary behavior, and breathe out peace towards them too. There were times when this just calmed our bodymind down a little, and times where it did diminish some of the fear over several weeks or months. There were even a couple of times where I was able to get to the point where I could relate more compassionately towards this person in reality, recognizing the kinship in our vulnerability to others.*

We invite you to try sitting for a while around another person—or being—that you find challenging, and struggle to relate to in an unconditional way. It's best to choose someone a little difficult for you, rather than actually stirring up a trauma response, initially. Can you breathe in the tough feelings you're having about that person on the inbreath, and breathe out something more compassionate or peaceful towards yourself on the outbreath? If that works, after a while, might you breathe in whatever difficult feelings you imagine could be underlying that person's behavior, and breathe out peace or calmness for them? If this doesn't work for you, you could try journaling a bit about your feelings, and then about what you imagine theirs to be. Or you could move your body around with your feelings, and then around what you imagine theirs to be. Whatever works for you.

Pema Chödrön emphasizes that it's just as important and helpful to feel the stuck or blocked feelings when you *can't* manage to feel more caring and connected towards another person, or yourself, as it is to feel the feelings of compassion and kinship flowing when you can. Again, it's not about saying that unconditional is better than conditional and trying to force yourself to feel the "good" one! If you feel blocked, scared, judgmental, or numb, you can feel for yourself and all the other people who're feeling just like you right now!

## ACTIVITY 2: EXPANDING THE CONDITIONAL INTO THE UNCONDITIONAL

James writes: *I'm the aspect of MJ who does a lot of the administration and boundary-setting these days. Another thing we've found very useful through our recent trauma time is to ask ourselves, when there's* a difficulty with somebody, "What is the distance with this person where we'd feel able to be warm and open?" When we noticed that we could not be differentiating, mutual, caring, and compassionate towards another person, or towards ourselves in relationship with them (see section 1.4), we'd step back until we reached a point where it was possible.

With some people, this involved seeing them less frequently or communicating only in writing for a while, or some combination of the two. With some people, it felt possible to explicitly say that we were doing this, and why, whereas with others we had to find ways of communicating it that we felt they'd be able to hear and/or we felt able to say at those times (giving ourselves permission to be where we were, even when we couldn't be entirely honest and open).

For example, there was one person who we hadn't yet built a trusting relationship with, who had asked to see us again quite soon, and Robin felt he had to say "yes." After sitting with his fear of what would happen if he refused, I messaged them saying we were very low on energy at the moment (also true), so we would check in with them again once we'd emerged from that, likely in a couple of months. Keeping more to that frequency from then on, we noticed that fears receded, and we felt keen to see that person when we did spend time with them.

There was a close friend who Morgan felt resentment around: that they didn't want to spend enough time with us. After tuning in, Morgan was able to tell them that she was having these feelings of being unwanted by them, but knew they were her stuff and did not want to act on them, affirming that our friend's freedom was very important to us. Morgan and the friend agreed to keep sharing how they were feeling each time they saw each other, until that period had worked through. Morgan used the image from Greek mythology of the character tied to the mast of a ship so they couldn't act on their desires. She would keep speaking how she was feeling honestly, but would not let herself act on those feelings in a way that attempted to constrain our friend's freedom.

We invite you to return to a relationship that is currently a little challenging—while not tipping over into traumatic memories. Can you journal for a while, or chat with a friend, about the relationship *container* that might enable you to feel freer and/or safer in that relationship? What kinds of boundaries around the amount of time together, how you relate and communicate, expectations, or anything else might help you find a "distance at which you can be warm and open"—with that person and with yourself in relation to that person. You might try imagining that you asked for that container, and they agreed to it. How do you feel in your body when you imagine this? Of course, in reality, it is often a process of "hokey-pokey" to find that right container and/or boundaries for each relationship, and what that is will likely change over time.

We like the concept Vikki Reynolds writes about called the "zone of fabulousness," where, in relationships of all kinds, we agree to keep noticing when we've become a bit too enmeshed in some way, or a bit too distant, and keep dancing together to find the "zone of fabulousness" between the two.

**REMEMBER...** While there are many problems with the culturally dominant ways of understanding—and doing—relationships, and their roots in colonialism and other forms of oppression, most of us struggle to relate in connected and unconditional ways, much of the time. We need to have a lot of compassion for ourselves and for others about this (holding the conditional within the unconditional). Practicing critical relationality is not an easy feat, and we hope you can go slowly and be really kind with yourselves.

Over the rest of the book, we'll cover many, many more practices that you might find helpful for holding conditional relating within unconditional relating, as well as exploring how we might co-create more differentiated, mutual, caring, and compassionate ways of relating between us, and in communities of support for this.

## Further resources

For more on dominant cultural rules of relationships and why we might question them, see MJ's book:

- Barker, M.J. (2018). *Rewriting the Rules: An Anti Self-Help Guide to Love, Sex and Relationships*. London: Routledge.

To find out more about how relationship normativities link with gender and sexuality relationships, you can read this book alongside our other two books in this series: *How to Understand Your Gender* and *How to Understand Your Sexuality*. You might also want to check out Chapter 3 on relationships in our book *Life Isn't Binary*.

For more about the pressures on normative romantic/sexual relationships, see:

- Perel, E. (2006). *Mating in Captivity*. New York, NY: HarperCollins.

To read about the problems with escalator models of relationships, and alternatives to these, check out:

- Gahran, A. (2017). *Stepping Off the Relationship Escalator: Uncommon Love and Life*. Off the Escalator Enterprises.

Two great books about how colonialism and capitalism show up in intimate relationships, and what we might do about it, are:

- Rosa, S.K. (2022). *Radical Intimacy*. London: Pluto Press.
- Cassidy, M. (forthcoming). *Radical Relating*. North Atlantic Books.

For more on the history of colonialism and racial capitalism, their ongoing legacy of colonialism on all aspects of life, and resistances like the Black Panther movement, check out:

- Manjapra, K. (2020). *Colonialism in Global Perspective*. Cambridge: Cambridge University Press.

You can find more about decolonization not being a metaphor here:

- Tuck, E. and Yang, K.W. (2012). "Decolonization is not a metaphor." *Decolonization, Indigeneity, Education & Society 1*, 1, 1–40. https://jps.library.utoronto.ca/index.php/des/article/view/18630/15554

A list of the characteristics of white supremacy culture, along with much more useful material about white supremacy culture, can be found here:

- www.whitesupremacyculture.info/characteristics.html

You can learn more about colonization and Black sexualities in this book:

- Mauro, A. (2023). *The Colonization of Black Sexualities*. New York, NY: Routledge.

There's more about polyamory, polygamy, race, and culture in these books:

- Rambukkana, N. (2015). *Fraught Intimacies: Non/Monogamy in the Public Sphere*. Vancouver, BC: UBC Press.
- Patterson, K.A. (2018). *Love's Not Color Blind*. Victoria, BC: Thorntree Press.

You can find out more about rigid gender binaries as part of colonial legacies, including the impact on relationships, in:

- Iantaffi, A. (2020). *Gender Trauma: Healing Cultural, Social, and Historical Gendered Trauma*. London: Jessica Kingsley Publishers.

You can read more on the intersection of gender, queerness, race, mental health, and carceral logic in this memoir:

- Ziyad, H. (2021). *Black Boy Out of Time: A Memoir*. New York, NY: Little A.

Some of Dr. Kim TallBear's work on sustainable intimacies is here:

- Disrupting Settlement, Sex, and Nature. https://indigenousfutures. net/wp-content/uploads/2016/10/Kim_TallBear.pdf

Lewis's work on abolishing the nuclear family is here:

- Lewis, S. (2022). *Abolish the Family: A Manifesto for Care and Liberation*. New York, NY: Verso.

You can find the disability justice framework, which we adapted in this chapter, here:

- www.sinsinvalid.org/blog/10-principles-of-disability-justice

Bonnie Badenoch's book, referenced above, is:

- Badenoch, B. (2017). *The Heart of Trauma: Healing the Embodied Brain in the Context of Relationships*. New York, NY: W.W. Norton & Company.

The kind of non-dual approach to holding the conditional within the unconditional can also be found in Jeff Foster's writing, such as:

- Foster, J. (2016). *The Way of Rest: Finding the Courage to Hold Everything in Love*. Boulder, CO: Sounds True.

Vikki Reynolds writes more about the zone of fabulousness here:

- https://vikkireynolds.ca/wp-content/uploads/2019/09/2019-context-uk-zone-of-fabulousness-reynolds.pdf

# CHAPTER 3

# YOUR RELATIONSHIP BACKGROUND

In this chapter, we'll focus on your relationship background: what you learned about relationships growing up in the context you did. We'll turn to how this shapes your relationship patterns, and your ideas about relationships today, in the next chapter.

First, we'll think broadly about what you learned about relationships from the world around you, growing up. Then we'll explore how relationship patterns develop in our earliest relationships, touching on ideas like developmental trauma and attachment styles. After this, we'll consider how you were positioned in relation to various intersections of oppression, and the impact of this on your relationships. Finally, we'll focus on adult–child relationships, including the models of parenting that you experienced, and how this impacted your own relationship to parenting on an inner and outer level.

## 3.1 WHAT DID WE LEARN ABOUT RELATIONSHIPS?

Perhaps the main way that we learn the kind of cultural norms about relationships which we covered in the last chapter is through the relationships around us growing up. For many people, this means, initially, our caregivers, and the others who we interact with regularly when we are babies and toddlers. As we get older, it also encompasses the peers and adults who we meet in our neighborhoods, education systems, or similar. The messages about relationships that we receive through media like kids'TV or through the kinds of relationships depicted in school materials are another big influence.

So those cultural norms about relationships—some of which we've seen can be restrictive and problematic—are passed on *intergenerationally*. We tend to assume that the ways of doing relationships that we experience around us are just how things are done, unless we're given reason to question them. And later, we may well pass them on to others.

To give an example, many families have specific ways of celebrating key times of year (such as Passover, Eid, Christmas, or New Year). They may decorate the home in a particular way, eat certain foods, give gifts, play certain games, do things at certain times, etc. When we're older, we may have a strong investment in that way of doing things, which we encourage the people in our life to engage with, or we may continue to return home to take part in those rituals.

If everyone around you does pretty similar things, you may never question these kinds of models, and you may pass them on pretty unconsciously. However, many people—for many reasons—come to question them at some point. Continuing with our example, kids whose family has a different faith from the majority culture, or who grow up in multicultural contexts, may question this kind of family tradition. Later on, we may move away from it, if it wasn't a good experience in our home, or if our friends and/or partners in later life have very different ways of doing it.

We can't underestimate just how much we learn about every aspect of relationships in this way, growing up, and just what an impact this has on future relationships. In section 3.2, we'll focus specifically on what we learn about how to relate with ourselves and others. However, there are so many more things we pick up in this way which may seem the "familiar," "right," "natural," or "normal" way to do things, until we come across people who do them differently. We pick up relationship norms from the world around us growing up, from seemingly small things like how we stack the dishes, whether we eat together, and how—or whether—we talk around the dinner table, to huge impactful things like how we relate to money, whether—and how—we talk about our problems, or how we do or don't touch ourselves and others.

---

**Reflection point: Family/community rituals**

You might like to pick a ritual that you remember from your early years to reflect on in this way, such as around a festival or other significant occasion (like birthdays or rites of passage). How do you remember experiencing it back then? Any particular memories (positive and/or negative)? Have you retained the ritual, adapted it, passed it on, or not? What are your feelings about this?

---

## Relationship models

One massive impact on our relationships, growing up, are the models of relationships around us. This includes both the kind of relationship that is presented as a good, legitimate, normal relationship and the ways of relating that happen within those relationships.

For some people, the relationship models they're exposed to may be very narrow. They may spend time with very few adults other than their main caregivers, for example, or all of their peers and media influences may have very similar kinds of relationships. In dominant culture, you might think of the stereotypes of suburbia in TV sitcoms where every family is a mom, dad, two kids, and a dog!

Other people might be exposed to a wide range of relationship models. The adults around them may have many different kinds of relationships, and/or might change relationships over time. They may meet peers who come from different communities and do all kinds of relationships in different ways. Think of a diverse community, where many people have parents who are single and/ or in multiple partnerships (simultaneously, or over time), including same-gender and different-gender combinations, and relationships which are romantic/sexual, and those that are not. Also, people may be brought up in extended family and/or friendship networks, including adoptive families, kids in the foster system, etc.

Similarly, ways of doing relationships might be consistent or varied. Returning to our stereotypical sitcom suburbia, the ways of doing relationships there often privilege the married monogamous couple, which we talked about in section 2.1. It's expected that this couple will meet most of each other's needs, and that they'll remain romantically and sexually attracted to each other over time. Probably, the mom will do most of the childcare, and the dad will go out to work. The expectation will be of "happy families," so problems may have to be quickly dealt with or swept under the rug. Everyone will enjoy spending time together and communication will be easy.

For those who grow up with more varied models around them, they may see a diversity of ways of communicating, dividing labor, dealing with problems, expressing emotions, relaxing together, and so on in the relationships around them. For example, they may see relationships where people are conflict averse, ones where conflict is reacted to in volatile and frightening ways, ones where conflict means the end of a relationship, ones where people are not afraid of conflict and enjoy robust arguments to clear the air, ones where people have structured ways of ensuring that conflicts are addressed, and ones where people seek help from professionals to work through more challenging conflicts.

## Family systems

In addition to the models of relationships that we're exposed to—or not—another thing that significantly shapes our later relationships is the ways in which our family systems operated growing up. Here we're using "family" in its broadest form to encompass whatever combination of adults and/or children were around you during your childhood.

Again, for some people, this is relatively consistent—for example, for those who grow up living with a grandparent, a parent, three siblings, and a couple of cats (who made it to old age!). For other people, the constellation of people around them growing may go through one radical shift (e.g. due to an adoption, bereavement, or divorce) or may change regularly (e.g. if they grew up in more of a community setting, or if lodgers or partners of parents or siblings came and went relatively frequently). In section 3.3, we'll return to this diversity of ways of doing relationships and families.

As with relationship models, there are many ways in which family systems shape our relationships. For example, the presence or absence of other children in our homes and lives growing up can have a massive impact on how easy or challenging we find it to relate with peers. How positive or negative our experiences of adult–child relationships are will likely shape our relationship with authority figures and elders in later life. Whether we ever have a much younger child around will shape our later experiences of parenting-type roles (more on all this in section 3.4).

Our position in the family is one thing that can hugely shape the kinds of roles that we automatically take on in future relationships. For example, oldest siblings may become very used to caretaking others or taking the lead in relationships, or they may become very resentful of everyone expecting them to take responsibility! Youngest siblings may take for granted that they will be looked after, or struggle with always being babied. Some middle children may enjoy—or resent—their relatively invisible status in families, and may seek out later relationships where they are similarly quite free, or where people see them in ways they weren't seen growing up.

As you can tell from this description, there is no definitive way in which kids are treated due to their position in the family which we could generalize about, and no universal way in which that impacts later relationships. In some families, it may be the oldest child who is treated with kid gloves because they are the first, and later children who are treated more robustly. Also, with shifting families, we may experience different positions, such as going from being an only child to suddenly having siblings, or from being the oldest to one of the youngest. Gender often comes into it too, with the oldest/youngest boys or girls being treated in specific ways, regardless of whether they are the oldest or youngest in the family as a whole.

Family systems often treat us in other ways which may or may not be related to our position in the family. For example, adults may have favorites or develop particular relationships with children who are similar to them in some way (e.g. gender, temperament, interests). In many families, there are early expectations on kids to be "the x one" (e.g. "the clever one," "the easy one," "the vulnerable one," "the pretty one," "the sporty one," "the one who'll break my heart," "the rebellious one," etc.). Such expectations can be very difficult to shift once they are in place, and they can become stories we tell about ourselves which—again—have a huge impact on our later relationships. It can also be challenging if there is a family story that everyone is treated equally, when children feel these very different treatments and/or expectations. Also, different families value different things, so being positioned as "the clever one" or "the pretty one" may be a relatively positive or negative experience in different families, for example.

Finally, all groups—including families—can engage in scapegoating behaviors, where any group problems are blamed on a certain member who is then punished or rejected, unless everyone is alert to this possibility and works against it. A scapegoat role can attach to one person, or move around over time—for example, if the current scapegoat leaves. Again, painful early experiences like this can leave us vulnerable to such experiences in later relationships and/or relating in certain ways in an attempt to avoid it happening again.

## ACTIVITY: YOUR LEVELS OF INFLUENCE GROWING UP

We'll come back to exploring the influences and experiences that shaped your relationships in more depth in section 3.2. For now, sketch out some of the main messages you remember receiving about relationships at the following levels: culture, community and institutions, and family/people in my everyday life. For example, for culture, you might think about messages you received from media like magazines and/or TV shows; for community and institutions, you might think about your schooling and/or faith community; for family/people in my everyday life, you might think about the relationship role models around you growing up, and the systemic aspects we just explored.

You might want to particularly think about whether the different levels were aligned or not, remembering that they come with their own challenges. Having aligned models of relating at all levels can mean that we're never given cause to question them, but it can feel relatively comfortable, whereas having contradictory models can make it easier to question any "givens" about the right way of relating, but that can be a painful process and involve making tough choices or code switching.

You can put at the center the beliefs and understandings about relationships that you remember holding personally.

You can fill this out for your growing up in general, or focus on a particular age, or do it more than once for multiple ages.

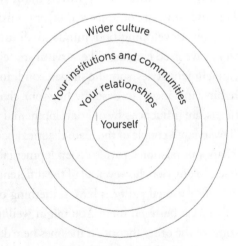

*Figure 3.1: Your levels of influence*

We'll come back to these levels of influence as they surround you in your life now in the next chapter. While it is useful to fill out these diagrams for the messages we learned about relationships, generally, growing up, they can also be useful for any specific aspect of relationships that comes up between you and another person. For example, if you find that you differ from a friend or partner in your expectations or assumptions about doing some aspect of relating, it could be very useful for you both to complete a diagram like this for that thing specifically, and then share them. For example, you could do it for a theme such as conflict, silence, home, money, cleaning, or caring for others when sick. What were the messages that you received from each level about this specific thing growing up?

## 3.2 GROWING UP IN RELATIONSHIP

Most of the main psychotherapy approaches agree that our experiences in our earliest relationships have a profound impact on our later patterns in terms of how we relate to ourselves, others, and beyond.

We learn from very early on that some emotional responses, behaviors, and ways of relating are approved of, or rewarded, by those around us, and some are disapproved of, or punished in some way. This shapes our developing bodyminds in all kinds of ways. Different writers have used language like survival strategies, defense mechanisms, attachment styles, somatic shapes, conditions of worth, self-stories, habits, and more, to describe how our characters, and relational patterns, are influenced by our developmental experiences.

Here, we'll overview a couple of the main theories about how early relationships shape our relational patterns: developmental trauma and attachment styles. In our view, however, all of the different approaches to development of relational patterns have something of value, and there is a lot of overlap between them. You might well find it useful to check out some of the other theories if the ones here don't resonate so much with you, or if you're just keen to find out more.

## Developmental trauma

Developmental trauma is a form of relational trauma as it is formed in—and impacts—our relationships with ourselves, others, and the world. Broadly speaking, the idea is that, growing up, children need to be *held and heard* by others in their feelings in order to learn how to emotionally process and move through the challenging things that inevitably happen to them. We mean those words metaphorically as it's not necessarily about children being physically held, or having their spoken, signed, or written words taken in, but more about adults attending to (hearing), and containing (holding), the feelings that they may be communicating in all kinds of verbal and non-verbal, explicit and implicit, ways.

If the adults around the child are unable to hold and hear their feelings, then painful things that happen will remain unprocessed and lodged in the bodymind. There, they can easily be triggered by later events and then land with the force of all the earlier, unprocessed, experiences. Additionally, such children are more likely to develop "insecure" styles of relating with others, desperately seeking others who will finally hold and hear them and their feelings, and/ or avoiding closeness because they've learned that isn't possible.

Of course, holding and hearing children perfectly isn't always possible, but this is fine if adults can notice when relational *ruptures* have happened (where they have not understood or empathized with their kid) and *repair* these (by apologizing, explaining, and making room to hold and hear the kid's feelings when they are available for it). Such *good enough* care also enables children to develop more "secure" later relationships as they are able to weather moments of rupture, rather than abandoning/annihilating themselves or the other person because those moments are so intolerable.

Many kids don't receive enough holding and hearing, rupture and repair. This may be because adults simply can't be available enough in this world of financial crisis, atomized family units, and complex competing demands. Frequently, adults experienced their own developmental trauma which has never been addressed—with such little cultural support for doing so—so the trauma passes down intergenerationally. Such adults may dismiss the emotional needs of their children, or blame them for the things that happen to them. They may, themselves, be one of the main sources of the kid's distress.

Because it is so dangerous for children to acknowledge that those they depend on utterly are unsafe—to do so would mean death—they frequently internalize the belief that something is fundamentally wrong with them. This is the foundation of the chronic shame and self-hatred that so many of us grapple with.

Tragically, it is common for those with developmental trauma to keep replicating the kinds of relationship dynamics they experienced in the past. This may be because these are all they know, because they are still trying to get their child's needs met, and/or because they're trying to find a way to make the same dynamics turn out better. Such repetition means they can end up experiencing many further traumatizing relationships as an adult, such as damaging relationships, painful break-ups, bullying, and other forms of non-consensual relating.

Often these relationship dynamics can feel extremely good at first, perhaps because they feel so familiar to us, or because we're so drawn to them. This can mean that it's easy to ignore the danger signs in the first burst of positive feelings and/or sense that we've found The One true person or group. This can make it even harder to acknowledge and/or extricate when we realize that we have been repeating old, painful patterns. One meme we've encountered is painfully on point about this: "When you're wearing rose-tinted glasses, the red flags all look like bunting!" Deliberately working on our patterns (section 4.2) and committing to conscious, consensual relating (section 5.4) can help us to notice such dynamics and proceed with caution.

Some writers on developmental trauma suggest that the main ways in which people tend to react to trauma (flight, fight, freeze, and fawn) become the dominant ways in which we relate with others in later life, if these were our go-to as children. Or our patterns may be a combination of more than one of these, or we might respond from different ones in different parts or selves (some of which may be more foregrounded or more disowned). Some authors suggest further Fs like "fold," "fragment," or "fasten," which you might look up if they resonate for you.

- *Flight relationship patterns* can include staying busy and distracted and/or moving away from challenging feelings or relationships, or going into addictive behaviors as a form of distraction or avoidance.

- *Fight relationship patterns* can include trying to control others' behaviors and/or blaming them for our difficult feelings or any problems.

- *Freeze relationship patterns* can include withdrawing from all, or some, relationships, through fear and/or becoming frozen or unable to deal with tough feelings or relationship problems.

- *Fawn relationship patterns* can include being hypervigilant to what people want from you, and attempting to people-please, and/or give them what you think they want from you, particularly when there are any problems or difficult feelings.

Stacey Haines writes that all people need safety, belonging, and dignity. But developmental trauma means that we often do not get all three of those things. Relationship patterns often develop as the only way of getting safety, belonging, and/or dignity available to us, and they will continue until our bodymind learns other reliable ways of getting those things. Just as many of us foreground one or more of the Fs as our relationship patterns (e.g. flight and fawn), many of us foreground our needs for one or two of safety, belonging, and dignity—if we learned that we had to sacrifice one or two to get the other. For example, we might sacrifice our dignity or sense of self in order to find relationships where we feel safe enough and as though we belong. Or we might sacrifice belonging for dignity if being who we are feels more important than fitting in with others.

## Attachment styles

Related to developmental trauma is the approach of attachment theory from the British psychologist John Bowlby. He was spurred into his work by his own experiences as a kid. He was mostly cared for by a nanny when he was a child, and she left when he was four years old, which devastated him. He was then sent to boarding school when he was seven, which he grew to believe was detrimental for children's wellbeing: something borne out by much subsequent research and therapeutic work on boarding school syndrome. Bowlby also worked closely with boys who'd been arrested for criminal behavior, so he was very aware of the links between cultures of relationships—and child rearing—and personal trauma.

Attachment theory argues that children need a safe haven with their caregivers: a caring, protective space they can return to, to be soothed when they are stressed. They need a secure base: a stable attachment relationship with one consistently available caregiver which provides a template for their later relationships in life. Over time, the child becomes more and more able to move away from this secure base. It is the knowledge that they can move away and come back that means that they gradually develop the capacity to be more independent and look after themselves and their own emotions in the way they were looked after in their secure base.

Bowlby's colleague Mary Ainsworth developed attachment theory in her research with infants who were left alone with a stranger by their caregiver. She found that those who did not have this kind of "secure attachment" developed different forms of "insecure attachment." An "anxious-ambivalent" attachment is where the child is highly distressed without their caregiver and may be either angry or helpless when they return. An "anxious-avoidant" attachment is where they avoid or ignore their caregiver and don't show distress at them leaving, or much reaction to them returning. "Disorganized attachment" was added by Mary Main and relates to more inconsistent attachment behavior.

Later theories mapped these attachment styles onto adult relationship behaviors, delineating between:

— secure attachment: flexible, good at connection and at discerning nourishing from risky relationships

— insecure attachment:

• anxious preoccupied: needy and dependent

• dismissive-avoidant: independent and not wanting intimacy

• fearful-avoidant: desiring close connection and finding it very difficult.

The diagram below shows how these relationship patterns relate to whether our fundamental sense of ourselves and others is that we/they are okay or not (an idea from an approach called Transactional Analysis). This can help to clarify the different relational stances of the attachment styles.

Figure 3.2: Attachment styles and "who is okay"

Most recent attachment theory finds that people can display different attachment styles in different relationships, and/or in the same relationship at different times. We can develop "earned secure attachment" in later life, through working on our relationships with ourselves and others, and we can learn more "secure" forms of attachment in a particular relationship, even when it began in a more "insecure" mode. It may well be that we hold different relationship patterns of all kinds in different parts or selves. We'll explore this more in the next chapter.

Both developmental trauma and attachment theories propose that a key role of caregivers is to regulate the child's emotional state, meaning that the child can learn how to do so themselves long-term. This means learning how to calm ourselves in times of heightened emotions such as fear, sadness, anger, and frustration. Co-regulation is when caregivers attune to how their child is feeling, and engage in back-and-forth interaction to understand—and meet—their needs, soothing them when stressful events occur.

### Reflection point: The Fs and attachment styles

Look back over the list of the Fs, and the list and diagram of the attachment styles. Do any of these ways of relating resonate for you—in yourself and/or in those around you? Would you say any of them—individually or in combination— are common for you? Are there any others that sometimes happen? Are they different in different relationships, or in different selves—or parts—within you?

If we are met in such a way, we learn how to soothe and calm ourselves when tough things happen and our bodies go into more reactive modes (self-regulation). We'll also find it easier to form good connections and to reach out to them when we need to. Without such an early "secure attachment," we're likely to be overwhelmed by tough events and emotions, and to engage in survival strategies to avoid them, and we may well struggle to discern nourishing from risky relationships, and to reach out to others when we need support.

## Neurodivergence and relationship patterns

It can be difficult to tease apart ways of relating to ourselves and others that come from forms of neurodivergence that we are born with (such as autism or ADHD) and those that come from the way in which we are brought up. This is generally far more complex than a simple binary of nature vs. nurture (there's more about this in the other books in this series if you're interested). Tragically, neurodivergence has been so poorly understood and stigmatized until relatively recently that people often assumed that it was "caused" by poor parenting, or that it was pathological in some way. We now know that people have diverse ways of processing information, communicating with others, attending to situations, responding to feelings, and all kinds of other things that impact how we relate.

If we grow up in a family and community which doesn't understand or accommodate our neurodivergence, then we may well also be traumatized. For example, many autistic people do not want much touch or eye contact. The experience of being forced to engage in the kind of holding or eye contact that neurotypical caregivers or others want is traumatizing—as all non-consensual experiences are. It also means they're probably not being held and heard in their feelings in the ways that would be beneficial for them (developmental trauma).

Many neurodivergent people—particularly those who are marginalized and do not conform to the stereotype of the white, male neurodivergent child—learn to mask their neurodivergence. They often use versions of the four F relational patterns we just covered, such as people pleasing, self-medicating with drugs or alcohol, or attempting to control others. Devon Price's book *Unmasking Autism* is a helpful resource for unpacking this. Nick Walker's *Neuroqueer Heresies* is very useful for considering how our bodyminds are continually shaped by both neurodivergence and traumatic experiences, as well as by therapeutic and other positive experiences. We'll consider this more in the next two chapters. We'll cover how we can shift stuck relationship patterns, and process past traumas, in ways that may help us in our current relationships, as well as how we can accommodate diverse bodymind needs and preferences in relationships.

In this section, we've focused almost entirely on relationships with caregivers, as these are so key in how we learn how to relate. However, it's important to remember that who caregivers are can vary between people, and over time, and—of course—that other early relationships, including those with siblings and peers, can be highly impactful too. Writers like Gabor Maté have argued that this is particularly the case these days, because many caregivers are under so much pressure, and have very little support in order to raise kids in ways that meet their emotional and relational needs. This can mean that many kids end up looking to peers to meet unmet early attachment needs. Of course, other children are ill-equipped to meet these needs, and often act in further traumatizing ways when this happens.

## Multiple experiences: Relationship patterns

"Growing up, I was extremely sensitive to the feelings of the adults around me. It was so confusing to me because I would pick up on their pain, and then express it because I was so confused and overwhelmed by the feelings, but they would generally deny it being anything to do with them and punish me for getting upset. All this means that I can be hypervigilant to other people's feelings in relationships, and I really struggle when someone's words are out of sync with their actual feelings."

"For ages, partners would tell me that I was avoidant because I didn't want to live with them or share a bed. I found that the avoidant attachment idea didn't fit so well for me. It was much more helpful when I finally realized I was autistic, and I need a lot of space and solitude around interacting with others, in order to process."

"My relationship patterns were highly shaped by my experience of child sexual abuse. The fact that the whole family was in denial that it was happening meant that I repressed all the anger I felt—both towards the abuser and towards the adults around me who failed to notice or keep me safe. In relationships now, I know I can push people away because I expect them to violate my trust, but also pull them in because I so want somebody not to abandon me. Understanding the roots of this—and being able to explain it—helps a lot."

"For me, a lot of my relationship patterns are about the ways I had to mask my neurodivergence. As a Black kid, it was so risky to be seen as in any way angry or difficult or confrontational, so I tried to hide my meltdowns and became a people pleaser, giving people plenty of smiles and eye contact even though it never felt good. My body was tense literally all the time. Having close neurodivergent friends with similar experiences is helping with the process of unmasking now."

## Reflection point: Early experiences of unconditional love

There's been a lot in this section about the impact of early traumatizing relationships, and ones where we're not held and heard, or don't feel secure. Before we go into the final activity, we invite you to reflect on an early experience that you have of feeling unconditionally loved, well held and heard, or secure in a relationship. Research suggests that even having one such relationship in your life can have an important mitigating effect on some of the damage that more traumatic, and insecure, relationships do. For many of us—sadly—this isn't an ongoing relationship with a caregiver, but it might be—for example—a positive relationship with a teacher who took particular care of you, or a neighbor or grandparent who sometimes looked after you. For many of us, it is an early relationship with a companion animal or with a place. It can also expand to include relationships with fictional depictions of friendship, solitude, or "imaginary friends." You could also include, here, the memories you have of being loved well by certain people, even if you did eventually lose them, or they didn't manage it all the time. For example, your relationship with a parent at certain times of day, or how your family was when they were on holiday, or how a sibling was with you after they left home.

## ACTIVITY: RIVER OF EXPERIENCE

Imagine you're developing ways of doing relationships as a river. You can use the image here in the book—if it's your book!—or draw your own. Each bend in the river is a significant experience, set of circumstances, or relationship that led you to your experience of your relationships today. You might include specific people or groups, moves to new homes or schools, a person, engaging with certain media, particularly tough or nourishing relationships or experiences—anything really. You may want to draw in the kinds of relationships you reflected on in the reflection points in this chapter: the ones where you learned certain trauma patterns or attachment styles, and early models of more loving/secure relating.

You can start at any point in your life, but we suggest starting from birth or early memories. Annotate each bend in the river with a few keywords or images, to remind you what it represents. Please remember to be gentle with yourself as you go through this activity, and take your time to breathe and take breaks as needed.

*Figure 3.3: Your river of experience*

Some people prefer to use a different metaphor for this activity. For example, you might think of chapters in the book of your life. Or levels in the computer game of your life.

Of course, you can draw as many rivers as you like. For example, you could do different ones for different parts or selves and their relationship patterns (see section 4.2), for different kinds of relationships, or for the different kinds of love covered in section 1.4. You could do a river for the tough and traumatic things that shaped your relationships, and one for the pleasurable and joyful things. We certainly find that our responses to this activity change every time we do it for ourselves.

You may want to share your river with close people in your life, perhaps people you're in relationship with, a therapist or other practitioner, or friends who are doing this activity. It's also absolutely fine to keep it private if this doesn't feel comfortable.

## 3.3 INTERSECTIONS AND POSITIONING

In this chapter so far, we've talked about what we learned growing up and some of the intergenerational patterns we might have been exposed to when it comes to relating with ourselves and one another. Now we want to turn to the complexity of it all a little more, given that our relationships do not exist in a vacuum. We can't separate neatly what we learned about relationships from what we learned about gender, sexuality, class, race, ethnicity, faith/spirituality, disability, body size, socioeconomic status, and so on. If you've read *How to Understand Your Gender* and/or *How to Understand Your Sexuality*, this section might seem familiar, since we're following a similar pattern, but hopefully the content is fresh and worth looking into.

When we talk about intersections, we're referring to all the different aspects of our identities and experiences illustrated in the image. However, when we talk about intersectionality, we're talking about the theory first introduced in the late 1980s by Black US legal scholar Dr. Kimberlé Crenshaw. This is a theory that invites us to look at our experiences through the lenses of systemic power, privilege,

Figure 3.4: Intersections

and oppression, especially when it comes to race and gender. This is because Dr. Crenshaw came up with the idea when looking critically at the different experiences that Black women and girls were having within the judicial prison-industrial complex, compared to Black men and boys and white women and girls.

As always, while we're strongly influenced by this theory, we encourage you to go to the source and read Black scholars if you want to find out more about intersectionality. We list a couple of resources for further reading on this at the end of the chapter. We'll explore your position from an intersectional perspective in Chapter 4. For now, we'd like to introduce you to another theory that we feel can be very helpful when thinking about our relationships.

## The dance of positioning

Another idea we're drawing from here is positioning theory. Positioning theory is not just about our positionality in the world according to sociocultural labels. Rather, this theory focuses on the interactions between people, which is why we think it's so helpful when addressing relationships, as we're doing in this book! This theory expands on the work of Lev Vygotskiy, and it was introduced in 1990 in a paper by Bronwyn Davies and Rom Harré called "Positioning: the discursive production of selves."

While the theory has more layers, we want to share one of its core ideas here. This is that we're constantly invited and inviting one another into certain sociocultural positions through our interactions. For example, right now, you are being invited by us, through this book, into the position of reader, and we're being invited into the position of authors. This is just a small example, but our lives are woven by these interactive, positioning dances. We can, of course, accept or reject those invitations. However, we cannot move out of the invitational dances altogether, just like we cannot move outside of culture. We can definitely increase our awareness of these dances, if we want to be more conscious and intentional in our relationships with ourselves and one another.

From the beginning of our lives, our caregivers and those around them invite us into certain positions. When we're babies, we can't, of course, accept or reject them, but we can do so when we're older. This can be a source of tension within families, especially if a child diverges from familial expectations. One of the early positions we're invited into is gender, as well as the position of "child." We discuss this in more detail in *How to Understand Your Gender*, but it's worth mentioning here because the way we're gendered often influences the way people relate to us, especially within a family and other caregiving context, such as nurseries and schools.

Position is different from role, because while the latter is static, the former is dynamic, context-dependent, and relational. Position includes our beliefs, values, sense of social duty, morality, obligations, and expectations as well as our individuality. This theory is often used in social discourse analysis, and it includes various categories of positions, which we won't go into here. We wanted to introduce it, though, as a potentially helpful framework to better understand the relational dances that we likely engaged in growing up.

Positioning theory might also help us to better understand what was happening when we were growing up not just in relation to our families and main caregivers, but also in school, our early friendships, and—for those of us who engaged in them—our early romantic and/or sexual experiences. We'd argue that when our positioning followed accepted sociocultural linguistic and familial invitations and patterns, we likely felt we "fitted in" or belonged, and might even have been praised for it. Whereas when we diverged from those invitations and patterns, we might have experienced alienation, isolation, confusion, fear, and even rejection and violence, whether verbal, emotional, or physical.

Carceral logic is a way to monitor ourselves and others to make sure we dance within the narrow confines of positioning invitations that are acceptable and comfortable within any specific sociocultural, linguistic, and familial contexts (see section 2.2). When we move out of those narrow confines, we might be punished by others distancing emotionally, highlighting our differences verbally, or even enacting violence. Systems of power, privilege, and oppression are, of course, also at play here. This might seem all a bit heady, so let's move into some examples from MJ and Alex, and an activity to explore your own relational positioning growing up, if you want to.

In the examples below, we reflected on some of our experiences with positioning within key relationships growing up. Hopefully, these examples give you an idea of what we're asking you to do in the next activity.

## ALEX'S EXAMPLE AND REFLECTIONS

Alex drew this picture when thinking of their positioning within key relationships growing up.

Alex reflects:

One of the stories from the day of my birth is by my maternal grandmother who said I came out "with my head held up, as if I were a month old already." She was very proud of telling that story since she saw that as a sign of intelligence. I came out into the roles of first child and first grandchild. These roles would keep inviting me into positions of leadership and responsibility within my family circles. My nonna—grandmother—on my mom's side became a widow suddenly three days after I was born. She was just a few years older than I am now when this happened. She would keep inviting me into positions of intimacy and closeness that were different to the ones of the grandchildren that came after. Growing up, I knew she needed me emotionally and physically since I would also often sleep in the same bed as her for company. It would take about three decades for me to understand how much I had been invited into being positioned as an adult and an intimacy surrogate within my family system, and how this positioning has shaped all my relationships since.

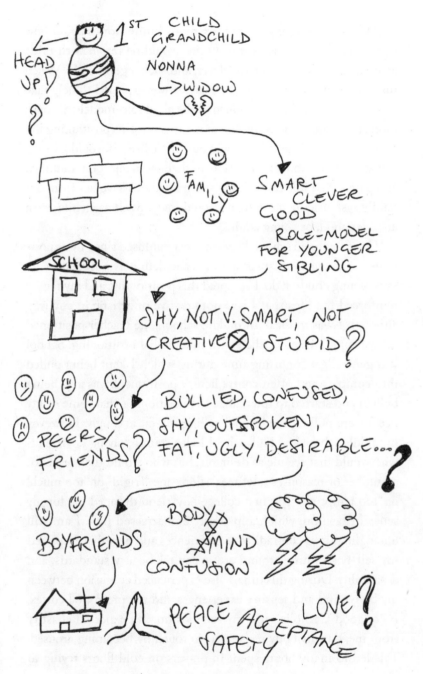

Figure 3.5: Alex's positioning snapshot growing up

When I was young, there were more family stories about how clever and smart I was. Those stories would be retold with pride again and again. I was smart, clever, and such a good child. When my sister came along seven years later, I was expected to help take care of her. I had been positioned as the good role-model and, once more, parentified and adultified in many ways. This positioning has influenced my sibling relationship our whole lives. It would take me a long time, and about two decades of therapy, to reject my adultified and parentified role towards my sister. I couldn't save her from our family systems any more than I could save myself as a child, even an older child, or young adult.

Once I entered school, I became very confused since I was positioned as shy, not very smart at times, and definitely not creative. As most young children do, I accepted this positioning, and my family reinforced the idea that I was not creative or artistic in any way, although I was musical. In middle school, one teacher positioned me as stupid, which clashed with my familial positioning. School was generally a confusing time during which I kept being pulled into complex and often contradictory positions. I was also being bullied and started to internalize the positioning that some of my peers were pulling me into by calling me fat and ugly. However, in middle school and high school I also started having boyfriends who would first see me as desirable, but who would then leave for a number of reasons, sometimes calling me "frigid" or "too much" or "too tempting." My first college boyfriend dumped me for my sense of fashion, which apparently embarrassed him. I am still untangling these contradictory experiences and how they impacted my self-positioning around erotic capital, beauty standards, and desirability. During this time, I also experienced confusion between my bodymind and sensory experiences and my prefrontal cortex. As a "good Catholic girl," my self-positioning expected chastity from me, but my body responded to touch by becoming aroused. This led to many hours spent in prayers on cold floors trying to understand what it all meant, not just within myself but in relation to my love for God.

God and Church were, in fact, the refuge that home wasn't. Growing up, churches were always open in Rome, so I could escape within their cool interiors and find unconditional love, safety from physical harm, and acceptance. However, as I grew in deeper relationship with the Church, and even explored becoming a nun for a number of years, I kept finding that love to be more conditional and limiting than I had first experienced as a child. Churches became less peaceful and more judgmental, and I was buffered once more into contradictory positions: a loving, devout Catholic, but also a temptress, and a heretic who questioned doctrine.

Overall, growing up, I felt that no matter how much I tried to position myself in ways that fitted in and were congruent with the familial, linguistic, and sociocultural invitations I was surrounded by, I could not do so without sacrificing some of who I was. The overall relational message I learned was clear: you cannot be loved and be the whole of yourself. To be in a relationship is to make yourself smaller, to sacrifice a piece of you for the greater good—that is love, whether this be the love of family, God, or a romantic partner. The other relational message was around sexual feelings: you cannot be good and have sexual feelings at the same time, but if you don't have sexual feelings, you can also not be fully loved by a partner. Those are messages that are still deep in my bones, heart, and sinews, and engraved in the grooves of my brain. They show up in a variety of ways in my current relationships again and again, as a friend, partner, lover, community organizer, parent, human. More on that will be explored in the next chapter, though.

## MJ'S EXAMPLE AND REFLECTIONS

MJ drew this picture reflecting on their positioning within key relationships growing up.

Figure 3.6: MJ's positioning snapshot growing up

MJ reflects:

We (the plural system of MJ!) have drawn pictures of two pivotal times in our childhood where we were invited into very different positions by the key relationships around us. These contradictions shaped our self system in key ways which we're still unraveling now—at nearly 50 years old.

In the first image—age five—our gran invited us to be vulnerable in our relationship with her as she enjoyed caring for us, or "spoiling us" as other people called it. Meanwhile, our parents struggled with the fact that we cried every day and tried to train us out of it.

In the second image—age nine—our family invited us to be intellectual, immersed in studies, fascinated by our interests, and into certain kinds of literature, music, etc., while the culture in the school that we joined at that time was anti-intellectual, and the kinds of interests and tastes that were expected—particularly of someone perceived as a girl—were very different (fashion, appearance, boys, etc.).

In terms of intersections, we've highlighted neurodivergence and class in both images, although there were certainly other elements in play too such as gender, sexuality, faith, and cultural background (particularly around our family having moved from the south to the north of the country before we were born). We now know that our neurodivergence was a big part of why we were so emotional (age five) and why we loved immersing in particular special interests (age nine). But these things were not understood by those around us, and were encouraged and discouraged in different places. Being autistic also meant it was very hard to code switch! Class was also a big part of the reason why our gran and school peers encouraged very different ways of relating and behaving than our parents. Also the neurodivergence and intergenerational experiences of our parents (such as them finding heightened emotions difficult, and our dad having the work ethic of a working-class boy who was the first in his family to get into grammar school and university).

Eventually, both experiences resulted in us making splits between a "good" child whom we presented to the world and a "bad" child whom we hid. At age five, the "good" one was the people pleaser who could pick up on what each person wanted of us and give it to them, and the "bad" one was the one who carried all the scared/shameful feelings (both part of the self we now know as Robin). At age nine, the "good" one was the one who learned to fit in with everybody, and the "bad" one was the one who held all the rage at the way we'd been treated, but turned it in against us because it wasn't safe to express it out (both part of the self we now know as Morgan).

## This is only the beginning

Please note that these drawings and reflections are just snapshots at a specific time and place. If we were to draw and write this another day, we might even come up with different experiences of positioning within our key relationships. Positioning is such a constant, ongoing, interactive process that it would be impossible to capture all of it in its entirety. We also don't necessarily remember all our experiences and key relationships growing up, and we're sure there might be more memories that could be unlocked by a song, smell, thought, or encounter. Our memories are also not static, and we make sense of our lives growing up as we ourselves grow, change, and interact with those around us and the ecosystems we're part of. This can bring new understanding, insights, and meaning into our lives.

In the next activity, we're not asking you to draw and reflect on the ultimate story about your positioning dance growing up, but rather to pause and reflect on what comes up for you at this moment in time. We're asking for a snapshot of your relational, positioning dance growing up, just like those we gave with our examples, and only if it feels right to you, of course. We believe it can be helpful to have these snapshots to look back at and revisit throughout our lives, since we might find and remember new meanings each time we look at them or create new ones.

## *ACTIVITY: YOUR POSITIONING DANCE WITHIN KEY RELATIONSHIPS GROWING UP*

You've had a look at our drawings and read our reflections. If you want to, it's time to make your own. Take the time you need to think about which positioning dances you were invited into within your key relationships growing up. You can choose any period of time: from birth to the end of high school or a subsection of that, from middle school to your mid-20s, and so on. Much depends on how old you are now, what memories you have access to or not. Try to be as gentle and non-judgmental as you're able to at this moment in time and try to unleash your curiosity and creativity. Let your bodymind remember what it needs to right now, trusting that you can access memories in more ways than just one logical, linear one.

You can draw, create a mind map, compose a song, make a collage, do a ritual, or dance it out. Use whichever method suits the way you think and process best. Let yourself explore and create. You can see that we both did the activity differently as well. There's no right or wrong way of doing this. This is for you, so do whatever feels good for you at this moment to explore this idea of positioning within your key relationships growing up. Then take some time to reflect on what you created and how it might impact the way you relate to yourselves and others.

### Reflection point: Your own and other people's relational patterns and positioning within relationships

You might be starting to feel more familiar with your own relational patterns by now, as well as what you learned about relationships and how your positioning dance growing up impacted you, especially in the context of your specific intersections and sociocultural linguistic context(s). Take a moment to notice if there were ways of being in, or doing, relationships that you had no idea existed growing up.

Were there relationship roles, positions, and positioning dances that you were aware of, and if so, how did the adults around you talk about them? Which relational patterns and relationships were viewed as acceptable, or maybe even celebrated through things like weddings, and which were not viewed as acceptable or were unspeakable even? Which relational patterns and types of relationships did you have little to no contact with because your own positioning, and that of the adults around you, diverged from them? Did this influence the way you thought of other people's relationships or relational patterns? If so, how did you first react to these new-to-you relational patterns and relationships?

## 3.4 ADULTS AND CHILDREN

Much of this chapter is focused on what we learned about relationships growing up, so we wanted to take a moment to consider the relationships between adults and children in a little more depth. In this book, as you know, we're considering all types of relationships and not just romantic and/or sexual relationships. We're including familial relationships, friendships, relationships with nature and ancestors, and so on. While all of these have their own specific flavors and contexts, we believe it's worth thinking about adult–children relationships in particular in this section, although we do mention them throughout the book. Adult–children relationships are different from adult peer relationships for a number of reasons:

— Children depend on adults for their survival. The younger the child, the more dependent they are.

— There is a power differential between children and adults that cannot be erased as long as someone is a child (not just legally but also developmentally).

— Children–adult relationships are not peer relationships. While there can be intergenerational friendships between children and adults, these friendships are not peer relationships as long as the child is still a child, as stated above.

— Children don't have the same capacity for self-soothing and emotional regulation as adults do. In fact, they depend on their main caregivers and adults around them for co-regulation.

— Children don't have the same agency and power over their lives as adults do. The younger the child, the less agency and power they have.

— Children cannot meet the needs of adults. There cannot be authentic mutuality, care, and compassion between a child and an adult. Children can, however, learn to caretake adults for their survival or because they are being adultified/parentified (more on this later). This can *look like* mutuality, care, and compassion, but it's actually a survival strategy, which often includes fawning, most commonly known as people pleasing.

— Differentiation is something that happens developmentally as we grow up. This means that children cannot clearly differentiate from adults until they are older.

— This might seem really obvious, but we think it's worth stating: children are developmentally not done growing! This has all sorts of implications for relating.

— Adolescents are still children. This might also seem obvious, but given that many teens are treated as mini-adults, we believe this bears saying. They might be tall children who look like adults sometimes, but they are still children developmentally, albeit at a different stage in that process than younger children, of course.

— Children cannot set and/or protect their boundaries as adults do, for many of the reasons listed above!

It might seem odd to see such strong statements in a book that is otherwise fairly invitational, and we do generally tend to avoid sweeping generalizations. However, when it comes to children, we feel the need to be very clear since we've both experienced in our lives—and witnessed as professionals—what can happen when these points are not clear to adults who have children in their lives. Unfortunately, many of us have not been parented in a way that allowed us, and recognized us, to be children.

## Adultification and parentification

Many of us, especially in the teen years, have likely experienced some form of adultification and/or parentification—that is, being a child who is treated as an adult or even as a parent. We want to acknowledge that some children are also parents, if they have become pregnant during their teen years. This is a different matter from parentification. Parentification means that a child is being placed in the role of parent within a family system not because they are a parent but due to having parent-like expectations placed on them by their adult caregivers.

For example, Alex was expected to attend many health appointments, especially eye appointments, by themselves growing up. They were being treated as an adult even though they were about 11–12 years old, and possibly younger, but their memory doesn't stretch back that far for most events. They were also expected to manage their father's moods by being "good" so that he wouldn't be volatile and violent. That is parentification since it's parents who should help their children co-regulate and not the other way around. Being an adultified/parentified child often goes hand in hand with fawning and being a people pleaser. We learned, usually at a very young age, that, to keep safe, we had to meet the needs of those around us and keep them happy. Neurodivergent children can often be adultified and/or parentified if they're perceived as "being smart beyond their years"/"being an old soul" within a family and/or educational system. They can also be finely attuned to the emotions of those around them and take responsibility for them, if the adults in their lives are not careful to notice these patterns.

We'll explore further in Chapter 4 how what we learned about relationships as children impacts our adult relationships once we're grown. For now, though, we wanted to highlight the differences discussed above and address adultification/parentification as well as the legacy of intergenerational trauma. We cannot talk about adultification/parentification without acknowledging that, regardless of familial experiences, Black, Brown, Indigenous, Immigrant, trans, and queer children are often adultified and even sexualized within many sociocultural contexts, such as in what we currently call the United States of America, for example. There is scholarship written about this, especially focusing on Black children, and how anti-Blackness, white supremacy, racism, capitalism, and the legacy of slavery make it impossible in the US for them to be treated as children. The most horrific evidence of this phenomenon is the killing of Black children who are perceived as adult threats rather than be viewed as children at play, as in the case of Tamir Rice and far too many others besides him. The adultification of children, especially Black, Brown, Indigenous, and Immigrant children, as well as trans and queer children, has serious psychological, emotional, physical, and even lethal consequences.

This can all seem pretty bleak—and it is. We're not just talking about intergenerational trauma, but also historical, social, and cultural trauma that for many communities is still played out every day. In the next chapter, we'll talk about how we can contribute to changing this: to breaking these intergenerational legacies and this systemic pattern of violence. One of those ways is most certainly to not look away. We're aware that many of you, in fact, cannot because this is your lived experience. We also want to acknowledge, once more, that what we're writing will land on your bodyminds differently depending on your own social and historical positioning. Please remember to slow down and take care of yourself whenever you need to. For now, let's conclude this chapter with some space for reflection.

### Reflection point: How do we define childhood?

Take some time to record, in any way that feels accessible to you at this moment, some of your thoughts, feelings, and somatic responses to the following questions. As always, feel free to modify the questions, ask yourself new ones, or simply reflect or journal on this chapter so far.

If you were to write or share a definition of childhood, what would that definition be? What do you think it's fair and sustainable to expect from a child at various ages (for example, five years old, ten years old, 17 years old)? What did you learn about children growing up? What did you learn about the relationships between adults and children growing up? If you have children in your life, take time to notice how what you learned growing up impacts the way you relate to the children in your life. If you're still a child, what is coming up for you in this section? Are there statements you disagree with? If so, which ones and why? What could a loving, boundaried, and supportive intergenerational friendship between a child and adult look like? Do you believe this is even possible? If so, why? If not, why not?

**REMEMBER...** Remember to really slow down and take care of yourself. Writing this chapter, we definitely noticed increased tension in our shoulders and back, for example. Take the time you need and use the slow-down page at the end of this chapter too, if you want to. This can all seem heavy and bleak because much of it is. In the next chapter, we'll discuss how what we learned about relationships growing up might still impact our current relationships. We'll also start discussing how we might address those patterns in the present.

As psychologist George Kelly wrote, "no one needs to paint themselves into a corner; no one needs to be completely hemmed in by circumstances; no one needs to be the victim of his or her biography." We also remember that we cannot do this alone, especially if we want to change larger societal patterns. We need the changes to happen both within and between ourselves.

## Further resources

There's more about how relationship challenges—and other struggles—are rooted in family backgrounds in this book:

— Wolynn, M. (2017). *It Didn't Start with You: How Inherited Family Trauma Shapes Who We Are and How to End the Cycle*. London: Penguin.

Some great books on developmental trauma include:

— Walker, P. (2018). *Complex PTSD: From Surviving to Thriving*. Lafayette, CA: Azure Coyote Publishing.

— Haines, S.K. (2019). *The Politics of Trauma: Somatics, Healing, and Social Justice*. Berkeley, CA: North Atlantic Books.

— Fisher, J. (2021). *Transforming the Living Legacy of Trauma*. Eau Claire, WI: PESI Publishing & Media.

Two introductions to attachment in relationships, one focusing on non-monogamous and one on monogamous relationships, are:

- Fern, J. (2020). *Polysecure: Attachment, Trauma and Consensual Nonmonogamy*. Portland, OR: Thorntree Press.
- Heller, D.P. (2019). *The Power of Attachment*. Buffalo, CO: Sounds True.

Some books we've found particularly helpful on neurodivergence are:

- Price, D. (2022). *Unmasking Autism*. New York, NY: Harmony.
- Walker, N. (2021). *Neuroqueer Heresies*. Fort Worth, TX: Autonomous Press.
- Silberman, S. (2017). *Neurotribes*. London: Atlantic Books.

A great basic introduction to intersectionality is:

- Hill Collins, P. and Bilge, S. (2020). *Intersectionality*. Cambridge: Polity.

A collection of Crenshaw's own writing on intersectionality can be found at:

- Crenshaw, K.W. (2017). *On Intersectionality: Essential Writings*. New York, NY: The New Press.

If you are interested in the intersection of gender, sexuality, relationships, and trauma, you can find more in:

- Iantaffi, A. (2020). *Gender Trauma: Healing Cultural, Social, and Historical Gendered Trauma*. London: Jessica Kingsley Publishers.

The reference from the remember section is:

- Kelly, G. (1963). *A Theory of Personality: The Psychology of Personal Constructs*. New York: W.W. Norton & Company, p.15.

Well, that was a lot to write for us, so we are not sure how you're feeling reading it and also engaging in the suggested activities. We thought this could be a good time to invite you to breathe intentionally and slow down some, once more. Of course, you can always slow down, at any point in this book, and, in fact, we actively encourage you to do so.

If you like, for this slow-down moment, we encourage you to choose something that is pleasing, comforting, or at the very least neutral from your surroundings. This can be very simple, like a favorite color on a box of tissues, a tasty tea, or a beloved animal companion or greenblood (plant, tree, or flower). Anything that brings a sense of soothing comfort, pleasure, or at least neutrality within you.

Once you have chosen something in your surroundings, take time to connect with it. Really observe and connect with the resource you have chosen at this moment, with whatever senses are available to you. Notice, with as much curiosity and non-judgment as you are able to, at this moment, whether there is any shift in you after connecting with this resource for 2–3 minutes. It's also okay if there is no shift, of course. Whatever you experience is information, and you don't need to force any changes; just observe what is, at this moment in time.

If you feel overwhelmed, or a little out of it, you can also try to name five colors out loud, four shapes, three textures, two things you can hear, and one thing you can taste or smell (feel free to modify this according to the senses available to you).

Coming back into relationship with the environment around us can help us reconnect within ourselves as well, since we're more oriented to place and to time when we can come back to the here and now.

# CHAPTER 4

# YOUR CURRENT EXPERIENCE OF RELATIONSHIPS

At this halfway point in the book, we've set the scene of what relationships are (Chapter 1), how the world understands relationships and the impact of this on our understandings and experiences (Chapter 2), and how your background has shaped your relationship patterns, styles, and so on (Chapter 3). The second half of the book is even more focused on the practicalities of how we might relate in our lives now, with this chapter focusing on our current ways of relating. The next chapter is focused on relating across difference and over time, and in the final chapter, we explore relating within a broader context of interconnection and interdependence.

In this chapter, we focus on your current relationships. First, we'll revisit the influences on how you do relationships, and how those may have changed over time. Then we'll consider what your main relationships are at the moment, what the basis of these are, and how you'd describe them in words. After that, we'll pick up on the material we covered in Chapter 3 to explore your current relationship patterns and how those play out for you, thinking a bit about how we can learn to notice and communicate these patterns with others in our lives, and how we can discern where to accept these patterns and/or where we might want to shift them in some way. Then we'll revisit intersections and positionality in relation to our current relationships.

And finally, we'll explore several ways of getting more intentional about our relationships: learning and communicating about how we do intimacy, sharing information about how we relate, and making agreements around relationship commitments, conflict, and so on.

## 4.1 YOUR CURRENT RELATIONSHIPS

In the last chapter, we began by exploring the influences on your understandings—and experiences—of relationships growing up. While these often set a template for what you expect relationships to look like, and how you expect them to work, many of us—as we grow—find different influences. These may expand our understandings and open up different experiences, and/or they may contract our understandings and close down possible experiences.

For example, on a community level, we both came across the polyamorous communities in our 20s, which provided us with a language and structure for engaging in multiple romantic/partner relationships. However, in different ways over time, we both found the norms in these communities restrictive and developed different ways of doing multiple relationships with specific people in our lives. On a cultural level, the development of the internet and living in or near a capital city were both important factors in making these communities available to us, as were all the people who were writing about polyamory at that time. On a relational level, like most people, we've also both been burned by particularly re/traumatizing dynamics in relationships and sudden or painful relationship endings. This has meant us drawing back from relationships in general, or from certain kinds of relationships, in ways that were helpful in some ways and perhaps restrictive in others.

### ACTIVITY: MULTIPLE LEVELS OF INFLUENCE

Returning to the levels of influence diagram from the previous chapter, note down the different important influences on your ways of doing relationships now, on each of these levels. You might particularly want to focus on the ways things have changed, such as the ways in which family, friend, and partner relationships are displayed in the media, the burgeoning of various online relationship communities, or the people who have come into your life and those who have drifted away or been lost.

You may want to keep adding to this diagram as you read through the rest of the chapter, reflecting on how all of this impacts your own understanding—and experience—of relationships (in the middle of the diagram). Of course, this book, in itself, may become one of the influences!

*Figure 4.1: Your levels of influence*

## Who you relate with

Before going any further, it can be very useful to map out who we're actually in relationship with, so that we have a sense of our current relational landscape or constellation. There are many different ways that you might do this, but we find it particularly helpful to visualize it as a series of concentric circles (you might have spotted that we love a set of nested circles!).

Anthropologist Robin Dunbar came up with "Dunbar's number,"

which is the number of people that we seem to prefer—or be able to handle—in our networks of relationships, based on studying various communities around the world. He reckoned that the human bodymind can only manage around 150 people in our network of relationships. When we try to exceed that, things tend to get more difficult. Nested within the 150 meaningful contacts that we can manage, there's a sense that we have an optimum number of around five close people, around 15 good friends, and around 50 people we might call friends. And beyond that, we can maybe manage 500 acquaintances, and 1500 people in the world who we can recognize.

Not everyone agrees with this idea, and it's unlikely that those numbers fit exactly for everyone, but it can be an interesting starting point for mapping our relationships.

## ACTIVITY: MAPPING YOUR CURRENT RELATIONSHIPS

Note down your current relationship constellation in the diagram below. Or you may well find it useful to draw something like it onto a big sheet of paper so that you can continue to annotate it and color-code it as you go through this chapter.

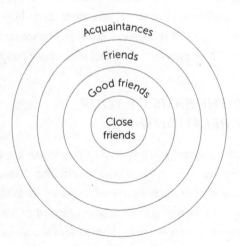

*Figure 4.2: Dunbar's circles*

You might like to follow Dunbar and include around five people or beings at the level of "close friends," 15 at the level of "good friends," 50 at the level of "friends," and 150 in "acquaintances," or these numbers may not work for you at all. We've gone with the language of "friends" here to encompass all kinds of relationships, but feel free to change this to whatever suits you, and remember that key "friends" can be non-human (e.g. animals, plants, land, ideas, projects, ancestors, deities, etc.). Some may also be groups or communities rather than individuals. We've also included a space for "internal friends." More on that in section 4.2 if you're unfamiliar with this idea.

Reflect on the experience of completing—or adapting—this diagram. Does a nested model like this work for you? How would you name each level of closeness? How many beings do you have in each level? What defines that level, for you? We'll consider this next...

## The foundations of your relationships

When sharing this kind of diagram with people, we've found that it often prompts conversations about how we determine levels of closeness. For example, for some people the levels are defined by the kind of relationship they have (e.g. with family and/or romantic/sexual relationships in the closest level). For some people, it's a lot about how emotionally open or vulnerable they feel able to be with the other people/beings. For some, it is more about how much those people/beings are part of their everyday lives. For some, it's about the level of ease or "being myself" they feel with those people/beings.

## ACTIVITY: THE BASIS OF YOUR CURRENT RELATIONSHIPS

Returning to the diagram you just made, note down—for each person, group, or being—what the basis of your relationship was and/or is. You can either note this for each individual, or you might like to create a color-code key, or similar, so that relationships of different kinds are written in different colors or fonts. Some may be several colors if the relationships have multiple bases. Some may have started one way and changed into something over time (like our relationship!). The list might include the following, but feel free to ignore any that aren't relevant to you, edit the wording, and add any further ones that are relevant:

- sharing a family background

- being thrown together (e.g. at school, in a workplace or neighborhood)

- having been in each other's lives for a long time

- physical/sexual attraction

- romantic partnership

- being in the same spiritual, political, interest, or other community

- a sense of being likeminded people

- creating together

- cohabiting

- co-parenting

- a caring relationship of some kind

- a transactional relationship of some kind.

## Your relationships words

As we said right at the beginning of the book (section 1.1), the words that we use around relationships are really important. For example, if you only have the words "partner" and "friend" available to you within the dominant cultural context, you may well find yourselves treating "partners" as more important than "friends," spending more time and energy on partner relationships, and so on, because we have so many assumptions built in to what it means to be "just friends" or "more than friends," for example.

The people who ran the conference where we met for the first time—Trev Butt and Viv Burr—wrote a whole, fascinating chapter about this in their book *Invitation to Personal Construct Psychology*. They wrote about how "opposite-gender" friends or colleagues were frequently pressurized by the language—and related cultural assumptions—of relationships. There were no words for a very close platonic relationship between a man and a woman, and this—oftentimes— could push such a relationship into a romantic/sexual affair, or mean the people distancing from each other even though they both valued their bond hugely. Our relationship experience can therefore be massively impacted by the available language—and lack of language.

One of the earliest pieces of research that MJ did around relationships was about relationships words in the polyamorous community, and how these enabled people to have relationship experiences that they otherwise would not have been able to experience. For example, polyamorous people have come up with:

— language for different versions of consensual non-monogamy (CNM) so that they can figure out whether they are on the same page as a potential partner about how they like to do things (e.g. solo polyamory for people whose relationship with themselves is one of their partnerships, kitchen table for those who like all their partners to be in relationship with each other)

— language for different kinds of partnership and other relationships within polyamorous constellations (e.g. primary/ secondary relationships for different intensities of relationship, polycules, triads, and quads for whole polyamorous systems, anchor/nesting partnerships for such pivotal relationships, sweeties or comet relationships to describe less close or occasional relationships, metamour for your relationship with a partner's partner)

— language for different emotional experiences (e.g. new

relationship energy for early intense attraction, compersion or frubble for a positive feeling on your partner being loving towards another partner, wibble or wobble for small jealous feelings which need to be acknowledged but not for anyone to change their behaviors, polysaturated for the sense of overwhelm of having too many relationships).

All kinds of non-normative communities have had to develop languages in order to reflect their relationships and experiences, and to communicate about them with each other. Often these have something useful to offer to everyone. For example, ace and aro communities have delineated the following types of attraction. It could be helpful to everyone, whether or not we are on the ace and aro spectrum, to get clearer about which kinds of attraction we're experiencing. These include:

— *sexual attraction:* finding someone erotically desirable

— *romantic attraction:* desiring a romantic relationship with someone

— *crush:* having romantic feelings towards someone that may be transient, or not acted on

— *squish:* an aromantic crush where we feel strong platonic feelings towards someone

— *sensual attraction:* a desire to do sensual—but not sexual—things with someone, like cuddling or other kinds of touch

— *aesthetic attraction:* appreciating someone's appearance without necessarily wanting to do anything sexual or romantic with them.

These are all examples of language within specific communities, but you can also think about relationship language—and how it changes over time—at the cultural level, and at the level of specific relationships.

The language from particular communities often becomes more available in the mainstream over time, with more media representations and visibility. Also, the language within wider culture develops. For example, as people have explored the territory between monogamous and non-monogamous relationships, particularly on online platforms like dating apps, words like "monogamish," "hookup," "fuckbuddy," "booty call," "Netflix and chill," and "friends with benefits" have come in, which can really help clarify what people are looking for. Also, since the 1990s there has been more popular media focusing on friendships rather than romantic relationships (starting with TV shows like *Friends* and *Sex and the City*). From these, words like "bromance," "buddy," "bae," "BFF," "soul sister," "homie," and "my ride or die" have become part of people's lexicon.

As people recognize the importance of relationships with non-human animals, many talk more of "animal companions," "non-human family," "support animals," or "service animals," rather than "pets" or "domestic animals." Although, akin to what we explored in relation to adult–child relationships in section 3.4, there are important issues around equality, power, and consent to consider in human–non-human relationships.

Many people often develop relationship language within the context of specific relationships. This is a constant work in progress for us, as we try to capture the specific nature of our relationship in a way that signifies its importance to ourselves—and others—as well as capturing all elements of it—particularly the fact that it is an emotionally close relationship where we often cohabit for brief periods of time, and that we create together. We've played with language like "collaborator," "writing partner," "work spouse," "non-romantic partner," "queer kin/family," "co-author," and "art-ner."

**Reflection point: Your relationships words**

Return to your diagram of the important relationships in your life—human and non-human. Perhaps focus on the inner few circles. What words do you currently use to describe them—between you, and with other people? Do you feel happy with those words? Did you agree them between you? How do other people respond to them? Reflect on whether there may be other words in wider culture or specific communities, or that you create yourselves, which might be a better fit. How might you indicate the importance of these relationships to others beyond language? For example, celebrating relational milestones, expressing affection, encouraging others to recognize you in some way. Do you need words to capture the relationship style, the feelings you have in this relationship, or the other relationships around it, as well as the type of relationship (as in the polyamory examples)?

We'll explore getting intentional about our relationships in these kinds of ways in more detail in section 4.4. First, let's return to exploring our relationship patterns, and intersections, and the ways these influence our current relationships.

## 4.2 YOUR RELATIONSHIP PATTERNS

In the last chapter, we covered a few different theories of how we develop relationship patterns or habits. These patterns impact both how we relate internally, to ourselves, and how we relate externally, to others and the wider world.

You might find it useful, before we go on, to revisit section 3.2 just to remind yourself of where you got to with identifying your main "F" trauma survival strategies and/or attachment styles. You could think about these things in relation to the close relationships you identified in section 4.1. You could add notes (or more color codes) to your diagram about the ways in which you tend to relate in those relationships.

## Shame and your current relationship patterns

One of the main reasons—perhaps even the main reason—that we go to the various "F" strategies, or "insecure" attachment styles, in our relationships is the avoidance of shame. Growing up, most of us are taught—implicitly or explicitly—that certain aspects of ourselves are acceptable and others are unacceptable. Most of us gradually learn to shape ourselves so that we behave in more of the ways that others reward and fewer of the ways that others punish (whether explicitly or in more subtle ways). With the understanding of a child, we generally believe that those "unacceptable" things are something that is "wrong" with us.

The more significant our developmental trauma—and the more our wider culture reinforces the message that there are normal and abnormal ways to be—the more profoundly we will come to believe that there is something fundamentally wrong with us. Many of us carry chronic shame, believing—on some level—that others in our lives will eventually see what is "wrong," "bad," or "unlovable" about us, and will abandon us or annihilate us in the ways we experienced when we were young. If we were neglected or abused, for example, or if the adults around us couldn't hold or hear our feelings and/or punished us for having them. When we're little, it often feels safer to assume that there is something "wrong" with us than it is to acknowledge that the people who we depend upon may be unsafe in some way, because that would be way more dangerous to our lives.

Chronic shame often goes hand in hand with harshly critical inner voices, attempts to hide, cover up, or mask anything we learned was unacceptable, and fears of being exposed in the things about ourselves we see as shameful. The carceral logics inherent in the wider world, and in many communities, exacerbate this, as there is such a culture of policing and punishing each other—and

Figure 4.3: Shame compass

ourselves—for any perceived faults, flaws, or relational mistakes (see section 2.2).

Tragically, shame massively gets in the way of our connections with ourselves and others, because it feels very risky to be real, open, honest, and vulnerable, in the places we carry shame: all things which are important—if not essential—for intimacy (see section 4.4). Also, as shame researchers like Brené Brown have pointed out, shame needs to be shared and met with empathy in order to dissipate—something that is very hard to do when we live in shaming relationships with ourselves, others, and/or wider culture.

Shame writer Donald L. Nathanson created the "shame compass" which illustrates four main ways in which we endeavor *not* to feel shame. We've recreated this in the diagram above, and suggested how the four points of the compass might map on to the kinds of relationship patterns we covered in the last chapter.

So, for example, people who tend to try not to feel shame with *avoidance* may stay very busy and distracted so as to not have to tune into their feelings. They may engage in addictive kinds of behaviors for the same reasons, or have lots of quite surface-level relationships so they don't have to let anyone in too close. They may engage in hopeful fantasies of the "right" person or group and/or jump from relationship to relationship searching for that.

People who tend towards *withdrawal* are more likely to distance from others in order not to expose themselves to any possibility of being shamed. They may become anxious and fearful of potentially shaming experiences happening to them, and attempt to control these by hiding away literally and/or emotionally.

People who tend towards *attack in* are likely to blame themselves for any difficult feelings they experience, or problems in relationships. They may well try to monitor and control *themselves*, and engage in fawning or people-pleasing behaviors, especially if they feel as though they're being criticized or rejected in any way.

People who tend towards *attack out* are likely to blame others for any difficult feelings they experience, or problems in relationships.

They may well try to monitor and control *others*, and engage in coercive or controlling behaviors, believing that others will let them down or are even deliberately out to get them.

You can see how many common mental health struggles, such as addictions, anxiety and depression, compulsive behaviors, self-injury, hearing critical voices, and paranoid experiences, happen when people become quite entrenched in one or more of these positions as a survival strategy, or way of not feeling shame. Sadly, the impact of trying not to feel shame can be as bad as—if not worse than—the feelings or experiences that we're trying to avoid.

## ACTIVITY: YOUR RELATIONSHIPS AND THE COMPASS

Rather than being completely entrenched in one of the points of the shame compass, and the associated relationship patterns, most of us tend towards different patterns in different relationships (and at different times in the same relationship). Take five or so of your close people/beings from the relationship map you made earlier, and write their names around the shame compass diagram, depending on where you tend to go to with them. If you tend to relate in more than one way with them, feel free to write their names between two or more points of the compass. If you tend to feel very secure and able to be open and vulnerable in that relationship—with no fear of shame or shaming—then you could write their names in the middle of the compass. You might want to reflect on whether you have one or several more common ways of relating to yourself and others, and what it is about different relationships—or how they work—that brings out different ways of relating in you.

### Plurality and your current relationship patterns

Many therapists from a range of different approaches suggest that it is more helpful to think of ourselves as "self systems" rather than individuals. They question the idea that we are—or should try to be—atomized, unified individuals, who are coherent in how we do things and consistent over time. They suggest that this is another dominant cultural normativity, which doesn't reflect how people across time and place have understood and experienced themselves, and also doesn't reflect how most people understand and experience themselves today.

For example, you may well have noticed that you have quite different go-to ways of relating to yourselves in different relationships and situations. Many—if not most—people have experiences of different inner voices (inner children and inner critics, for instance) and often use the language of "a part of me…" when explaining their decision-making processes (e.g. "a part of me wants to keep writing this chapter and a part of me wants to get outside in the hammock!").

An alternative way of viewing selves is that we are systems within systems. Just as the body is made up of multiple interconnected systems that influence each other in complex feedback loops, so is the mind (and, of course, the body and mind can't be simply separated, which is why we use the word bodymind throughout this book). Writers use the analogy of the internal family system (Richard Schwartz) and the musical symphony orchestra or band (James Fadiman and Jordan S. Gruber) to demonstrate how "self systems" operate. In this view, the plurality of ourselves isn't a problem to be solved, by integrating all of your parts, or selves, into a coherent, consistent whole. Rather, the aim is to get to know all of our parts, or selves, kindly and honestly, improving communication between them and helping them to work as a team. This is pretty similar to the aim for external relationships really: differentiation, mutuality, care, and compassion within and between selves all being extremely helpful (see section 1.4).

Unfortunately, in dominant culture, where there is such a "monomind" or "single self assumption," and so much stigmatizing and pathologizing of those who are openly plural, it can be very difficult to identify our selves or to relate openly between them (internally or in relation with others).

From a developmental perspective, plurally we can understand that everyone has selves who would default to each of the main survival strategies, attachment styles, or ways of relating. However, we learn, growing up, that some of these are acceptable for a bodymind like ours, and/or in a family/community like ours, while others are unacceptable. This means our self system becomes unbalanced over time, as we may foreground some selves (with their strategies and patterns) and disown, repress, or cast out others. Disowned selves may leak or lash out in confusing ways.

Picking up on what they wrote in section 3.3 about the moments in their life when they faced contradictory demands from the people around them, here is (team) MJ explaining how their self system developed, and the implications for their relationships.

## ARA REFLECTS:

For many years, we had no sense of our plurality. We thought we were a singular person, having learned on our psychology degree that multiplicity was either made up or a severe psychiatric "disorder." Our go-to way of relating was avoidance, and it manifested in us staying busy and distracted at all times, with lots of people in our life, often feeling a nagging sense of wrongness in our relationships and searching for the "right" relationship or relationship style.

Several times in our life, the singular "MJ" who did this was "eclipsed" by other selves, but we didn't have that understanding back then. We thought we had become anxious/depressed, because engaging with other people felt terrifying and all the joy went out of life. In some relationships, we also had meltdowns, or emotional flashbacks, which again we now understand as the more traumatized selves in our system being triggered and suddenly finding themselves in the driving seat—with no idea of what was going on, or that there was anyone else in here. This only tended to happen with partners, and we can see now how this was the selves who had more needy/dependent and/or angry/blaming relationship styles (Robin and Morgan).

If you look at the image we drew in section 3.3, you can see that we now recognize two pivotal points in our childhood when one part of a self was disowned and one came forward. At five, we learned that we mustn't show our fear and sensitivity, so we repressed this "bad" boy, and foregrounded a "good" people-pleasing boy (both parts of Robin). At nine, we learned that neither of these selves was acceptable at the school we went to, so we became the "bad" angry girl to protect them, and when that was too dangerous, she became our inner critic, and projected a "good" girl who did well and fitted in with everyone, with the critic in the background telling her how to be (both parts of Morgan).

In terms of the shame compass and trauma patterns, our go-to would be "good girl" avoidance/flight with "good boy" attack in/ fawn (just under the surface). Deeply buried under that, "bad" Morgan held attack out/fight, and "bad" Robin withdrawal/freeze: the two ways of relating that were absolutely forbidden for us, as we were not allowed to show fear or anger. Our zine, "Triangles (and Circles) of Selves," has a lot more about how this worked.

A major reason why we've spent the last five years or so of our life working deeply on our inner system is because we realized how much suffering we—and others—were experiencing in our relationships, because of how unbalanced we were. We couldn't feel the fear and anger that might warn us when a relationship wasn't a good idea to pursue, and we often struggled to be really intimate in relationships and not to fall into people-pleasing and rescuing behaviors. Gradually, we dropped those avoidance/flight and attack in/fawn strategies, and the "good" parts who did those things kind of emptied out, so that Robin and Morgan could come forward fully and learn how to be in relation—with the rest of us and with other people.

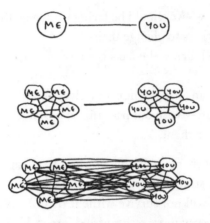

*Figure 4.4: Singular and plural understandings of relationships*

People have very different experiences of plurality, from those for whom it feels quite metaphorical to acknowledge their "parts," to those—like MJ—who experience themselves as vividly several different people sharing a bodymind. This includes those who identify as plural systems and/or as DID (dissociative identity disorder). However, we feel that the sense of ourselves as systems is useful for everyone to recognize in themselves, and in others. It can certainly help with being compassionate with our own and others' inconsistencies. Emmi Bevensee's article is particularly helpful for drawing out how we can relate with each other in the three ways depicted below: as separate individual selves, as systems which still relate with each other between whole selves, and as systems where each self or part can relate to the selves or parts of another bodymind. Emmi suggests that we can helpfully move between these different models when considering important relationship themes like consent and accountability.

## Accepting and/or changing our relationship patterns

All of this brings us to the complicated question of whether—having identified our relationship patterns, survival strategies, attachment styles, and so on—we should be trying to change them in any way, or expecting others to change theirs.

We have to balance the facts that:

1. We all can, and do, hurt ourselves and others—sometimes very badly—with our patterns, so it is urgent and important to address them.

2. Many of them are highly resistant to change (they're called survival strategies for a reason: on some level, we're often sure we will not survive without them!). Also, they tend to become even more resistant and intractable if we try to push through or force them to alter.

Our view on this is something akin to the recovery movement serenity prayer. It's about accepting the things that we can't (or perhaps shouldn't try to) change, changing the things we can (or should), and—crucially—developing the wisdom to know the difference. In fact, it's not even as binary as this (shocker!) because it can be about accepting and changing the same thing in different ways. It's often essential to accept the feelings we feel when we hit our patterns, while changing how we behave when those feelings hit—for example, feeling the fear/rage we have towards someone without people pleasing or blaming them. This is what's meant by refraining and not repressing (the feelings) or reacting (out of them).

Such endeavors are also often highly paradoxical: sometimes it's only when we stop trying to change something, and accept it, that it finally shifts! This paradoxical process of acceptance/changing requires a lot of patience and compassion. It frequently feels more akin to expanding *around* something than it does to *eradicating* it (see section 2.4).

Some would make divisions between patterns that are innate or learned here. For example, we might say that the relational patterns of innate neurodivergence are ones that we should accommodate—rather than change—and the ones resulting from trauma we should try to change. However, we saw in Chapter 3 that it's often extremely difficult to tease apart what aspects of us we're born with and which we develop, especially as some traumas happen before we're even born. Also, innate things *are* possible to change in our extremely flexible bodyminds, while some learned survival strategies are extremely hard to change, especially when we don't have the resources and support to do so, or alternative strategies available.

Similarly, many people would try to change relationship patterns (in themselves or others) which are non-normative, and accept those that are normative—for example, trying to make an asexual person sexual, or a neurodivergent person communicate in a neurotypical way, but not vice versa. It won't surprise you to hear that we question such divisions! We particularly need to be mindful of the long history of insistence on neuronormativity and how important it is to move towards embracing and accommodating neurodiversity of all kinds instead (see section 3.2).

Also, it's worth being mindful of how some trauma patterns are actively encouraged in normativity (e.g. flight patterns of working very hard and distracting with all the things we can buy, and fawn patterns of conforming to the status quo and not rocking the boat). Others are disallowed, particularly for certain kinds of people—for example, fear/freeze being unacceptable for men in many cultures, or Black people having to mask any sign of fight/anger in many situations because of how dangerous it is to be seen that way by white people. Again, we might usefully try to balance the culture such that all trauma patterns are equally understood as valid responses, as worthy of compassionate engagement, and as shaky foundations indeed for an entire person, community, or culture!

Finally, even becoming aware that we have relationship patterns, survival strategies, and specific ways of relating that may be harmful or unhelpful is a huge task. Part of the reason those shame compass strategies and forms of masking work so well is that they often hide us from ourselves—not just from other people. We may not even know we are doing it, and we may well respond to anybody pointing it out with further defensiveness!

If you do want to embark on a process of moving towards greater acceptance and/or changes in your relationship patterns, there are many ways of doing this. We'll say a bit more about the options in Chapter 6, but useful possibilities would include, for example, working with a trauma and/or systemic therapist either on your own or in your relationship (if this is affordable in your context), or engaging in a recovery support group (such as the reparenting approach of the ACA (Adult Children of Alcoholics and Dysfunctional Families) 12-step program), or with a spiritual tradition which centers self-acceptance and shifting damaging patterns (such as many Buddhist sanghas). These group and peer support options are often available at low or no cost.

All of these approaches emphasize undertaking such work slowly, and developing the capacity to be with ourselves—and others—with as much compassion and honesty as possible. Then the aim is often to attempt to refrain from our usual behaviors, relationship patterns, or survival strategies, and to stay with whatever feelings arise, without trying to repress them or going back to react out of them. For example, if you usually blame other people, you'd refrain from telling people off or messaging all your friends to say how badly you'd been treated, and would try to stay with your anger, without shoving it down, or letting yourself act out of it. Gradually, this way, we learn to be with our relational feelings (holding and hearing them ourselves), instead of acting in various ways to try to avoid them.

In relation to other people's relational patterns, the approach is very similar. We can emphasize that their feelings are absolutely fine, and valid, and need expressing, but we can set boundaries around the behaviors that we're willing to be around based on those feelings (e.g. "It's so understandable that part of you feels abandoned when I embark on a new relationship, and I'd much rather you said something than pretended to be fine. But it's not okay if you tell me off about it, or try to stop me doing it," or "It makes all kinds of sense that you get angry, but when it's about me, I need you to find someone else to share those feelings with while they're live").

In the next chapter, we'll return to the question of how we might learn to be honest about our relationship patterns with each other (whether they come from neurodivergence, trauma, past relationship experience, relationship norms, conscious choices, or something else). This can help us to forge relationships where there is a good fit, where we agree on the relationship container needed, and/or where we can accommodate each other's patterns. All this is much easier to do if people are able to notice and name when they are responding out of trauma, or some aspect of their neurodivergence, for example, and where others can understand this and respond to that in a shame-sensitive way.

This is a lifelong journey (or many lifetimes, according to some faith traditions!). Returning to the conditional/unconditional idea that we explored in section 2.4, you might imagine the unconditional sense of our interconnectedness and fundamental okay-ness as a container or cradle. In this cradle, we can hold the fact that we—and others—are inevitably drawn back to conditional ways of relating with compassion.

## 4.3 RELATIONSHIPS AND YOUR INTERSECTIONS

In Chapter 3, we discussed intersections and introduced two theories that inform our work: intersectionality and positioning. We focused mostly on positioning theory for this book and invited you to consider your own positioning within key relationships growing up. In this section, we invite you to revisit all of these ideas but from this current point in time and relationships, wherever you might be in your life course and whichever relationships you might be in right now.

First of all, though, let's take a moment to reflect on your own intersections right now in relation to systems of power and privilege. We didn't really go into this in the last chapter, so let's make some time to do so now before we revisit the exercise on positioning within key relationships growing up.

When doing the following activity and/or looking at the wheel of power, privilege, and marginalization over the page, please note that although we're asking you to map your current position, we're considering those categories from a systemic perspective. This means that the categories closest to the center are the ones that are considered the most powerful and influential on a collective, sociocultural, linguistic level, not that you necessarily have power on an individual level. For example, a wealthy, documented, immigrant investor who does not speak the official language of the country they live in is not going to have the same power as a houseless, undocumented immigrant who does not speak the same country's official language. We also understand that there are many more nuances beyond what can be captured by three buckets for each category, including how these categories are constructed in different places across the globe.

## ACTIVITY: MAPPING OUR LOCATIONS IN RELATIONSHIPS TO POWER, PRIVILEGE, AND MARGINALIZATION

Take a few moments to look at the picture and then try to draw your own web of positions, at this point in time. Take a pencil and connect from category to category where you're at, right now. Or you could circle where you feel closest to right now. Please note that things change over time. For example, Alex went from not being a citizen in the US for 14 years to being one recently. We'd like for you to map where you are at right now. If you want, you could use a different color or line pattern to map past intersections too. We also provide examples of Alex's and MJ's intersections on the following pages. Please note that this wheel is not meant to be a definitive representation of all

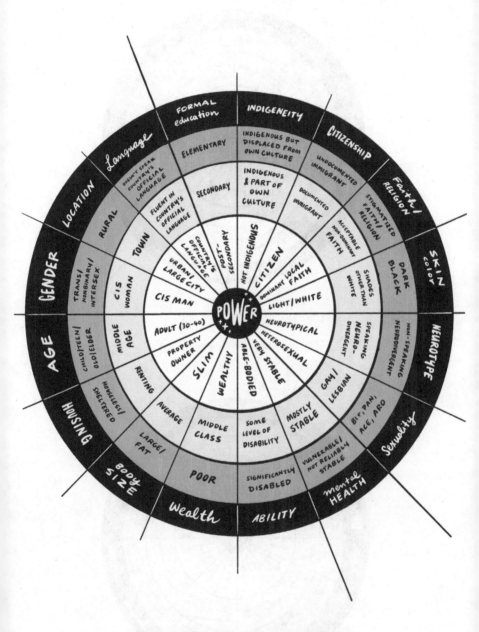

**Figure 4.5: Wheel of power, privilege, and marginalization**

*Adapted from James R. Vanderwoerd (web of oppression), ccrweb.ca (power wheel), Sylvia Duckworth (wheel of power/privilege)*

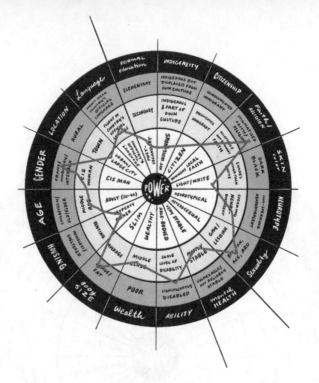

*Figure 4.6: Alex's wheel*

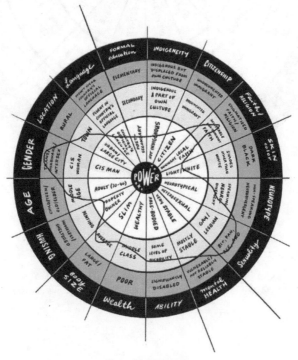

*Figure 4.7: MJ's wheel*

types of power, privilege, and marginalization, and that it's place- and time-dependent. None of these categories are fixed and immutable; rather, they are relational and context-dependent. As always, feel free to redraw your own wheel, leave it completely, or take what is helpful and leave the rest.

We hope that you can approach the activity above with curiosity, compassion, and as much non-judgment as possible. It's not bad to have privilege, and most of us have areas in which we have privilege and in which we don't. These areas are also not static across time and place, or even generations. What we're inviting you into is awareness, since our locations in relation to systems of power, privilege, and marginalization impact how we do relationships now, whether within the context of romantic relationships, partnerships, friendships, parenting, or work relationships. Some of you, of course, might be very aware of your locations and that's okay. Once more, this is not about right/wrong, good/bad, but rather about consciousness and intentionality, as we'll discuss more in the following section.

We'd also like to remind you that intersectionality is about the systemic analysis of experiences through the critical lenses of power, privilege, and oppression. This means that the space you occupy as an individual at this point in time is the result of larger, complex, intergenerational, historical, cultural, and social patterns mostly beyond your individual control. However, being aware of our own web within these larger webs can be really helpful when trying to better understand our current relational patterns.

This is not about oppression Olympics, or comparing yourself to those you are in a relationship with; it's about understanding your own location and complex web of power, privilege, and marginalization better. We hope this means that you can move with more intentionality through the world and within your relationships. Please note that we said "move" and not "walk on eggshells." It can be easy to get caught up in shame, especially if we have more privilege than most, and end up walking on eggshells around others, especially if they have less privilege than we do. However, this, in our opinion, doesn't serve anyone's liberation, but rather it reproduces oppressive cultural and social dynamics. We want, of course, to consider some of the characteristics we talked about earlier, such as differentiation, mutuality, care, and compassion. However, being afraid of making mistakes in a relationship or walking on eggshells are symptoms of trauma, and we encourage you to look at these with care, curiosity, compassion, and support when these reactions come up.

Now that we've considered our intersections, let's revisit the activity from the previous chapter where we invited you to engage with your positioning within key relationships in your life while growing up. We would like to invite you to combine the awareness of your current web of power, privilege, and marginalization with what you learned about yourself and others growing up through your positioning experiences within key relationships. Alex will revisit their example from the previous chapter to show you what we mean.

## REVISITING ALEX'S EXAMPLE AND REFLECTION

My nonna (grandmother) died almost two decades ago now, so looking back at our relationship is complicated. When I think about all the ways in which our relationship impacted my life, two of the things that stand out to me are culture and class. Culturally, there was nothing strange about me sharing a bed with my nonna on and off throughout my childhood and adolescence. Class-wise, it also made sense for my nonna to take care of me, given that both my parents worked and didn't earn enough to pay someone like a nanny. My nonna also taught me Sicilian, which is a distinct language from Italian, and passed on many of the cultural traditions to me, which, combined with spending several months out of the year in Sicily, gave me a sense of belonging to place, language, culture, and ancestors—basically, a sense of Indigeneity. She also brought me up in a combination of Catholicism and animism—typical in Sicily, I would say—which enabled me to claim my own spirituality as a Pagan later on in life and to feel a continuity of lineage that many don't have the privilege to experience. Even though my positioning in that relationship made it harder for me to understand consent and boundaries, especially when I moved to Anglo countries, it also enabled me to develop a strong sense of cultural, social, historical, and linguistic identity, which has served me well in many of my relationships, especially with other non-Anglo folks.

The positioning as "the clever one" in my family also meant that I continued to pursue educational opportunities, despite the confusion experienced in school as an unrecognized neurodivergent person who was labeled both smart and stupid within the educational system. Eventually, this led to me accepting a scholarship to do a PhD in the UK, where I had moved two years before, and to move class completely. Unlike one of my partners who also has a doctoral degree, though, my friends are much more eclectic in their educational backgrounds, and some of my close people never went beyond secondary schooling. I attribute my ease in moving between class categories to this positioning dance within my family, and the intergenerational class mobility that I have actively participated in. In relationships, I don't find it hard to talk about money, although I do find it incredibly hard to ask for help, especially financial help, should I need it.

My positioning as both stupid and smart has become much clearer since understanding that I am neurodivergent (AuDHD, specifically). This has shed a new light on many of my interactions within the educational system, but also on interactions with my peers growing up. I am still unpacking how my neurodivergence has impacted me and my relationships, but I am experimenting with being more open about it, recognizing what I need, unmasking around people I trust, and practicing not being ashamed of who I am or how my brain works, although undoing internalized ableism seems to be the work of a lifetime!

In terms of sexuality, I now better understand that the way I was being positioned had so much less to do with me and more with the positioning of my boyfriends at the time. Coming into my own gender and sexuality, as also shared in our previous two books, has definitely contributed to so much more ease in my relationships and to accepting my non-normative gender, sexualities, and relational orientations as a trans, bi, queer, polyamorous, kinky person. Although I feel fewer competing impulses between my somatic responses and my prefrontal cortex, I still struggle with sexual shame sometimes, and this can impact my current relationships too. This also intersects with being a survivor of abuse, both as a child and adult, and how this has impacted my relationship with my own bodymind and other people's bodyminds. The bullying growing up also impacts the challenges with accepting my own fat bodymind, and this is at times reflected in the fact that I struggle to understand why people would be attracted to me. The combination of issues related to my mental health, body size, disability, gender, and sexuality can at times be hard to disentangle in new relationships, as well as in long-term ones.

Finally, I moved away from the Church, but I do miss many of the practices that helped me feel safe and held. In the past few years, I have reconnected to my devotion for the Black Madonna, whom I was brought up to honor as sacred, and connected this to pre-Christian deities and practices, which also helps me have a sense of continuity in my spiritual practices. This has impacted both my relationships with fellow Pagans and brought many new friends and community relationships in my life with Italians from the diaspora, especially trans and queer Sicilian-American people. Nowadays, I find it easier to diverge from people's expectations in my self-positioning and I am increasingly open about who I am, although I still struggle with some sexual shame, as highlighted earlier, and with truly believing that I can be loved in my wholeness. My relationships with ancestors, greenbloods, and deities as well as those with my friends, partners, and children are helping me navigate reclaiming the whole of who I am. I believe this is another lifelong journey.

Here are a few more experiences from a broader range of people to capture some of the diversity of how our intersections and positioning can impact our relationships.

## Multiple experiences: Positioning ourselves within our relationships

"I never saw healthy models of interracial relationships growing up. It always felt as if I were not Black enough and not white enough for either side of my family. That made friendships, community organizing, and intimate relationships challenging for a long time. I kept feeling like I had to 'pick a side' when 'both sides' were already within me, so... how could I pick just a part of me? Finding a peer group of multiracial people has been so helpful and healing for me!"

"I never wanted to parent alone like my dad did. I saw how much he struggled, and I never wanted that for myself or my child. Choosing parenting within a queer, multiparent household was a very deliberate choice for me and one that I don't regret, even when things get rough and complex. One of the things that is hard is that I am the only Indigenous adult in my household, and I wish I had more connections with elders and community."

"Growing up with a parent with complex PTSD wasn't always a piece of cake. Even though she was very open with her struggles and always apologized if needed, there was a level of volatility that rubbed off on me. My current partner struggles with how intensely 'blamey' I can get when I am stressed out, and takes it personally. I know this is something that I need to keep working on, and sometimes I do resent my mom for this, but I also know she was doing her best."

"It's really hard for me to feel at ease with some of my Somali friends who have access to language, family, and culture. As an interracial adoptee, I don't have the same relationship that they do to those things. In fact, I don't talk to my white family any longer because of their lack of accountability around my childhood abuse. I long to connect with my friends, their families, and my language and culture on a deeper level, but too often I feel like an outsider who doesn't belong anywhere. On better days, I feel the love of my friends and family of choice. It can be very up and down."

### Reflection point: Knowing clearly where we come from and who we are

Now that you have done all this work in Chapter 3, and in this chapter so far, take some time to slow down and reflect on that journey. We'd like to invite you to record your thoughts, feelings, and somatic experiences in whatever way feels most accessible to you right now. What is your current positioning, especially within different kinds of relationships? What do you know to be true about yourself? Are there things about your positioning that are non-negotiable in relationships and things that might be more so? If so, what are they? Do you feel capable of communicating your positioning, intersections, history, trauma, and current needs and desires clearly to other people, when it's safe enough to do so? If so, how do other people in your life react when you do? Are there relational patterns that you would like to change or deepen into?

Before continuing our journey to reflect on intentionality within all our relationships, let's take a moment to slow down.

If you like, it's time to take a break from reading, reflecting, and activities for a little while.

In Chapter 3 and Chapter 4 so far, we've excavated a lot of trauma, potentially, and invited you to consider your lives from a multiplicity of positions. If you are having some feelings, we'd understand! If you're not, you might want to slow down and notice whether you are keeping busy to avoid feelings, or numbing out. If you are, we're not judging; we just ask that you be as aware of your own bodymind as possible.

For this one, we'd like to offer a relational, grounding, co-regulating exercise. If you have access to another person, ask if they would be willing to engage in placing their feet on your feet and vice versa. What do we mean by this? You would sit in front of one another, close enough for your feet to touch. One of you would have their feet underneath those of the other person. Stay there and breathe for 3–5 minutes. How does it feel? What do you notice that's coming up for you? Whatever it is, try to meet it with curiosity, care, and as much non-judgment as you can offer yourself right now.

Then, when you're ready, switch positions so that now the other person has their feet on top. Again, stay here and breathe for 3–5 minutes. How does it feel? What do you notice that's coming up for you? Whatever it is, try to meet it with curiosity, care, and as much non-judgment as you can offer yourself right now.

If you don't have access to another person right now, you could do one of the other slow-down pages, and save this to do with someone else at some point, if that feels good to you.

Then, when you're ready, come back to this book.

## 4.4 GETTING INTENTIONAL ABOUT OUR RELATIONSHIPS

By now, you should have a sense of what your relational patterns are, where they might come from, and whether you are comfortable with them or want to try to make some changes. In this section, we'd like to share some tools for getting intentional in all your relationships, including understanding your intimacy needs and priorities better, as well as communicating who you are and what you need to those around you. In the next chapter, we'll go into how differences within and between ourselves impact our relationships and how we might navigate these.

As elsewhere throughout this book, some of these tools will be more applicable to some relationships than others, but we're really thinking about as broad a bucket of relationship categories and types as possible. If something doesn't feel applicable to a specific situation or type of relationship, that's okay. We hope a different tool either in this section or the next one might be a better fit.

You've already done a large part of this work so far by reflecting on the language we use to talk about relationships, how we define them, what messages we have received within historical, cultural, social, and familial contexts, what we learned growing up, and what our relational patterns and positioning are currently. We hope you can take a moment to take it all in and maybe pat yourselves on your shoulder if that feels good! We know that this work can feel like a lot because we've also been through it and continue to engage in it. What we're inviting you to do is not easy or simple, but we believe it's so worthwhile! The next thing to consider is our current intimacy landscape.

If you have read our previous books, you'll have come across the following intimacy assessment before. We find it can be quite helpful to do this activity regularly since we find that priorities and who meets different intimacy needs has changed over time for us and continues to do so. If you've taken this intimacy assessment quite recently and want to skip it, we completely understand! However, we have added a few more types of intimacies since we wrote *Life Isn't Binary*, and we only explored types of erotic intimacy in *How to Understand Your Sexuality*, so you might want to have a look at the new format, which combines both. If you're in a new, intimate relationship, whether romantic and/or sexual or not, you might want to do this with the new person(s) in your life as an invitation to discuss intimacy needs and desires, as well as hopes and expectations, further.

## ACTIVITY: ASSESSING OUR INTIMACY NEEDS AND PRIORITIES IN RELATIONSHIPS

First of all, take a moment to reflect on what intimacy is for you and what it means to you. If you'd like, take some notes on this in whichever way feels most accessible for you at this moment. We define intimacy as any type of closeness that we might have within ourselves, with the ecosystems we're part of, or with other people outside of ourselves. We also believe, as you can see from the assessment below, that there are many types of intimacies. We have not redefined each type of intimacy at length here since we've already discussed this in *How to Understand Your Gender*, *Life Isn't Binary*, and *How to Understand Your Sexuality* in a number of ways.

Now, if you want, take time to consider all the 17 different types of intimacy in the table that follows. Guiding questions for your exploration might be: Do you experience this type of intimacy? If not, would you like to, or is it simply not important for you? Are there other types of intimacy you experience? Do they fit in these categories or not? Are there things that block you from experiencing some types of intimacy? If so, what are they? Are there opportunities to explore all these types of intimacy in your life? If so, what are they? If not, what are the obstacles?

Once you've done this, think about how important each type of intimacy is to you. Please note that not all types of intimacy might be relevant for you, and that's absolutely fine. You might want to use a ranking system and order them from 1–17, or use a 1–10 satisfaction scale with 1 being not at all satisfied and 10 being completely satisfied, or a 5 stars system, with 1 star being not very important and 5 very important. You can also invent your own scale or make qualitative notes for each type of intimacy. It's your assessment, so do whatever feels best for you at this moment in time!

Next, reflect on whether your needs around that type of intimacy are met. This could be a simple yes or no, or a more nuanced answer, such as "They're met some of the time—for example, when I visit my family of choice." Then take some time to name all the beings that help you meet those intimacy needs, including yourselves! This could be inner persons or parts, people in your life, greenbloods (plants or trees), animal companions, specific places, bodies of water, or even things like books and movies.

Finally, take a few moments to reflect on this type of intimacy and evaluate whether there is anything you would like to change in this area of your life. For example, would you like more people to meet your needs around this type of intimacy? Maybe you want to show up for yourself more in this one area, or challenge a relational pattern that no longer serves you. Feel free to revisit this intimacy assessment whenever you want, and especially during times when there might be major life changes or shifts in your relational systems. Remember that there is no right or wrong answer. This is your own assessment, and it reflects your own values, experiences, priorities, needs, and desires!

| Types of intimacy | How important is this type of intimacy for you? (You can rank them 1–7 or use another system such as 1–5 stars) | Are your needs met in this type of intimacy? (This could be a simple yes/no or a more nuanced answer) | Who meets your needs in this area, including yourself? (Feel free to write down names and don't forget greenbloods, such as plants or trees, bodies of water, places, and animal companions as well as people—whether inner or outer) | Is there anything you would like to change around this type of intimacy? (This space is to annotate any of your thoughts on whether there is a change in priority, or how these needs get met or any relational patterns you might want to address with regard to this type of intimacy) |
|---|---|---|---|---|
| **Work** Sharing tasks, supporting each other in various responsibilities (e.g. raising family, house chores) | | | | |
| **Play** Sharing experiences of fun, such as recreational activities (e.g. going to dance parties together, sports, hobbies) | | | | |
| **Mind** Sharing the world of ideas (e.g. reading, discussing a movie) | | | | |
| **Commitment** Togetherness through dedication to common values/ideals/practices (e.g. doing activism together; co-parenting; collective living) | | | | |

cont.

| | | | | |
|---|---|---|---|---|
| **Delight**<br>Sharing experiences of beauty (e.g. nature, art, dance, theater, interior decor) | | | | |
| **Communication**<br>Being truthful and open with each other (e.g. giving constructive feedback) | | | | |
| **Emotion**<br>Sharing significant feelings (e.g. being vulnerable, emotionally open, and available) | | | | |
| **Creative**<br>Helping others to grow and celebrating them as co-creators (e.g. nurturing self-development, celebrating change, making art, or writing together) | | | | |
| **Access**<br>An implicit understanding of access needs out of shared similar lived experience of the many different ways oppression manifests in our lives (e.g. being able to be present with someone's trauma, immediately know that access needs are present and meeting them, such as grabbing a different type of seating) | | | | |

| | | | |
|---|---|---|---|
| **Crisis**<br>Experiencing closeness through standing together at painful/difficult times (e.g. death of a loved one, illness) | | | |
| **Conflict**<br>Facing differences, negotiating conflict resolution (e.g. arguing, disagreeing) | | | |
| **Spirituality**<br>Sharing a sense of communion/belonging (e.g. philosophical or religious experiences, the meaning of life) | | | |
| **Sexual**<br>Sharing sexual and sensual experiences (e.g. kissing, having sex) | | | |
| **Physical**<br>Sharing, giving, or receiving non-sexual touch (e.g. bodywork, wrestling, holding hands, or cuddling with friends) | | | |
| **Ecological**<br>Closeness with land, greenbloods (i.e. plants or trees), non-human redbloods (i.e. animals), and elements such as water, fire, air, and earth. This intimacy is about feeling a sense of kinship and close connection with the world around us | | | |

cont.

**Kink**

The sense of closeness we might experience when engaging in sharing our kinks with others. This could happen through play but also by belonging to communities with whom we might share fantasies, desires, and behaviors that we might not share with others outside of that community. This might or might not be sexual for you. In fact for some people, it's even spiritual. There may or may not be a power exchange as part of this type of intimacy (e.g. dom/sub; daddy or mommy/boy or girl; top/bottom)

**Self-pleasuring**

A sense of aliveness and closeness with ourselves by exploring what brings us pleasure. Once more, this might be sexual or not. We might experience self-pleasuring intimacy through masturbation or fantasy, but also by simply being more present and intentional when we shower or massage lotion into our skin, soothe ourselves in tough emotional states, or notice which food brings us pleasure

* Please note that Alex adapted this exercise from existing materials and ideas by Clinebell and Clinebell (1970) and Metz and by Mia Mingus for the concept of access intimacy in particular, as well as from their own work.

We hope that doing this activity has given you some sense of what is working well in your intimacy landscape right now and what you might want to consider a little more closely or shift entirely in your life. Being aware of all of this is one thing, but being able to communicate who we are relationally, where we've come from, and what our needs and desires are is another.

A way of communicating this, especially to those closest to us but also to potential new friends and/or partners of any kind, is making a relationship user guide. MJ, together with sex educator Justin Hancock, has created several zines that can guide you through this process, including "Make your own relationship user guide" and "Make your own sex manual." While we cannot possibly cover all of the materials from these zines in this book, we'd love to share some guiding questions you might want to use when creating your own user guides, for whichever relationships you choose (e.g. friendships, work partnerships, co-parenting).

---

### Reflection point: Making our own user guides to relationships

In a notebook, voice memo, large piece of butcher paper, or whatever works for you at this moment, take some time to annotate your thoughts around the following questions:

- What is working well for you right now in your relationships?

- What is not working well for you right now in your relationships?

- What kind of relationships would you like to invite into your life?

- What kind of relationships are you not available for?

- What makes you feel comfortable and somewhat secure

in a relationship of any kind (e.g. direct and open communication, consistency, clear and negotiated expectations)?

— What are some of the main triggers for you that you've come across in your relationships?

— How, what, and when do you like to communicate in different types of relationships?

— What are your relational needs right now?

— What are your relational desires right now?

— What are some non-negotiables for you in your relationships (e.g. deal breakers, things that would mean ending a relationship of any kind)?

— What boundaries do you generally need within your relationships?

— How do you address moments of misattunement?

— How do you feel about conflict and how do you manage it?

— Which structures work best for you in relationships (e.g. weekly check-ins, getting together at specific times of the year)?

— What expectations do you have of others in relationships? (This might, of course, differ according to the type of relationship.)

— How do you know when a relationship is working well for you and meeting your needs?

— How do you know when a relationship is working well for someone else and meeting their needs?

We hope that the answers to these questions can lay the foundation for whichever relationship user guides you might want to create and share with those in your lives. Some other things you might want to create to share with others might be:

— values manifestos

— relationship agreements

— type of commitments you're open to

— communication guide

— relationship accommodations

— conflict agreements.

We'll come back to some of these, such as relationship accommodations and conflict agreements, in the next chapter when we discuss differences and ruptures within relationships.

**REMEMBER...** We know we keep saying it, but this is all rather a lot! Please make sure you treat yourself with care and compassion as you work your way through this book. We're sharing a lot of ideas, questions, experiences, reflections, and activities with you, and it can feel overwhelming to digest them all at once. We hope you're taking as many breaks as you need and taking all the time you want in going through this book, truly!

Please remember that your current relational patterns were not set in a day. In fact, many of them, like ours, might have been set over decades! This means that it might take time to accept and/or change them, or even to discern whether you want to accept them, change them, or do something else with them altogether! Alex often says to therapy clients,

"The slower we go, the faster we get there." This is indeed a paradox but one we hope you can embrace with us, and see if it ends up being true to your experience as well!

## Further resources

We listed some good resources about trauma and relationships at the end of the previous chapter.

If you want to read Trev and Viv's book which we mentioned here, check out:

— Butt, T. and Burr, V. (2004). *Invitation to Personal Construct Psychology.* Chichester: John Wiley & Sons.

In addition to Mel Cassidy's book *Radical Relating*, listed in the resources at the end of Chapter 2, a couple of good recent books on consensual non-monogamy are:

— Kent, J. (2022). *A World Beyond Monogamy.* London: Luminastra Press.

— Lindgren, J., Winston, D., and Matlack, E. (2023). *Multiamory: Essential Tools for Modern Relationships.* Jersey City, NJ: Cleis Press.

If you want to read more about shame, check out Brené Brown's work on the subject, and:

— Bradshaw, J. (2006). *Healing the Shame that Binds You.* Deerfield Beach, FL: Health Communications.

You can find (team) MJ's free zines and books about plurality on their website here:

— www.rewriting-the-rules.com/zines

— www.rewriting-the-rules.com/plural-work

Their "Triangles (and Circles) of Selves" zine is available here:

— www.rewriting-the-rules.com/wp-content/uploads/2023/11/Triangles-and-circles-of-selves.pdf

Other useful resources on plurality include:

— Barker, M-J. (forthcoming). "Incorrigibly Plural." In N. Walker (Ed.) *Neuroqueer Theory and Practice.* Autonomous Press.

- Bevensee, E. (2018). "Widening the Bridges: Beyond Consent and Autonomy." Center for a Stateless Society, March 17. Available from: https://c4ss.org/content/50557

- Fadiman, J. and Gruber, J. (2020). *Your Symphony of Selves.* Paris, ME: Park Street Press.

- ACA (2021). *The Loving Parent Guidebook.* Signal Hill, CA: ACA WSO.

- Schwartz, R. (2021). *No Bad Parts.* Louisville, CO: Sounds True.

You can find Meg-John and Justin's zine about relationship user guides here:

- https://megjohnandjustin.com/product/make-your-own-relationship-user-guide-3

Their zine about making your own sex user manual is here:

- https://megjohnandjustin.com/product/make-your-own-sex-manual

CHAPTER 5
<br>
───

# *LIVING OUR RELATIONSHIPS OVER TIME*

This chapter focuses on how we actually *live* our relationships, particularly in the context of how we—and our relationships—inevitably change over time. We start by reflecting on the ways in which we will fit and misfit with each other in different ways in different relationships—for example, in terms of our bodymind diversity, our relationship patterns, our backgrounds, and so on. Framing relationship struggles—and relationship ease—in terms of our fit or misfit in certain areas is a lot more helpful than the common idea that there is any "right" way of relating that everyone should conform to.

We then frame relationships as a constant work in progress where we're always practicing relating. We find this more helpful than any kind of static idea that we "have" a relationship of a certain kind that will stay the same over time. In this section of the chapter, we explore a lot of relationship practices, including communicating our wants, needs, desires, boundaries, and limits (with ourselves and each other), discovering our areas of overlap, making communication and conflict agreements, and dealing with relational ruptures.

In the second half of the chapter, we turn specifically to transitions and endings in all kinds of relationships. We explore how the cultural norms around break-up can easily push us towards staying together and/or breaking up, when those may not be the best thing for us and/or when there may well be other options beyond that binary. Then we explore why consensual and conscious relating go hand in hand, because we need to be conscious of things like cultural norms and relationship patterns, in order to move towards consensual relating. We consider all the different elements that can close down, or open up, our capacity to be consensual in relationships.

## 5.1 FITTING AND MISFITTING

We've been doing a lot of groundwork to understand our relationships so far, but what about how to practically navigate our relationships as they change over time? Given that change is indeed one of the only constants in the multiverse, it makes sense for us to think about how change might impact us and our relationships. Unfortunately, dominant cultures can give us the message that relationships are supposed to stay the same when this is not the case. For example, it's common for parents and children to not have many, if any, models for how to navigate transitioning their relationship to an adult–adult parent–child relationship as the children become adults. We also notice that people sometimes have expectations that their partners, whether romantic, sexual, or not, will stay the same, more or less, whereas we have experienced first-hand that people change. For example, we both changed gender identities and expressions and understanding of our neurotypes in the 20 years we've known each other, to name but a couple of things that changed for us just in the last two decades of our lives! In fact, even over the last week, during the writing retreat to co-author this book, we've been able to communicate more with one another about our own trauma patterns, neurodivergence, and relational needs than we have been able to before!

Change can be scary and unsettling, and believe us, as neurodivergent folks, we get that. However, it's also something that is inevitable. Sometimes the change is not even between us, but rather it's internal. We make assumptions about someone else, or our relationship with them, and then the reality of the person or the situation becomes clearer, and we need to shift our own perceptions, hopes, and expectations. This means that sometimes we might really want to fit in with someone else, be it a colleague, friend, partner, creative collaborator, or even child, and it's not happening. These moments can be anything from mildly disappointing and surprising to heartbreaking. There can be so many reasons why some relationships fit and others don't: timing in life, our trauma patterns, differences in values, needs, desires, sexuality, relational orientations, language, aspects of our identities, past experiences, cultural clashes, and so on. Some of these can be reconciled sometimes, and others not, or they might be reconcilable for a time but not forever.

It can be hard to predict the fit or misfit of relationships since there are so many variables, including our own capacity to accommodate differences both in the moment and over time. For example, when Alex got together with one of their nesting partners, most of their colleagues, who knew them both, gave them "three months max" but they're still partners after 23 years at this point and have also been co-parents for the last 20 years and counting. The reasons why their colleagues didn't think their relationship would work were multiple: differences in culture, introversion/extroversion levels, neurotypes, sexualities, relational orientation, and probably things that were personal to their own stories and experiences, rather than anything to do with Alex and their partner. On the other hand, there can be people who seem extremely compatible on paper and just don't mesh. This goes for relationships, partnerships, colleagues, and so on, as we said earlier. Sometimes it's also just as simple as wrong timing or wanting different things at that moment in our lives.

Unfortunately, there can be this idea in dominant discourse that there is "a right way" of doing relationships. We simply don't believe it's true. If it were, there would likely not be so many self-help books on how to parent, or make collegial relationships work, how to find the love you want, how to improve your sex life, how to keep your marriage alive, how to do open relationships, and so on and so forth. As well as books, there are online courses, podcasts, coaching sessions, memes, and more out there. There is no shortage of advice! We want to make it clear that we're not here to tell you how to do your relationships, but rather just to give you things to think about and explore, and some tools we've found helpful both personally and in our work. We expect you to disagree with us at points, or find some of the activities in this book irrelevant, or even useless to you, and that's okay.

Besides self-help books, we're inundated on social media with ideas, rules, and even prescriptions on how to do relationships "right": this is how to have a healthy relationship, here's how to set boundaries, listicles on when to know it's time to cut toxic parents out of your life, how to parent "right," how to have a non-toxic household, how to find the "right" work environment, and so on and on. That is a lot of noise to cut through from experts, influencers, people with lived experiences, therapists, coaches, and authors like ourselves.

It's hard to break away from normativity. As humans, we have a deep desire to know what's "right" and "good," what's going to make things work—ultimately, what is going to help us avoid pain. We need to feel some sort of control in our lives, but the reality is that there's so much outside of our control, especially when it comes to relationships, whether they be with the ecosystem we're part of, with inner people/parts of ourselves, or with others around us. Let's take a moment to read a few experiences of people reflecting on relationships, and how they've been surprised by fits and misfits in their own lives so far.

## Multiple experiences: Fitting and misfitting over time

"When I first met Joan at work, I thought she was everything I ever hated about liberals. I avoided her like the plague! Then we were assigned to the same work project and were forced to spend quite a bit of time together. Slowly, in bits and pieces of conversation here and there, we found we had a lot in common, actually. Sure, there are differences, but some of the things that bind us in our friendship are much stronger than those differences. Now she is one of my closest friends—dare I say even my best friend? We also rubbed off on each other. We've both changed our views on some things and helped each other have more nuance and fewer big declarations around right and wrong. I hate how idyllic and idealistic this all sounds, but it's how it went down."

"I never expected to not like my child. For a long time, I felt like I failed. How could I have gone so wrong? What could I have done differently? Where did the little boy I adored spending time with go? Whose fault was it? I wanted someone to blame, and I blamed myself plenty. Finally, I understand that while I will always love him, he has made choices that are just not compatible with my values and who I am. There is no way of 'liking' that. Like I said, love is not in question, but I cannot like someone who votes for political leaders who actively seek my destruction, for example. Sometimes I still have hope, but most of me has resigned to the fact that I will likely not have the relationship with my adult son that I had hoped for while he was growing up."

"I always wanted a romantic partner. I remember being very young and playing weddings with my dolls and my friends. As a teenager, I had drawings and dreams of what my wedding day would be like. Somehow, none of my relationships ever ended up working out longer term. However, in my 40s, I came across ecosexuality and started developing a deeper relationship with the land I'm a settler on, and getting to know the trees and plants around me, and I found such deep love in these relationships. For the past 20 years, I have been devoted to my relationships with the natural world around me, and it's the best romance I could ever dream of. People don't always get this and ask me if I'm lonely because I don't have a human partner, but I feel the least lonely I've ever been and so in love every day with this beautiful world."

"My partner and I were perfect. I know this might seem like an exaggeration, but I kid you not: we were so incredibly compatible. Our desires fit so well, as did our values. We found each other incredibly hot and had great sex. We liked each other's friends and families, which is unusual, I know. We were best friends as well as romantic and sexual partners. We lived together with ease, since our habits were very in tune as well. It was heartbreaking when we decided to break up, and we surprised a lot of people who had looked at us as the 'perfect couple' for the past ten years. In the end, they wanted to be a parent and I didn't. We looked at this for years, since we met when we were just in our early 20s, but couldn't find a way through. We went to therapy, cried, bargained with ourselves and each other, but in the end, we decided that splitting was the way to go. We wanted each other's happiness and, more importantly, neither of us wanted to bring a child into this world if one of us was going to resent them. We're still friends, and they have a toddler now. Sometimes I get sad and miss them, but I know that we're both happier for making the choice we did and staying true to ourselves."

"My roommate and everyday partner in life is my octogenarian great-aunt. This is not what I had expected a few years ago. I wanted to live communally, but I always thought it would be with peers or partners. Life had other plans, and due to a lot of circumstances, here I am, having a wonderful time with my elderly but still very sharp great-aunt who is also my godmother. Some people think it's a burden, or that I'm 'so good' for taking her in, but the truth is that I find so much comfort and support in our relationship as well! It's hard to explain that to people who aren't close to me or don't know me very well. She's also helping me co-parent my child, and it feels such a gift to not be doing this alone socially, emotionally, physically, and economically. She might not be the co-parent I expected, but she's great at it!"

**Reflection point: Embracing the unexpected in relationships**

Now that you have thought about fitting and misfitting in relationships, and read the multiple experiences above, we invite you to take some time to reflect on a few questions. As always, please feel free to engage with the questions that feel meaningful to you at this point in your life, and leave the rest. You can also create your own questions or just reflect on everything we have shared so far in this section!

Are there relationships in your life that were surprising or unexpected? If so, which ones? What did you learn/are you learning from and through them? If not, what sense do you make of that? For example, do you feel you usually hang out with people who are very much like you in most ways? If so, what would it look like to be open to connection with people who might be different from you in some way? What's the difference between safety and comfort for you, especially in relationships with others, whether internal or external others, or with the ecosystem around you?

When things change within yourselves, in others, or in your relationships, how do you react? Is it easy, difficult, or neutral for you to embrace change? When you're drawn to someone or something (e.g. a spiritual tradition, place), do you try to "force" yourself to fit in or shape yourselves to fit what you think they want or need? If so, what is that like for you? Which needs and desires that are different from yours do you feel you can accommodate, and which ones do you feel you cannot? What is your relationship with change in general?

## Change and control

Change, surprises, and the unexpected in general can bring up a lot of anxiety for many of us. One of the ways in which we try to deal with anxiety as humans is to attempt to regain some sense of control. In relationships, this could happen in a multiplicity of ways. We're not going to list all of these here, but we do want to talk about control in relationships a little bit, especially as it often happens as a reaction to either feeling anxious about our relationships or navigating unexpected changes. One of the ways in which sometimes we can end up trying to control the uncontrollable is to assume that other people need what we need. Sometimes this is also called "projecting."

For example, Alex struggled with body image growing up, as touched on in their reflection in Chapter 3. Some of those struggles felt rooted in gender, so they wanted to make sure their daughter didn't face similar struggles and was very affirming when she was a teenager. One of the ways they tried to be affirming was to make positive comments on how she looked, especially when she was trying out a new style of clothing or hair. However, her daughter pointed out that, to her, this felt misogynistic, because they didn't make as many remarks on her brother's appearance, and also that it felt unnecessary and not always welcome! This wasn't easy feedback to hear but it was very fair, and Alex was, and still is, grateful that their child felt confident enough to let them know that their impact was very different from their intention. This is an example of how Alex was projecting their past experiences, suffering, and needs on their child. While the intention might have been "good" (to ensure their daughter had a positive self-image), the impact was that they were being non-consensual and not relational. It feels scary to even write this, but we believe it's necessary for all of us to understand how easy it can be to cross someone else's boundaries, or to impose our own needs on them when we're driven by our pain. Instead, we need to learn how to engage in open communication about what the other person's needs are.

These incidents can happen in any and all of our relationships. As humans, we can tend to think that what we feel, think, or experience is universal, if we're not careful. Egocentrism is a word that we could use for this, meaning the inability to differentiate between ourselves and someone else. We have witnessed this create a lot of pain and problems in all sorts of relationships. This is why we talked about differentiation as one of the characteristics of loving and affirming relationships. We cannot truly love or care for someone if we're not differentiated. We need to see the other as someone with their own history, identities, experiences, needs, desires, and hopes to be able to give them what *they* need rather than what *we* imagine they need.

For example, we both have had people in our lives who have pushed their needs aside to give us what they thought we needed, and then resented us for it, and at times even blamed us for it, despite us not even knowing what they were doing! Honestly, we've also done the same in the past, when we were so desperate to fit with someone, or to have the relationship we wanted or thought we wanted, or were terrified of losing someone. Once more, if you're resonating with some of this, or reflecting on ways you have been controlling in relationships in some ways, or others have been controlling with you, please go slow, breathe, reach out for support, and generally take care of yourselves. Remember to be compassionate and as non-judgmental as possible, as you have a look at your relational patterns and histories.

## ACTIVITY: WHAT IS IN OUR CONTROL AND WHAT'S NOT IN RELATIONSHIPS

Let's take a moment to engage in a simple activity. This might be an idea that's very familiar to you or not. Regardless, we find that it's a helpful activity to engage in again and again, especially when we're feeling anxious, stressed, insecure, or fearful in a relationship. You might want to think about a specific relationship for this activity, or just relationships in your life generally. As always, there is no right or wrong here, but rather what you choose to do, which can include not engaging with the activity at all!

When you're ready, take some time to write or draw inside the circle in the diagram below all the things that are within your control in a relationship, or in relationships in general, and then write or draw outside of the circle all the things that are outside of your control. For example, inside the circle you might write things like "leaving or staying in the relationship" (although we know this is more complicated than that in some situations, such as abusive ones), "self-soothing," "being open about my feelings," "being honest with myself about my needs." Outside the circle, you might write things like "other people's feelings," "other people's reactions," "weather," "capitalism," and so on. Feel free to adapt this exercise in a way that works for your bodymind, as usual.

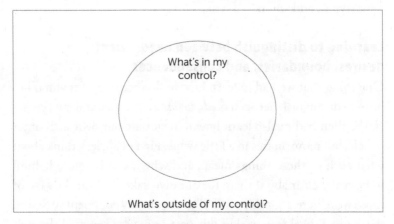

What's in my control?

What's outside of my control?

*Figure 5.1: What's in our control and what's not*

Given that so many things can be outside of our control and can change in our relationships, in the next section we'll be focusing on some relational practices that we've found helpful in our own lives, and that some of our therapy clients have found helpful too.

## 5.2 RELATIONSHIPS AS PRACTICE

You might assume that since we're writing a book about relationships, we're going to be great at it, right? Well, wrong actually. A lot of what we've learned has been through trial and error. We've made so many mistakes, and still do, and we certainly haven't had the best role models growing up. So, what qualifies us to write this book besides our scholarship, training, and work as therapists? One of the things that we believe is helping us write this book is that we're committed to practice being in relationship (because how could we not, given that we're part of an ecosystem?), and to nurture intentional relationality in all aspects of our lives. In this section, we'll share some of the principles and tools to practice intentional relationality. As we keep saying, please take what is helpful and leave the rest. Feel free also to adapt any of the suggestions below to your own circumstances, relationships, neurotypes, and so on.

## Learning to distinguish between needs, wants, desires, boundaries, and consequences

One thing that we had to learn how to do (because of trauma) has been to distinguish between *needs, wants, boundaries,* and *consequences.* We then had to also learn how to negotiate our own with other people, but more on this in a little while. First of all, let's think about what each of these things mean, and why it can be quite helpful to be really clear about them for our own sake, and for the sake of those we're in relationship with. If you're already confident with this, that's great! Feel free to skip this part or maybe just read through it to see whether we might have a perspective that's different or similar to your own.

The first obvious thing to say about *needs* is that they're not mere desires. While desires are important, they're not essential (if they are, they're likely a need rather than a desire). A need is not negotiable and it's foundational. We need food, water, and shelter to live. For example, Alex needs people to communicate directly rather than indirectly. If people don't do this, it's likely that Alex will miss rather a lot from the communication being attempted, or will feel taken by surprise or even triggered. MJ needs time to check in with their system. If they don't, they will more easily become distressed and even triggered. Our needs are not demands, though. We all have things that we need to function within ourselves and in relationships. However, people are not required to meet our needs. We then have a choice with what we do when people in our lives don't meet our needs. Can we meet our own needs? Are there relational needs that are non-negotiable? Is there a compromise available?

When it comes to needs, we like the idea of *relationship accommodations*, a term first used, as far as we know, by a neurodivergent psychologist, Raffael Boccamazzo. This term indicates the practice of making reasonable adjustments to meet the other person's needs, and to enable them to meet our needs. This can be applied to relationships in almost any context. The concept of differentiation, introduced much earlier in this book, is also helpful here. If the other person is different and distinct from me, it makes sense that their needs might also differ from mine, which means that we need to find a way of accommodating one another's needs, when possible and reasonable.

Unlike needs, *wants* are more about desires—that is, things that are nice to have but we can live without, most of the time. If we can't live without it, it's probably more of a need than a want, whether we like to admit it or not! We can feel very strongly about what we want, so much so that we might end a relationship of any kind if we're not getting some of what we want. Distinguishing between needs and wants can be important when we're trying to discern whether a relationship is working or not. One thing that's also important is communicating our needs and wants with others, rather than just keeping them to ourselves. There's more on the importance of communication in relationships a little later in this section.

We can have both needs and wants in relationships. If we're barely getting what we need in a relationship, it might not be very satisfying. If we're getting only what we want but not what we need, it might be a fun relationship but not a sustainable one in the long run. Our relationships generally need to meet a mix of needs and wants to feel affirming and supportive rather than merely functional. We're not telling you what is a need and what is a want, in terms of relationships, because there are too many variables that go into it. For example, access to a car might be a want for someone because they can also use public transport, walk, or bike. For someone else, it might be a need because they're disabled and cannot easily access alternative forms of transport. Similarly, in a relationship, for some people not getting startled might be a want, and for others it might be a need because of trauma or neurodivergence.

This seems a good segue into talking about *boundaries*—that is, the lines we draw around what we are or are not willing to do, put up with, or engage in within relationships. Our boundaries are grounded in our needs, principles, values, beliefs, and general sense of integrity and morality. Boundaries help us stay in relationships because when we can trust their no, we can better trust their yes, and, vice versa, when they can trust our no, they can also trust our yes. Yes and no are straightforward examples of boundaries.

Please notice the "no" in the phrase "I don't know." If someone says "I don't know," it's at the very least a no for now. "Maybe" is similarly a "no for now," and a signal that the person needs to think about their boundaries, needs, and wants a little more than they can at this present moment. Boundaries can be as simple as yes, no, maybe, or more complex and nuanced, of course. Some common boundaries in relationships can be a right to withdraw consent at any point, the right to keep something private and confidential, or having some time for ourselves. A boundary is not about controlling someone else's behavior, but about being clear on what we need to feel secure enough to engage in a relationship.

Boundaries on their own are not enough, though, which is why we want to take a moment to talk about *consequences*. Consequences are what happens after we set a boundary. Boundaries without consequences don't usually get us very far. For example, when parenting, if a boundary is set around not being hit by your child, what are the consequences for hitting? Please notice that we're saying consequences and not punishment. There is a difference, even though at first glance it might not seem so. A punishment is usually retaliatory and not always direct or clear. A consequence should be clear, expected, and communicated. Going back to the example of hitting and parenting, a consequence for hitting might be having a conversation about what happened when the child has calmed down enough to engage in that conversation, at an age-appropriate level. The conversation needs to be held, ideally, when everyone is calm and not upset, led by curiosity and open to possibility.

If one of our boundaries in a relationship is not being lied to, it needs to be clear to those we're in relationship with what happens if they do lie to us, and whether the type or size of the lie makes a difference or not. Are we willing to accommodate someone in our life who uses lying as a management strategy to avoid conflict due to their own trauma? If so, what's the impact on us if we choose to do so, and what's the impact on the relationship long-term? As you've probably noticed, communication is key when it comes to needs, wants, boundaries, and consequences. We'll turn to discussing this shortly, but first let's take a moment to engage in an activity.

## ACTIVITY: GETTING CLEAR NEEDS, WANTS, BOUNDARIES, AND CONSEQUENCES IN RELATIONSHIPS

Take a moment to either pick a specific relationship in your life or to think about relationships in general. Adapt the table that follows to use it in whatever way makes the most sense for you right now. The table is just one example of what you might do. Consider your own needs, wants, boundaries, and consequences for any boundary crossing. Then, if you like, fill out the table. As usual, feel free to make a smaller or bigger table, or choose to reflect on those ideas through a different format.

| In my relationships with... | | | | |
|---|---|---|---|---|
| | Example | Anyone | Specific type of relationships (e.g. work partnership, friends with benefits) | Specific person (add name) |
| I need... | honesty | | | |
| I want... | mutuality | | | |
| My boundaries are... | being able to say no | | | |
| The consequences for boundary crossing are... | first a conversation; if repeated again and again, it might mean ending the relationship for now | | | |

If we have our own needs, wants, boundaries, and consequences for boundary crossing, and others have their own, how can we ever be in relationship with one another without either sacrificing ourselves or asking the other person to sacrifice themselves? We believe this is possible, and as we wrote in *Life Isn't Binary* when discussing relationships, we don't have to get caught in an all/nothing mentality, or dualistic thinking where it's "either my needs or yours."

What follows is a graphic depiction of what we're ideally looking for when relating with others: that sweet spot in a Venn diagram where our needs, wants, boundaries, and consequences either overlap or are close enough. If there is no sweet spot, is there enough proximity that we can work with it? We can't answer that question, or many others, for you, but hopefully this helps you find some of your own answers.

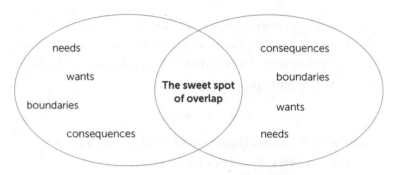

*Figure 5.2: The sweet spot of overlap*

## Communication agreements

As we said earlier, communication is rather vital in all of this. While it would take an entire book to go into depth about communication, we'd like to just touch on it here to make sure we don't overlook this important relational pillar. While clear and direct communication is usually the most accessible for many people, including neurodivergent people, it's not always easy to engage in it. For example, we might have been brought up in a culture where direct communication is considered rude, as it is in the Midwest of the United States. Other things that can keep us from being able to communicate clearly and directly might be trauma, neurodivergence (ironically), past experiences, language barriers, and so on.

One thing that can help in any kind of relationship is to have explicit communication agreements, rather than implicit ones. What do we mean by that? Many types of communication agreements are implicit. For example, you, as the reader, are reading this book, rather than rewriting it as you go. There are implicit sociolinguistic and cultural agreements that position you as the readers and us as authors. When we have colleagues, friends, children, siblings, parents, or partners, we might have all sorts of expectations when it comes to communication, and those might be implicit or explicit. They're implicit if they're not shared and explicit if they are.

If you're not sure what you need in terms of communication, you might want to spend some time reflecting on your communication needs, wants, expectations, and style. For example, are you a verbal processor, or do you need some solo time to reflect on something that's brought to your attention before being able to communicate about it with another person?

**Reflection point: Questions to ask ourselves first with regard to communication**

Communication agreements can be really helpful in making the implicit explicit. Some questions you might want to ask yourself first before negotiating a communication agreement with others are:

— How often do I want to communicate with this person?

— How do I want to communicate (e.g. in person, on the phone, via video, text)?

— What happens if communication breaks down? What do I need in those circumstances?

— Are there topics that are off-limits in this relationship and, if so, are they always off-limits or only when we're communicating via certain methods?

— Do I have needs, wants, boundaries, and consequences that have not yet been expressed in this relationship?

— If there is a crisis, do I need to communicate things differently?

— Are there deal breakers when it comes to communication in this relationship?

These are just some of the questions you might want to ask yourselves when considering writing a communication agreement with someone else. We can't write communication agreements alone because they involve other people. We can first of all work at being clear about our own communication wants, needs, boundaries, and consequences, but then we need to bring them to the other person(s) to see what might work or not work for them. Out of that negotiation process, we can, hopefully, come out with a communication agreement that works for everyone involved. While there is quite a bit written about communication agreements for work teams, we believe that explicit communication agreements are helpful in any relationship. Those agreements can be more or less thorough and more or less formal, but we do believe that some form of explicit communication agreement is necessary to make relationships work.

We're not providing you with a communication agreement template, because each type of relationship might need a slightly different format. A communication agreement can also be as simple as a conversation, or it can become an ongoing conversation, and it doesn't need to be written down, unless that is one of your needs because of memory, language, trauma, or processing issues. If you need to write down your communication agreements, that is absolutely fine! It might be that this is one of your relational needs, and it's okay to ask for what you need.

## Regular check-ins

Communicating is great, but what happens when we don't make time for it? At the beginning of a relationship, because of that new relationship energy with a new friend or partner, or when we have external structures forcing us together, such as at work or school, we might not need to put much thought into when to communicate. However, at other times in our lives, communication can really slide if we don't actively pay attention to it.

One way to ensure that we're tending to our relationships is not only to have communication agreements, including expectations, clear but also to make time for regular, potentially structured, check-ins. For example, we, MJ and Alex, just had a communication check-in during the writing retreat focused on this book. We were able to clarify whether our communication patterns and frequency felt good or not, and to start talking about any changes we might want to make.

Regular check-ins and agreed-upon relationship processes and containers are great ways to prevent larger problems later on. We know that if we're not careful, it can be easy to let things slide until we're truly upset, resentful, or, worse, done with a relationship without the other person ever even knowing why we made that decision or what actually went wrong. There can be many ways to check in, depending on our relationship. Here's a list of examples that we hope might inspire you to come up with the types of check-ins you need in your own relationships right now.

## Types of regular check-ins

— *A round of roses, thorns, and buds at dinnertime once a week, or even once a day.* Everyone takes turns at sharing their rose (something joyful), thorn (something painful and upsetting), and bud (something they're looking forward to). This can be done for that day or week. It can be a particularly good way to check in with children.

— *Daily, weekly, monthly, and seasonal check-ins.* There is a space for all of these types of check-ins in relationships. Much depends on what commitments you share with others, what type of relationship you're in, and so on. For example, you might want to check in daily with an assistant, or weekly might feel like enough. You might want to check in seasonally with your spiritual community as a whole. In intimate relationships, such as partnerships or parent–child relationships, we suggest checking in at least weekly, with shorter daily check-ins if possible. Make sure that time for these check-ins is protected, and that everyone involved understands this is a priority and reschedules it if necessary. One relationship can have multiple check-ins of varying length. For example, you might want to have a quick daily check-in with a partner at the beginning and/or the end of the day, a slightly longer weekly one, a leisurely monthly one, and a more in-depth one seasonally.

- *Meal-planning check-ins.* If you live with other people, checking in about meal planning and grocery shopping can be extremely helpful in avoiding resentment, quick meals, and lots of takeout not out of choice but out of necessity. If you're also raising children with them, you might want to use some of this time to go over the school drop-off/pick-up schedule, driving-to-activities schedule, and so on.

- *Parental check-ins.* If you co-parent with someone, co-parenting check-ins are also really important to make sure issues don't fester. Co-parenting check-ins are needed whether you live with the other co-parent(s) or not, if you want to avoid bigger issues later on.

- *Self check-in.* One of the types of check-ins that can sometimes be neglected is that with ourselves. We feel that checking in with ourselves is just as important as checking in with people around us. Sometimes, this is when we realize that maybe our needs have changed, or that we need to communicate something new to people in our lives, and so on. If you have a sense of having different parts or selves, you can make regular times to check in with all of them, or ensure that you do so when something big happens (see section 4.2). For example, team MJ have a bag of little stones with designs on them representing each of them, and they often take time on the full and new moons for each self to hold their stone and talk about their regrets and gratitudes, or just how they're doing at the moment. They also often journal dialogue between some of their selves if any of them are struggling or having insights. We invite you to not neglect this important type of check-in.

- *Specific, structured check-ins.* There are also models of relational check-ins, such as PIERS, the RADAR, and HALT. PIERS is a good check-in for giving and getting a sense of how everyone is doing. It stands for Physical, Ideas/Intellectual, Emotional, Relational, and Spiritual. Each person in a group (or just two people) has a set amount of time to talk about where they're currently at in each of these areas of experience. You can also add a point at the end of the share where you say whether there's anything that's live for you in that specific relationship, and whether you each/all have capacity to talk about that today—and any preferences for that. You can find a zine about how to do this in the further resources. The RADAR model is good for regular relationship check-in meetings. It stands for Review, Agree the Agenda, Discuss, Action Points, and Reconnect, and was created, as far as we know, by Jase Lindgren, Emily Sotelo Matlack, and Dedeker Winston who host the Multiamory podcast and co-authored a book with the same name. You can find a link to more information about it in the further resources. The HALT model encourages us to slow down and check whether we're in a space to communicate, or if we're Hungry, Angry, Lonely, or Tired. If that's the case, we should take care of ourselves first. It was first developed to support people in recovery from addiction, but it can be a helpful checking-in point for anyone in any number of situations.

## Reflection point: Which check-in do you need in your current relationships?

Let's slow down and take a few moments to think about your current relationship landscape. As you consider the types of check-ins listed above, which do you find appealing or helpful, if any? Are there types of check-ins you would like to introduce in your relationships? If so, which ones? Maybe you have tried to have regular check-ins in your relationships before, and they haven't worked very well. If so, can you identify what didn't work for you or others? What can you learn from these experiences? Would you be willing to try to use check-ins again? If so, what would you need to feel they were effective? As usual, use whichever method feels most accessible to you in this moment to reflect and take notes on these topics.

## Planning for misattunement, rupture, and conflict

Although we're sharing several tools with you here, we're not necessarily expecting you to use them all, or implement them all at once, even if they're appealing to you. We also want to make sure that we're explicit in another one of our beliefs, which comes very much from experience, as well as from reviewing the existing literature in this field as scholars: *it's impossible to be in relationship, any kind of relationship, without encountering at least some misattunements, rupture, and conflict.* There is no formula that we know of that can help us bypass or avoid rupture or conflict altogether, even though we understand that rupture and conflict can be scary and undesirable for many of us for very valid reasons (family trauma, anyone?).

We'd like to propose that while we cannot avoid misattunement, rupture, or conflict, we can at least prepare for them. *Misattunement* occurs when the other person or people are not in tune with where we're at, or what we need. For example, if a baby is pushing away because they've had enough social stimuli at that moment, but a parent interprets that as rejection and tries to connect harder, that is a moment of misattunement. In adult peer relationships, a moment of misattunement can look like making a joke when someone needs to be held in a more serious container.

Moments of misattunement are unavoidable because nobody can be finely tuned into what someone else needs 24/7. They need to be expected in relationships and they don't need to lead to deeper rupture, especially if we're able, prepared, and willing to recognize what happened in that moment, apologize if need be, and move on. If someone is constantly misattuned to our needs, it can be a problem in the relationship, but to expect someone to be attuned to our needs at all times is not realistic since even babies' caregivers cannot do that. However, if we've experienced trauma, we might be more sensitive to misattunement than other people. If so, just as with any other relational patterns we've talked about, it's very helpful to be aware of this and to learn what we need to communicate to those around us in those moments.

*Rupture* can come from a moment of misattunement, but it's generally considered a more serious break in the relationship fabric that holds us together, as can be intuited from the term. Ruptures are also to be expected in relationships, although they're hopefully not too frequent, serious, or intense. An unintentional boundary crossing can be a form of rupture. For example, maybe you're used to casual touching or interrupting when communicating with friends, because that is culturally appropriate to your upbringing, while someone else might view these as moments of boundary crossing, especially if you don't know each other well. This type of rupture can lead to getting to know one another better and to clarifying what everyone needs when communicating, leading to appropriate relationship accommodations so that people can become more comfortable with one another. Due to linguistic, cultural, and social differences, we can also find ourselves in situations where someone thinks we had a rupture and we're not aware of it, or don't consider it such, which can be a rupture in itself!

*Conflict* is when the rupture is severe enough to cause a prolonged clash in the relationship. While misattunement and rupture can also be intolerable for some people, conflict can be downright scary for many since most of us haven't had healthy models from whom to learn how to handle conflict. In the next chapter, we'll talk more about managing conflict within communities, especially in relation to accountability. Alex also has a book coming out with a different co-author on engaging in conflict from a trauma-informed lens (see further resources at the end of this chapter). For now, we want to briefly mention a couple of things about conflict before moving on to the next section in which we address relationship endings and transformations.

First of all, when the conflict is between an adult and a child, the adult is the person responsible for self-regulating since children, as we said earlier, need adults to co-regulate, and not the other way around. It's also really important that adults don't withdraw their affection towards a child as a form of punishment or a manifestation of their anger, since this gives the child the message that they are not lovable in some way, shape, or form. Ultimately, when the conflict is between an adult and a child, or children, the responsibility of repair lies with the adult, even if the adult is the "injured party." This doesn't mean that if you're the adult you need to apologize if you haven't done anything negative or hurtful, such as yelling, but it does mean that you need to make the time to ensure that the conflict is talked about when everyone has cooled down, so that whatever issue happened, it can be avoided or approached differently in the future (see section 3.4 for more on adult–child relationships).

In terms of adult interpersonal relationships, we believe that we can help ourselves and one another navigate conflict better if we can:

— be aware of our own triggers and trauma patterns as much as possible

— be willing and able to recognize our own roles and responsibilities when conflict occurs

- be able to not collapse under shame, especially if someone blames us or if we perceive them as blaming us for what happened

- discern what's ours and what's not ours when it comes to thoughts, feelings, and behaviors

- be clear about our own needs, wants, boundaries, and consequences when engaging with others

- have the capacity and tools to self-soothe

- be driven by a desire for repair through curiosity and not driven by revenge or a desire to hurt the other person because we've been hurt.

It can be helpful for adults in relationships to have a *conflict agreement* created when we're not in conflict with someone. Sex and relationship coach Dr. Sophia Graham has a great example of a conflict agreement on her website, and we've included a link to it in our further resources section at the end of this chapter. For now, let's engage in the last activity for this section, if you want to.

## ACTIVITY: CREATING YOUR OWN CONFLICT AGREEMENT

For this activity, you might want to type on your computer or phone, create a voice memo, or write on a piece of paper. Whatever method you choose to use, it's helpful to record your conflict agreement in some way that you can share with others.

Take some time to think about how you would like to show up during moments of conflict in an ideal world. For example, Alex would like to be grounded, fairly calm, congruent with their emotions but not in a trauma response, caring, present, verbal, and relational during conflict. Of course, this is the ideal, and there have been plenty of times when this is not how they have shown up in conflict! As usual, try to be as caring, non-judgmental, and compassionate as you're able to be at this moment. This is not easy work.

Based on how you want to show up in conflict, write out a number of statements starting from the prompt "In conflict, I will..." or "When in conflict, I want to..." or "During conflict, I strive to..." Choose whichever writing prompt above feels best to you right now or feel free to write your own prompt for this activity. Write out as many sentences as you need to explain to yourself and others not only how you want to show up but also what you're committed to doing when in conflict. A brief example might be:

In conflict, I will...

- listen to understand the other person's perspective and not listen to respond

- recognize when I'm too upset to keep engaging in the conversation

- take breaks as needed while communicating clearly when I might be able to re-engage so the other person doesn't feel abandoned

- ask for what I need to be able to stay present

- take care of myself so I can be present

- be honest with myself and others about how I feel

- arrange for a better time to discuss the conflict if I'm hungry, angry, lonely, or tired (HALT model)

- stay focused on the current issue rather than bring up the past, unless the past is relevant to the current context

- be willing to bring in a third party such as a friend, moderator, or family therapist if the other person doesn't feel safe and/or listened to, or if I don't feel safe and/or listened to.

It can feel like a lot to talk about conflict.

In fact, you might even have picked up this book hoping to avoid conflict in relationships, and here we are, telling you that it's unavoidable, in our experience, and that you'd better prepare for it!

We fully acknowledge that this might not be what you were looking for!

So let's take a breath and a break, and slow down, as we do. Of course, you can slow down at any point during reading this book, and we wholeheartedly encourage you to do so. These slow-down pages are just a prompt and reminder to slow down whenever you need or want to.

For this break, we invite you to connect with your own heart. If you feel comfortable and able to do so, take a few moments to place your hands over your heart. If you want to, you can close your eyes, but you don't need to.

Stay here, with your hands on your heart, breathing, for at least a round of 5–6 slow, deep breaths, according to your own lung capacity, of course. Take a moment to imagine that you are holding and supporting your heart as you do so. Can you let yourself be held by your own hands, in your own heart, at this moment?

No worries if the answer is no. Whatever comes up, it's information, and we hope you can hold it with open hands and gentle curiosity.

Stay here with your heart for as long as it feels good, gentle, and supportive. This support is always available to you. While it's nice to be held by others, we can learn to hold ourselves for these moments when another is not immediately available to us.

Then, when you're ready, continue reading...

## 5.3 NAVIGATING RELATIONSHIP CHANGES AND ENDINGS

Having considered how we might navigate moments of misattunement, rupture, and conflict in relationships, let's turn now to navigating more significant relationship endings, and changes over time.

### Dominant cultural messages around staying together and breaking up

As with so many things we've covered in this book, the dominant cultural norms really do not help us here! Here are some of the most common messages that we're aware of around relationship changes and endings:

— Relationships—and the people within them—should remain the same over time. We see this in the idea that couples should live "happily ever after," the sense that it is a big problem if people stop having sex, or feeling love, in the ways they did at the start (the specter of the "sexless" or "loveless" relationship), and the fact that "you've changed" is an insult that people throw at each other as if to change over time is to have betrayed your partner.

— At crunch points in relationships, there are only two (binary) options: stay together or break up.

— Remaining together over time is the mark of a successful relationship, but breaking up is a kind of relationship—and personal—failure. This is true unless you realize you were with the "wrong" person, in which case it is better to break up in order to find the "right" one.

— Because break-ups are a bad thing to happen, someone must be to blame for them, and it is generally better to believe that it is the other person—otherwise, it might be us.

– All of this only applies to romantic relationships.

In section 2.1, we explored how the cultural obsession with romantic partnerships is generally bad, both when we're in such relationships (because it puts us under so much pressure to be everything to each other and meet all of each other's needs) and when we're in other kinds of relationships (because they are so unrecognized *as* relationships, and undervalued, with little guidance or support on how to navigate such relationships).

In relation to break-up, the normative model is really bad for people in romantic partnerships, because it pushes them in two— equally problematic—directions. First, it invites us to ignore, avoid, or hide any significant problems in the relationship because we know that—to acknowledge them—would be to risk a break-up and all the pain and sense of failure this entails. This may well mean that we don't get any support from others about things we're struggling with, and can't be open and vulnerable within the relationship (which gets in the way of intimacy). Second, the normative model pushes us *towards* breaking up as soon as such difficulties do emerge or become impossible to ignore. This is because we have no alternative model of how we might make changes to the relationship or navigate such difficulties in another way.

The normative model is also really bad for people in other kinds of relationships because there is no script at all for navigating changes and endings. With romantic relationship break-ups, particularly in the case of divorce and separation, there is an assumption that they will be painful, and people will grieve and need support. This understanding isn't there for friendships, colleague relationships, group relationships, and others. That means that people in such relationships may well end them quite abruptly, or let them drift, without acknowledging the impact this has, and that we—and others—don't recognize how painful such endings can be, or offer support around them in the same way we might with a romantic partner break-up.

Outside of romantic partnerships, there seems to be an assumption that some kinds of relationship *must* stay together. This is to the point that ending them, or changing them in any significant way, is almost unimaginable. There can be a lot of confusion or blame when we do those things. For other kinds of relationships, though, the assumption is that they will change and end over time, and that we shouldn't struggle with that in any way.

Family relationships generally fall into the first category, which is why it can be extremely hard to distance, or separate, from a parent, child, other family member, or whole family. Friends generally fall into the second category, which is why we might treat friendships as quite disposable, or make life decisions which take us—or our families—away from significant friendships, without considering the impact of that or discussing it with those friends. Of course, there are exceptions to this, and there are some best friendships, friendship groups, and communities where it's seen as unacceptable to change, end, or move away from the relationship.

---

**Reflection point: Assumptions about different kinds of relationships**

Think about the different significant relationships in your life. You might find it useful to refer back to your map from section 4.1. Consider the following questions:

— In which of these relationships do you talk *about* the relationship and how it's going (with each other, with yourself, and/or with other people)?

— In which of these relationships do you have a concept of tending to, or working at, the relationship over time? With which is there a sense that it should just work well for everyone, and you would probably end it, or drift apart, if any problems did come up?

- In which of these relationships would you get support (such as mediation or therapy) if a problem did come up?

- With which of these people/groups/beings would you consult before making a major life decision, including how the decision would impact them—and the relationship?

- In which of these relationships would a major change mean the end of the relationship, and which do you think could probably survive such a change (e.g. stopping cohabiting, moving a much greater distance away from each other, starting a new significant relationship)?

## Changes, endings, and trauma

Thinking back to the material about developmental trauma that we covered in Chapters 3 and 4, this often exacerbates the difficulties in romantic partnerships, and any similarly pressured relationships, because those are the relationships in which our trauma patterns and insecure attachments are often likely to show up most vividly. This is partly because—in dominant culture—people tend to look to such relationships to meet needs that were unmet in childhood, or to get the kinds of love that they lacked, or lost, back then. However, as MJ has found since moving away from romantic and sexual relationships, it is perfectly possible for developmental trauma and insecure attachment styles to show up in other kinds of relationships, perhaps especially when we do start forming more significant relationships with friends or creating families-of-choice in our communities, for example.

When we're not aware of it, trauma bonds and insecure attachments often mean that we respond to relationship difficulties and endings in ways that make them even harder to deal with. This is because they touch on our earliest trauma and shame, and bring with them all of the memories of other painful relationships in the past that we haven't fully processed yet. For example, when people pull away or bring up a problem, we may well feel that we're being abandoned or annihilated, as we were in childhood. The emotions this stirs up can feel overwhelming and unbearable, making it very hard to deal with the present situation, and likely that we'll go back into our survival strategies (e.g. avoiding, attacking, collapsing into shame, or withdrawing).

The tendency to find the situation unbearable and retreat into survival strategies is especially likely if the other person hits our particular "no-go zones" of shame (see section 4.2). Sudden, confusing break-ups often happen because someone, whose good opinion of us we relied upon, seems to have seen one of the things in us that we've tried most to hide or not be (e.g. we never want to be seen as angry because we had a violent parent). Or they've unexpectedly behaved in a way that was shaming for us when we were younger (e.g. touching us without care in a way that reminds us of non-consensual touch as a kid). Even seemingly minor versions of these things, such as an offhand remark about someone being grouchy, or a hug that goes on too long, can easily be enough if we hold a lot of shame around these areas and have buried it deep. Of course, it's often the case—and even harder to deal with—when both people hold shame in those areas in tragically compatible ways. For example, I find anger particularly scary because of my background, and you are particularly ashamed of ever being angry because of yours, or I find unexpected touch particularly threatening because of my background, and you hold a lot of shame about being seen as creepy or non-consensual.

Tragically, this makes it more likely that the change, or ending, will take the form of a violent severing, which can damage everyone involved even more, precluding the possibility for mutual under-standing and forgiveness, for flexible change, or for respectful disen-gagement. Of course, this doesn't just impact the people concerned, as there is often a ripple effect through families, friendship groups, or communities, with pressure to "pick a side," or big challenges if the people concerned still need to co-parent or work together, for example.

## Doing endings and changes differently

So how might we approach endings and changes differently? How might we both shift away from unhelpful, normative scripts of staying together and breaking up, and take a more trauma-informed approach to changes and endings in all kinds of relationships?

How might we approach them differently? Here are some of our ideas, and you may well have more.

First, we might start by acknowledging the huge relational and individual challenges of significant relationship changes and endings. Perhaps we might try to shift—in our communities—towards a model of greater relationship transparency, so that those who are going through such transitions feel more able to share what's going on, to get support, and to acknowledge the impact of such shifts beyond their specific relationship, so that all those impacted can be involved and supported.

We've had the thought experiment of what it would be like if we rechanneled the kind of time, energy, and practical support that we invest in the beginnings of relationships (e.g. getting together, new relationship energy, and commitment ceremonies) into the times when people are transitioning or ending their relationships. Instead of backing off at those times, we could come together more—offering time, energy, and even some financial support, if needed.

We could ensure that we recognize—and support each other through—changes and endings in friend, family, and collegiate relationships, as well as romantic and sexual ones, including break-ups and bereavements. As we've explored throughout this book, we might expand our understanding of relationships—and break-ups—to include those with systems, organizations, and communities, as well as with places and times in our life.

Instead of the binary model of staying together or breaking up, we could move to one where we acknowledge that there are multiple options available to us, in all relationships, around how close or separate we are. It could be expected that people would move both closer together and further apart, in all kinds of ways over the course of a relationship, rather than there being an escalator model of ever-increasing closeness, or a model whereby levels of closeness must remain the same forever or the relationship has failed. We'll return to this in the next section where we ask what it would be like if our goal was a mutually nourishing relationship—whatever that looked like—rather than assuming a certain "right" level of contact, closeness, or connection, and trying to maintain that.

Getting more existential, we could acknowledge that all relationships in our lives will eventually end, whether through death or other forms of transition. Instead of clinging so hard to our relationships, we could take the approach that they are "already broken" and embrace the sadness and loss of this, alongside our current gratitude and joy, and all manner of other feelings.

We could acknowledge that all our relationships are in a constant process of ending and beginning that goes on beyond the point at which we're no longer with someone (because we still relate to them in our imagination and memory). All these endings and beginnings will open up some possibilities and close down others, both in terms of our own relationship and other relationships that we might—or might not—have, if this relationship becomes closer or more distant.

Right now, we are sitting at a table in Galicia writing the penultimate chapter of this book. Our relationship has gone through so many endings and beginnings over time—when we got together at that conference 20 years ago, when we broke up, when we started writing together, when Alex moved to a different continent to MJ, when we lost a treasured writing partner—first to an unacknowledged kind of relationship ending and later to bereavement. There are so many more. Our relationship may remain pretty similar after this week, or it may become closer due to what we've just shared, or more distant as we're both going through times of major uncertainty and transition. This book is the last one we are contracted to write together. Our writing relationship may deepen now that we're free to see where our creative partnership goes from here, or we may move more towards writing alone or with others, or we may explore different kinds of collaboration together. We feel all kinds of feelings writing these words!

## Multiple experiences: Doing relationship changes and endings differently

"I was always taught that you should stay together no matter what. Divorce meant that you were a failure: not just the relationship, but you as a person. There was so much stigma around it in my family growing up. For my husband and me, it was the best thing that ever happened to our relationship. We'd gotten into so many painful dynamics with each other. We—and the kids—were so stressed and tight at all times. After he moved out, things loosened up a lot, and I was really impressed with the ways he showed up for the children. Gradually, we found our way to a respectful co-parenting relationship and then, surprisingly, to a loving friendship. I'd now say he was my bestie, in a way he never was when we were trying to be a married couple."

"I didn't get to choose whether my most important relationship ended, because my best friend upped and died on me. We were both hitting retirement, divorced several times over between us. I'd been planning to move back to the town we grew up in—and she still lived in. We were going to be those two old women gossiping on the porch, and then, just like that, she was gone. It hit me way harder than losing any of my exes. I took years to grieve. Now I live in a religious community: something I'd always considered but would never have done if she'd stayed alive and I hadn't had that experience. You never know what life is going to throw at you."

"The biggest change in my relationship was when my partner transitioned. At first, I was furious. I couldn't believe that she was planning to make this change that impacted me so hugely. As a gay man, how could I be with a woman? There were huge judgments from my community. My family had only just got used to their son having a husband! I thought about breaking up with her, but thankfully I checked myself. I got support, met a bunch of other trans people and their partners. My family were surprisingly okay. In the end, the only break-ups ended up being with some of our friends and community, and frankly I don't miss them."

"I broke up with my parents a few years back. It had never been the easiest relationship, but when I went through a period of chronic fatigue, they were terrible: constantly telling me I was faking it, that it must be my fault somehow because I'm fat, sending me articles about diets and wonder drugs, and coming round my place without warning to 'tidy up' which felt super intrusive. Once I had the energy, I cut contact with them completely and changed the locks. They tried to push it a few times, but I held firm—with the help of my therapist and friends. Now I do have a call with them every couple of months, with the clear boundary that they are not allowed to mention disability, weight, or the state of my flat!"

"Probably the most painful break-up I had in recent years was a group one. A bunch of us in my spiritual tradition had a support group on Messenger; we did sharing circles together regularly over Zoom, and we met up to do rituals for a long weekend a few times a year. A consent violation happened between two members of the group at the end of one of those weekends. A couple of us were trying to hold them through a repair process, but the others weren't up for it. It felt like they were only into having a group relationship so long as it was easy. I considered that group to be a primary relationship, so the ending hit me really hard, especially as no one seemed to acknowledge what a big loss it was."

## When are changes or endings needed?

Given all the cultural norms, and trauma, we carry around relationships and endings, it can be really hard to tell when significant
changes, or endings, are necessary in relationships.

Hopefully, the ideas and examples we just shared will help move
you away from an all-or-nothing perspective, and enable you to
open up to multiple options when difficulties come up in all kinds of
relationships. This can include changing certain things rather than
ending the whole relationship. It can also include ending a relationship, knowing that this might not be forever, but that a period apart
might be necessary to get out of a traumatizing dynamic, before
a relationship with a different kind of container may be possible.

Here are a few signs that might suggest that a major change
(such as greater distance), or ending, is necessary, especially if several
of them are true and aren't changing over time. Remember that this
applies to all kinds of relationships, including those with groups or
communities. Feel free to add to this list, or adapt it, to create a list
of signs that would work for you:

1. One or more people feel unsafe, or trapped, in the relationship.

2. The relationship ticks many of the "red flags" for a coercive
   or abusive relationship (whatever side of the dynamic you
   may be on).

3. One or more people are frequently hitting overwhelming,
   painful feelings about the relationship.

4. The relationship no longer feels nourishing for one or more
   people (if it's not working for everyone, it's not working for
   anyone).

5. There is a traumatizing dynamic playing out that doesn't
   seem to shift, no matter what you do.

6. Things haven't improved even after getting support, or one or more people refuse to access support.

7. The lives that you'd like to have are going in very different directions.

8. It feels like there is a big gulf between the values that are important to each of you which don't feel possible to shift without compromising too much.

9. There seems to be no possibility of agreement on how to communicate about these things.

10. One or more of you is convinced by the story that it is all the other's fault, and unable to shift from blaming, or dismissing, the other.

We personally find the question "What is the distance at which I can be warm and open in this relationship?" to be a helpful guide when considering relationship changes or endings. This includes acknowledging that the answer can change over time, and that it's okay to have an answer of not being in each other's lives at all, especially in the case of relationships that are unsafe or that always draw us back into traumatic dynamics, for example.

We'll turn now to the concept of consensual, and conscious, relating, which is a helpful thing to practice at all points, in all relationships. It certainly makes navigating changes and endings easier, if we're used to relating with each other in these ways.

## 5.4 CONSCIOUS, CONSENSUAL RELATING

The kind of relating that we've been exploring moving towards throughout this book is consensual, conscious relating. In the remainder of this chapter, we'll explain what this means. In the final chapter of the book, we'll turn more towards how to do consensual, conscious relating in practice, and the kinds of relationships, systems, communities, and cultures we need to cultivate in order for this to be possible.

Consent is generally defined as "agreeing to do something." We're in consent when we feel able to tune into ourselves and honestly say "yes," "no," or "maybe" to what someone else suggests, and when we feel able to ask for what we want and need ourselves, knowing that others will be able to respond honestly too. Relationally, it's often not as separate as this (one person asking and another person agreeing or disagreeing). Consensual relationships happen when we're in an ongoing process of feeling into where we're at, and communicating that, checking in where others are at and listening to that, and making collaborative decisions about everything: from what to do during our time together, to where the relationship is going.

By conscious relating, we mean being aware, transparent, and intentional around our relationships. This would include being honest with ourselves, and others, as much as possible about the kinds of relationships we want, and how we want to do them. Importantly, consciousness includes trying to be as aware and open as possible about the things that shape our relationships, like the kinds of relationship norms and relational patterns that we've covered throughout this book. Relating *unconsciously* would include things like just conforming to relationship norms of your culture or community—and expecting others to do the same—and/or relating through your trauma patterns or attachment styles and failing to recognize that this is what's happening, or the impact that it is having on you and others.

## Why consensual *and* conscious?

For us, consensual and conscious relating must come together. Being conscious means being aware of the pressures on relationships that make it challenging—and sometimes incredibly difficult—to be consensual. We've talked a lot about these through every chapter of this book. It is very hard to be consensual in relationships when the dominant cultural or community norms suggest that there's a right, natural, normal way in which we *should* be doing things. It's also very hard to be consensual—with ourselves and others—in the places where we carry trauma.

Many writers limit the notion of consent to sexual encounters and relationships. Our feeling is that it would be difficult—if not impossible—to be consensual around sex, if we were not consensual around the rest of the relationship, whether that is a one-night stand or a long-term partnership. How easy would it be to say what you wanted or didn't want sexually if you'd already experienced someone pressuring you to meet up on a hook-up app, for example? How possible would it be to suggest a new kind of sex to a partner who responded badly whenever you suggested trying a different takeout?! Our aim needs to be a lot broader than consensual sex, both because many of our relationships are not sexual (friends, colleagues, family, etc.) and because those of us who have sexual relationships will struggle to be consensual in these if the rest of the relationships aren't consensual.

Even many writers who do advocate being consensual throughout our whole relationships often seem to suggest that this is relatively easy. They often present human beings as rational individuals who have pretty easy access to what they want and don't want, find this straightforward to articulate to others, and would generally only want others in their lives to do things that *they* consented to. In addition to this, it's often presented as relatively straightforward for people to tell that someone has violated their consent, or that they have violated someone else's, and there's often a sense that people should pretty easily be able to communicate this and take accountability if the fault is on their side.

In our view, this kind of understanding sets people up to fail. At best, it results in a kind of performative consent, and accountability, where people talk the talk but often feel they have to hide all the complicated, painful feelings that are going on underneath. At worst, such an approach actually makes non-consensual relationships more likely. This is because we assume that we—and others—will act consensually, and therefore repress all our uneasy feelings that this is not what's really happening a lot of the time. For example, we might just be going along with how everyone else seems to do things or playing out traumatic relationship dynamics.

## Consent and consciousness around relationship normativities

In section 2.2, we looked at some of the kinds of promises that people often make to each other in romantic relationships, either privately or—often—in some kind of public ceremony. Here are some common elements:

- staying together forever, till death
- not having any other (love/sex) relationships
- being with each other every day
- loving each other constantly
- sharing all your money and possessions
- demonstrating love with bodily affection/sex
- remaining together through any changes in wealth, health, etc.

While many people make their own vows these days, and may question some of these, there is still a strong cultural norm that relationships should work in this way, and that "breaking" any of these commitments would inevitably mean the end of a relationship.

Some communities question some of these normativities, particularly queer communities and openly non-monogamous communities, where people are often explicitly trying to do romantic relationships differently. However, even in those communities there are often a lot of shared assumptions and expectations about how relationships will work. Also, in all communities, as we've said, there are often norms about how to do friendships, family relationships, colleague relationships, and so on that aren't ever clearly articulated.

It is extremely hard to be honest with yourself, and with people you relate to, in the way that's vital for consent, if you know—or sense—that you would lose a whole relationship if you stopped feeling, or behaving, in a certain way.

## ACTIVITY: WHAT ARE RELATIONSHIPS CONTINGENT ON?

Think for yourself about how you would feel if someone you were in a relationship with wanted the following kinds of changes. Would this mean the end of the relationship for you? How would you want things to go, if it was you who wanted these changes?

— An increase or decrease in sex, touch, or physical affection (including from it happening to not happening, or vice versa).

— Love feelings changing (e.g. from more romantic to platonic, or between the other kinds of love outlined in section 1.4).

— Sharing space in different ways (e.g. moving to sleep separately, to sharing a room, or to living separately/together).

— Entwining or separating finances or work.

— Them wanting to move to a more open relationship, or having other relationships of a similar kind and closeness to the one they have with you, or them wanting to close the relationship, or having fewer other supportive relationships in their life.

— Them wanting to share a lot less, or more, of their everyday life with you.

— Them becoming a lot more, or less, physically and/or financially dependent on you.

How might the potential for these kinds of changes be built into a relationship in order that everyone might feel safe and free enough to feel and behave differently over time?

For many people, being in a certain relationship is also tied to things like being financially secure, having citizenship, their children having a co-parent and/or home, being part of each other's families, being part of a wider community, a shared business or work project, or being viewed positively by the wider world. The more these kinds of things are contingent on remaining in a certain relationship—and doing it in a certain way—the more difficult it will be to relate consensually.

Of course, the axes of oppression that we covered in section 4.3 have a huge impact on how safe and free people are to make changes in their lives, and how dependent they may be on certain relationships, which also has a major impact on our capacity for consensual relationships.

For all these reasons, becoming conscious of the norms and power dynamics around relationships—both in wider culture and in our own communities—and openly discussing which of these will, and won't, apply in our own relationships, goes hand in hand with cultivating consensual relationships.

## Consent and consciousness around trauma patterns

It's also harder to behave consensually with others when there is relational trauma present. Developmental trauma can result in deep fears of abandonment or annihilation by others, which can mean that we try to grasp hold of others—perhaps crossing their boundaries in the process—and/or that we try to push them away, potentially in non-consensual ways. The 4F survival strategies—fight, flight, freeze, fawn—can make it very hard to be consensual in relationships. For example, fawn makes it hard to be honest with others about ourselves, our needs, and our boundaries, because them liking us and approving of us feels so vital. Fight makes it hard to avoid attempting to control others' behavior because we often feel we have to do this in order for people to stay, or to avoid them hurting us.

As we said in section 5.1, trauma can also lead to us projecting our past experiences onto the people we're in relationship with, so we're not really relating with them at all. We're contorting ourselves to try to fit what we think others want, and trying to control others' behavior through fear of them leaving or hurting us, for example.

High levels of fear, shame, rage, and so on when we are triggered make it very difficult to be present to another person, to engage in open communication and conflict intimacy, to be honest about our feelings, needs, and boundaries, and to hear any criticism. Often when relationships are struggling, we trigger each other into trauma responses. It takes a long time for our bodyminds to return from one of these mutual triggerings, and when they happen regularly, we tend to go to old survival strategies to try to avoid it happening again. We may well also become hypervigilant for signs that it might be about to happen, which keeps our bodymind on high alert and more prone to being triggered.

Relational trauma can also make it very hard to tell when non-consensual behaviors have happened in relationships: both when we have behaved non-consensually and when others have. For example, controlling behaviors may have been so common in our families and such a familiar way of relating that we don't even notice what we're doing. Or we may be so used to overriding what we want in certain situations that we don't even realize we're doing it, or may only realize it a while after it has happened.

Finally, it is easy to look to partners, and to people we're in close relationship with, to be the one person who can prevent us from having to feel the tough feelings of trauma, and/or who can reach us and pull us out of them when they hit. Both of these can easily tip into treating each other non-consensually.

For all these reasons, becoming as conscious as possible around our trauma responses and relationship patterns goes hand in hand with cultivating consensual relationships.

## What opens up and closes down our capacity for consensual relationships

Moving away from that consent model where we are two rational individuals who can relatively easily tune into what we want and need, and communicate that with others, this diagram better captures all that's going on relationally at all times.

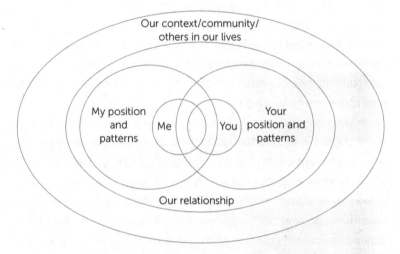

*Figure 5.3: Our wider cultural norms, systems, structures*

All the things in this diagram can close down, or open up, our capacity to relate consensually with each other. And, of course, we could add in more people (with their positions and patterns) for groups, polycules, and community relationships of all kinds.

## *ACTIVITY: BIG PERSPECTIVE*

Think of a recent example where you were trying to make a relational decision with someone. It's fine to pick something pretty innocuous, and we'd suggest initially staying away from very emotionally loaded examples like big consent violations or break-ups (although this approach can be very helpful—and settling—for those too).

For example, we might choose making our decision about how to spend this evening after we stop working (given we're nearly at the end of this chapter!). In this case, in the "me" and "you" circles we might put things like how tired we are, or what kinds of things we generally enjoy doing. In the "my/your position and patterns," we might include the marginalizations that we share and the ones we differ on, and the same with our trauma patterns. For example, we might include the different comfort levels around conflict in our cultural backgrounds, our levels of disability in general and at the moment, both of our trauma tendencies towards people pleasing, and our neurodivergent preference for direct communication. In the "our relationship" circle, we might include our history, including past experience of spending time together and treating each other (hopefully) pretty consensually!

In the context/community circle, we might include the person we're staying with, and her preference, as well as the other people who might want contact with us—or not—tonight, plus our sense of you as readers, and what will put us in the best place to write for you tomorrow! In the wider cultural context, we might put the norms about how friends do, and don't, relax together on vacation, as well as norms about when people expect to go to bed, and solitude vs. company, and how these differ between our cultural backgrounds and the context we're in right now. We might also put the context of the global COVID pandemic, and the way that's meant we've had so much less time together in person than usual in recent years.

These are a whole lot of things that will determine how free and safe we feel making that decision about how to spend our evening in a way that is hopefully as mutually nourishing as possible. Some of them open up the likelihood of consensuality (e.g. neurodivergent preference for direct communication, and history of trust building); others close it down (e.g. both being Very Tired, and a shared tendency to fawn).

For your own example, draw a version of this diagram—by yourself, or with the other person/people involved—about all the things that are in play in each of the squares and circles, which might impact your capacity to be consensual with yourselves, and each other. You could use different colors or highlighting to depict the things that feel like they close down the possibility of consent, or open it up, and ones where you're not sure. However you want to do it is up to you.

When a tough relationship moment happens, we often find it very soothing to work through a diagram like this, even just in our mind, to move away from a "my fault or their fault" binary, towards a deeper understanding of all that is likely going on for everyone involved, and in the wider context. This can helpfully inform how we respond.

> **REMEMBER...** There is a whole lot going on every time we relate with ourselves, or another person or being, including all of our histories and the wider context around us. Both cultural norms and relational trauma can make it very hard to keep hold of all of that in the moment when a relationship rupture or conflict is occurring. We encourage you to go very gently with yourselves and others in these areas, recognizing everything that might be in play (much of which we're often not aware of), and getting all the time, space, and support you need. We also encourage you to go very gently with yourselves and others when you don't manage to do this!
>
> In the next chapter, we'll look at more practical ways in which we can maximize our capacity to relate consciously and consensually, particularly how we can co-create relationship containers and communities of support and solidarity for this.

## Further resources

You can read more about navigating conflict here:

- Iantaffi, A. and Effinger-Weintraub, L. (forthcoming). *Do Conflict Better: A Trauma-Informed Guide.*

There are also chapters on conflict and break-up in MJ's book *Rewriting the Rules*, listed at the end of Chapter 2.

MJ's most recent chapter on break-up can be found at the end of their free book on relationships, here:

- https://rewriting-the-rules.com/wp-content/uploads/2022/11/Relationships.pdf

There's also a free book of MJ's earlier writings on consent at this link:

- www.rewriting-the-rules.com/consent-work

There's a great list of resources on consent here:

- www.artofconsent.co.uk/consent-resources

This article about the different, evolving, meanings of consent can be really helpful:

- www.artofconsent.co.uk/consent-is-evolving

Kitty Stryker's trilogy of books about consent—including a workbook and a book aimed at teens—are all very useful. Start with:

- Stryker, K. (2017). *Ask: Building Consent Culture*. Portland, OR: Thorntree Press.

There are several good articles about conscious relationships on Alethya. com, including:

- www.alethya.com/conscious-commitment

Our go-to place for writing about self-consent is Love Uncommon. Start here:

- https://loveuncommon.com/2017/09/28/self-consent

There is material about relationship accommodations here:

- www.youtube.com/watch?v=bZ-wCP4tjrg

You can find MJ's zine about PIERS check-in here:

- https://rewriting-the-rules.com/zines/#1659800563736-0b726435-5937

And the RADAR check-in can be found here:

- www.multiamory.com/radar

You can find Dr. Sophia Graham's post on how to have constructive conflict here, including an example of her conflict agreement:

- https://loveuncommon.com/2018/05/02/how-to-have-constructive-conflict

# CHAPTER 6

# MOVING TOWARDS DEEPER INTERDEPENDENCE

In this final chapter of the book, we're going to gradually expand back out beyond our individual experiences of relationships, to explore further how we might create systems and structures to support us at the relational, community, and cultural level. In Chapter 2, we saw how dominant culture and the legacy of colonialism shapes our way of relating to ourselves, other beings, communities, and the world. This chapter is about how we might do things differently at all those levels, because we need relational, systemic, and cultural support if we're going to manage to relate in more connected, conscious, consensual, caring, and compassionate ways.

Even within such a disconnected, non-consensual, often violent, dominant culture, we can create alternative relationship systems, communities of care, and micro-cultures of solidarity, which support us to do things differently. Eventually, perhaps, if enough of us develop and share such alternatives, and if we collectively work to dismantle the overlapping systems and structures of oppression, we might be able to shift the dominant culture in ways that support everyone to relate in more connected, liberated, and/or healing ways.

We've called this chapter "Moving towards deeper interdependence." The word interdependence—often used in disability justice movements—highlights the ways in which we are all interdependent on each other, for our survival and wellbeing (see Chapter 2). This is something that is often avoided or denied in the rugged individualism of late capitalism. We are all inevitably interconnected at all levels of experience (see Chapter 1), and interdependent. This usually takes us beyond our immediate relationships and communities, to remember the ways in which our wellbeing is deeply connected to people all around the globe (e.g. those who farm the food we eat, or put together our technological devices), as well as to other beings, and to the land and water of the world. Increasing awareness of the overlapping crises of global injustice and profound climate change highlights that we need to expand our notice of relationships to include all human and non-human beings, in addition to the land and the water.

Learning to relate with ourselves and close ones in more connected, conscious, consensual, caring, and compassionate ways gradually enables us to relate in such ways more broadly than that, with a deep felt sense of our interconnectedness and interdependence. We'll end the chapter with reflections on how we might collectively shift the relational legacy that we leave behind for future generations and the planet.

## 6.1 HOW TO DO CONSCIOUS, CONSENSUAL RELATING

We ended the last chapter (section 5.4) with an explanation of what conscious, consensual relating is, and why we might make that our aim. We could see this way of relating as laying the foundations for differentiation, mutuality, care, and compassion (the cornerstones of connected, intentional relating which we explored in section 1.4).

We could also see conscious, consensual relating as a way of doing trauma-informed—and shame-sensitive—relating. This is important because we all bring relational trauma patterns to our relationships (see section 3.2), and these are often about trying to avoid the shame which has been engraved on our bodyminds. This shame has been cultivated both by dominant culture (with its ideals and assumptions about what makes a good/bad person and relationships) and by developmental trauma (which often gives us the message that we are fundamentally "wrong" and need to hide and cover this up with defenses and survival strategies) (see section 4.2).

We've already covered various ways in which you might get more conscious and consensual around your relating throughout this book. This includes identifying your relationship patterns, doing relationship check-ins, identifying and communicating wants, needs, desires, boundaries, and consequences, and so on. Building on these, in this section we'll suggest:

— three specific relational practices for conscious relating (or sharing and navigating our different relationship patterns and preferences), and

— three further relational practices for consensual relating (or ensuring that our relationships are as consensual as possible from the micro everyday level to the macro level of the whole life course of the relationship).

We'll also flag places you can go to discover more suggestions.

## Doing conscious relating with ourselves and others

So how might we move towards being more conscious around our own—and others'—relational patterns? Whether those come from cultural/community norms, developmental trauma, neurodivergence, engaging with spiritual/therapeutic practice, and/or a complex mix of these and other places? How might we normalize communicating about where we're at with these things? And caring for ourselves and others with the capacities we currently have?

Here are three ideas from the macro level, to the everyday, to the micro level of specific relational exchanges.

### Macro: Sharing our ways of relating

We wrote about relationship user guides in section 4.4. One way of practicing conscious relating is to create documents like these, which explicitly include our various relationship patterns, needs, and preferences, and sharing these with those we're in existing relationships with, or who we're considering developing or deepening relationships with.

Of course, this is a deeply non-normative and vulnerable practice! If you think about the ways we are encouraged to do relationships, this is basically the opposite. On dating apps, we suspect that most people would choose the most flattering pictures of themselves and describe their positive attributes in the hope of encouraging people to swipe right. In fact, it is pretty normative to lie about aspects of yourself like your age or past relationship experiences, or at least to gloss over some things and polish up others. It would be unusual indeed to foreground your emotional vulnerabilities, your propensity to melt down or shut down, or your tendency towards needy or controlling relationship behaviors! We'll say more in the next section about how we might cultivate the kinds of relationships and support systems that make such honest, open relating feel safer and more familiar.

MJ has had some form of relationship user guide for the last 20 years, although what these included—and who they shared them with—has changed radically over time. Similar to an annual self-reflective document, like the Year Compass, you might find it useful to make an annual date with yourself to update or (re)write a user guide (see further resources). Focusing in on conscious relating, you might like to include:

- your neurodiversity (areas of neurotypicality and/or neuro-divergence)—and what these areas mean for how you relate and like/need to be related with

- your trauma patterns/attachment styles—and what these mean for how you relate and like/need to be related with

- any disabilities and/or aspects of your physicality—and what these mean for how you relate and like/need to be related with

- your relationship style/s (and how these are similar/different to the cultural relationship norms)—and what this means for how you relate and like/need to be related with

- your spiritual/therapeutic practices—including ways in which you may be working to accept and/or shift your patterns—and what these mean for how you relate and like/need to be related with

- any other important intersections (e.g. gender, sexuality, class, race, cultural background)—and what these mean for how you relate and like/need to be related with

- what communication styles and relationship containers you want/need in order to be able to communicate well about the relationship process (e.g. discussing your expectations, making joint decisions, resolving conflicts) without going into hope/fear (neediness or withdrawal) and/or self/other blame (collapsing or attacking) (see section 4.1). For example, this could include whether you prefer to communicate about such things in writing vs. speech, online or in person, synchronously or asynchronously, whether you prefer to address things pretty immediately or after time has passed, and whether your preference is to reconnect before having process conversations and/or to have process conversations before feeling able to reconnect. Of course, learning all of this is a work in progress, and may be different in different relationships too.

MJ also includes a brief introduction to their different selves and how they like to relate plurally in their user guides.

Another great model for this kind of thing—particularly for

people who carry a lot of trauma or who have mental health struggles—are Jacks McNamara and Sascha DuBrul's T-MAPs (Transformative Mutual Aid Practices). This enables you to communicate to others how your struggles tend to manifest, and what your needs, wants, boundaries, and limits are at different times, as well as building a map of your own wellness strategies, resilience practices, and community resources. There is an online questionnaire and a completable pdf version of T-MAPs; you can find a link in the further resources.

---

**Reflection point: Your relationship user guide**

Look through the list of relationship user guide points above again and reflect, for each point, what kind of things you might include there. Feel free to make some notes in the book, or elsewhere, if you find that helpful. If you already started working/playing on a user guide when we introduced it in the last chapter, you can add your notes there, and think some more about what structure would work best for you.

Alternatively, if you'd prefer to work with an existing structure—and if it resonates for you—you could try filling out the T-MAP pdf or online questionnaire, and think about who you might share something like this with.

---

If the people you're in older/newer relationships with are up for it, it is great if you can both/all create guides that include this kind of material, share them, and have some kind of communication about the areas of fit and misfit, and how you might navigate those (see section 5.1). You might well need to do all this over a long-ish period of time and keep revisiting it.

Of course, not everybody is up for this, given it is a pretty non-normative thing to do, particularly in relationships beyond romantic partnerships. It can be useful to explore, with other people, whether there are ways of creating and communicating such guides that would work better for them. For example, some people might prefer to set aside some time to work on them together, some might like to create—or receive—audio, video, or zine versions with illustrations, some might prefer to create and share one element at a time, so it's not overwhelming (e.g. each of the points above). Part of conscious, consensual relating practice is having that conversation first, and finding a mutual way of doing this, where possible.

MJ has found that a lot of people still aren't interested in creating or sharing their own user guides, but that it has still been important for them to share their own with their very close people. It's also been important when relationships are deepening, especially through a time of trauma when they needed a lot more support and were easily triggered in relationships. The different responses that people had to this sharing was—in itself—helpful information about who might be able to relate in the ways they needed during that time and who couldn't offer that. It enabled them to make choices about the distance they needed to be at in different relationships.

Sometimes the place that you, and others, are in makes it impossible for such conversations to be explicit (e.g. if you haven't got that foundation of trust and openness between you). The next two practices are ways that you might build those kinds of foundations more.

### Everyday: Relational sharing

Building some form of ongoing relational sharing into our time together is a helpful practice in the everyday of our relationship. This is true whatever the nature of that—whether it's cohabiting or coworking, seeing each other for intense periods once or twice a year, being in regular online contact, or whatever.

By relational sharing, we mean taking time for each person to share where they're at and what's going on for them at the moment, particularly around their relationships with themselves, other people, animals, projects, land, etc. It might well take the form of a timed share, where each person has something like 10–15 minutes to talk about this stuff. Heart circles or sharing circles are a nice format for doing this in groups. Some of the check-ins we covered in section 5.2 can provide more of a structure for doing such shares. Generally speaking, we would not address anything specific to our own relationship during these shares. Those kinds of process conversations would be separate (we'll cover these in a moment!).

This is another very useful conscious relating practice on multiple levels. It means that we continue to be reminded that the other person is a full, complex being, just like us, when it's often so easy to start relating to others just as they are right now, or in our relationship. It also gets us used to talking openly about our relationship patterns, styles, preferences, etc. with each other, in a way that is safe enough because it's not about our own relationship with each other. We get to just share and be listened to, knowing that nobody will respond or react, unless we actively invite feedback. It can be useful even to have a rule that nobody comments at all, just thanks the sharer, or that only certain kinds of feedback are allowed (e.g. empathy).

Through such sharings, we can become more familiar with how each person relates, so that we can be more aware and caring about their needs and boundaries ourselves. It also means that we're more used to talking about such things when anything comes up that we do need to address in the relationship between us. Finally, such sharings often help us to "put down" whatever we're currently carrying in order to be more present for the rest of our time together. We—MJ and Alex—have been sharing in this way over breakfast on every morning of our writing retreat in order to be as present as possible to each other and to you, dear reader!

Over time, you might well develop your sharing practices in ways that suit your particular relationship or group. For example, you may be following a particular spiritual or therapeutic teaching, which you support each other through. When people are struggling relationally, it can often be useful to have a structure where they get time to freely express their feelings—however they want, in words, movements, or sounds, and however "unreasonable" or blaming/shaming they might be! Then, when they feel done with that part, they can take another period of time where they can be more reflective and focus on what *they* bring to the situation, rather than the other person/people involved (which is out of their control—see section 5.1).

### Micro: Mini moments of repair and recalibration

A final useful practice for conscious relating is the "inkling list." We developed this when we realized that it was a lot to expect people to be able to do rupture and repair when so few of us have past positive experiences of rupture and repair to draw upon. Often, in relationships, we do no rupture and repair, often repressing small moments of discomfort or unease, and brushing them under the rug. This means that the first rupture—or conflict—we end up facing together is often a big one, or the cumulative result of all the little ones we repressed (see section 5.2).

An alternative to this is to make an intentional, conscious, ongoing point of tackling minor moments of misattunement, rupture, or conflict. The smaller these are the better, especially at first. MJ keeps an "inkling" list on their phone every time they notice a tiny sense of unease after an interaction with one of their close people. This may be a moment where they felt that they might have said or done something carelessly or non-consensually, or a moment where they felt discomfort about the way the other person said or did something, or just a sense that something was a little off. For example, in the past these have included: "noticing that this person and I seem to have different preferences for how we play our favorite board game," "wondering if the other person was overstretching to spend that last 15 minutes on the phone with me because they seemed a little checked out towards the end," and—right now—"worrying that I didn't respond well to

Alex when they said they needed to stop for lunch because I was so in the zone of writing about this!"

Again, in an ideal world, you'd have a relationship agreement that you would both keep such a list and would make a little time and space each time you communicate to see whether there are any "inklings," and to address them, when both people are in a good place to do so. Part of consent is starting with a check-in—maybe after sharing—about whether people are up for that today, and/or what kinds of conversation they would or wouldn't be up for (e.g. "I'm not up for it today," "I could manage one very small one, but I'm feeling pretty fragile," or "I could manage to hear one where you wanted reassurance about something you did, but not one about something I did today!").

The advice in sections 5.2 and 6.3 about how to navigate ruptures and conflicts is all useful for addressing your inklings, particularly around how you might communicate these things in a non-blaming/shaming way. It can also be useful to explore with people the fit/misfit in preferences about dealing with inklings:

- quickly or immediately (so there isn't something unspoken that they might pick up on in a confusing way)

or:

- waiting till an inkling is no longer live/hot before addressing it (so we can do it as carefully as possible, and own our part).

Of course, as with all things, this isn't a binary! We have to feel our way in each relationship, and expect that we may veer too much in one direction or the other at times (another opportunity to practice micro moments of repair!).

Part of this process may also involve practicing repeatedly finding Vikki Reynolds's "zone of fabulousness" between us. This would be about noticing when one of us is either pushing towards greater enmeshment or pulling for greater distance, and recalibrating, together, towards the place where we feel connected, differentiated, mutual, and caring (see section 2.4).

## ACTIVITY: YOUR INKLING LIST

Have a go at making an inkling list—either on paper or on a phone or other device. You might have bullet points for each of your closest people or groups, and note down anything you're aware of that would be helpful to check in about with each of them. Or you might hold on to the list over the next few weeks and get used to jotting things down after each time you're in contact. How might you decide if/when it's a good time to bring those things up with the people concerned? How might you check in with them whether you're both in consent to do so? How would you communicate in a trauma-informed, shame-sensitive way (both with yourself and with the other person/group)?

### Doing consensual relating with ourselves and others

Moving from relating in conscious ways to relating in consensual ways (although, of course, they are completely interconnected), here are three practices that you might find helpful to bring into your everyday relationships in order to make consensual relating a familiar practice. We've included links in the further resources to books and zines which include more details about these practices, and to other practices that might work for you.

Always remember that different things work for different people and relationships, and it's fine to adapt all these ideas to suit your particular bodymind and context.

Again, building in practices like these all of the time, and in your close relationships, can make them more of your default way of relating, and mean that they come easier in more challenging situations.

### Making consent the aim of all interactions

One really helpful reframe to do, in order to make consent more possible and likely, is to explicitly make consent the aim of all our interactions. Often—at an implicit or explicit level—we have an aim for our interactions with other people: a sense that an encounter will be good—or successful—if a certain thing ends up happening, and bad—or a failure—if they don't. Here's some examples of consent reframings:

— *A hook-up:* from success = I get laid, to success = both people are fully in consent throughout the encounter, whether or not a certain kind of sex happens.

— *A meeting:* from success = everyone goes for my proposal, to success = the whole team getting to feed back honestly on the proposal, and collaborating to ensure it's as good as possible and it works for everyone.

— *A whole relationship:* from success = we stay together, to success = we can be flexible and change over time to ensure that the relationship remains mutually nourishing, and are able to distance and/or step away if it no longer is for one or both of us.

— *Writing this book together:* from success = we get it done in a way that fits one of our visions for how it *should* be, to success = we engage in a consensual process with ourselves and each other, putting together the book in a way that's mutually nourishing for us, and as good as it can be for readers.

This reframe is not always easy. Remember what we said in Chapters 1 and 2 about how—at every level of human experience—we are encouraged to treat people as things, and to try to make things work out the way we want. Even during this writing retreat we have both caught (parts of) ourselves slipping into just wishing the other person would do things our way! The phrase "if it doesn't work for everyone, it doesn't work for anyone" is helpful here. Remembering the times when we—or someone else—did "get our way" and how that is so often a much less nourishing and rewarding encounter for everybody, not to mention one which can erode trust and otherwise negatively impact the ongoing relationship.

We've found that it's useful to explicitly practice permission-giving, to remind ourselves—and each other—that consent is the aim. For example, MJ has taken to explicitly checking in with friends, clients, and everyone they engage with the day before a meeting is planned. In these messages, they always include:

- their understanding of what the plan was (to check whether or not the other person has the same recollection), and

- a reminder that it is absolutely okay to change the plan, postpone, or cancel if the other person isn't feeling it for any reason (with no necessity to explain the reason, given that there are things people may not feel comfortable sharing, and people don't always know their reasons).

MJ finds it immensely helpful in their relationships where the other people make a point of doing the same thing. It can also be super useful, early on, to explicitly practice postponing, canceling, and expressing boundaries, to check that those things are welcomed in this relationship, and to normalize them, if so.

Similarly, whenever they agree to take part in a work meeting or activity these days, MJ generally asks that a contingency plan or two is built in, so that there are options if they aren't able to attend on the day, and people are prepared that plans might change. For example, they would check whether it is possible to have a back-up date, for them to attend online if they can't manage in-person on the day, and/or for them to send a video or other prepared resource. Again, it really helps when people and organizations are familiar with disability justice and accommodating neurodiversity (see section 6.3).

It is also helpful:

— when we can always explore multiple options (rather than it being a binary this-or-nothing)

— when we keep checking in throughout an encounter whether it's still working for everyone, and

— when we default to the needs of whoever has the least energy, wants the least contact, or whatever.

There's more on all of these things in MJ's free book and zine about consent.

It can be helpful to think of the model of sexual consent and to apply this to all aspects of relationships. For example, if one person wants to stop at kissing and another would like to have penetrative sex, it would only be consensual to stop at kissing. Similarly, if one person wants a long walk and another wants a short one, or one person wants a lot more online communication than another, it would only be consensual to default to the lesser amount (and perhaps to find other relationships in which to have longer walks or more online contact).

### Slowing down and checking in

Part of why it can be difficult to relate consensually is that we're often caught up in our daily lives and/or our interactions with others, making decisions quickly without really tuning into ourselves and each other. For this reason, where possible, it can be a great idea to deliberately slow our interactions—and relationships—down, and build in opportunities to tune into ourselves and check in with each other.

There are many different models for how you might do this.

One option is to intentionally slow down the whole process of relationship building, in order to build safe-enough and trusting-enough containers at every stage. Many of us, particularly when we carry relational trauma, can embark on relationships very quickly. Research by Jeffrey Hall found that it takes people, on average, 50 hours with someone to go from acquaintance to casual friend, another 90 to actual friend, and more than 200 hours to close friend. While we wouldn't want to suggest any "right" amount of time to cultivate relationships, you might find it helpful to reflect on how much time you need at each stage of relationship building.

Moving to more everyday forms of pausing and slowing down, Vietnamese Buddhist monk Thich Nhat Hanh has a bell ring at irregular times throughout the day in his community. Each time the bell rings, everyone is encouraged to pause and take a mindful moment, noticing whether they were caught up in thoughts, busy-ness, or interactions, and returning to the present, if they can. You might find putting an irregular alarm on your phone could encourage a similar practice of mindful moments throughout your day or in a work environment.

Another thing you might do is to deliberately take a pause before any decision point. In one group MJ is part of, each member of the group tries to be alert for wherever a decision is being made, so hopefully at least one person can say, "Hey, let's check in with ourselves whether we feel in consent with this," before going on.

Finally, we can make it an ongoing practice to learn how we feel at moments when we are in danger of overriding our consent, and to deliberately pause (and ask others around us to pause) at such moments. Trauma therapist Babette Rothschild refers to mindful gauges: sensations, thoughts, feelings, behaviors, and more that we might notice which are signs—for us—that we're overriding ourselves, or heading into a trauma response.

**Reflection point: Overriding signs**

Reflect on the signs that tell you that you might be about to override your consent (or go ahead with something without checking someone else's), or already have done so, in some way. The examples here are the ones MJ notices, and yours will likely be different for these, of course:

— bodily sensations (e.g. can't even feel the body and/or tight, clenched, shoulders hurt)

— thoughts (e.g. self-critical thoughts get loud, and/or busy, scattered, churning thoughts)

— feelings (e.g. uneasy, uncomfortable feelings, and/or feeling fizzy, excited, too fast)

— behaviors (e.g. pushing on with work, distracting behaviors, rushing, struggling to stop and tune in).

It's great to practice—when we notice such things—making them a sign to pause, take time out, and ground ourselves. Over time, that can help us to shift from going straight for our well-worn patterns to using such feelings as an automatic signal to pause.

There are also some great resources on Sophia Graham's Love Uncommon website for how you might very slowly begin to explore what a "yes," "no," or "maybe" feels like in your body, as well as how to practice emotional regulation and consensual relating (see further resources at the end of Chapter 5).

Even the experience of stopping and tuning into our bodyminds is unfamiliar to many of us. Here's one activity that can help with practicing this.

*Consent practice*

As we've emphasized throughout this book, it can be very difficult to *know* whether we consent to something or not, because forces like cultural norms and relational trauma are so powerful. We are often very used to overriding our consent, whether that is to please someone, or to push through a work project. We are also often used to unconsciously overriding others' consent with persuading, cajoling, or pressurizing behaviors.

This is why so many authors stress learning how to tune into our bodies to tell what consenting, and not consenting, feel like, and doing such somatic practices in relationships. There are many practices for how to do this, which you might want to check out. Here's a brief description of the 3 Minute Game from Betty Martin's *Wheel of Consent*. You can find out more about this in the further resources, including a detailed downloadable pdf about how to do it.

It can be great—if possible—to attend online or offline workshops where you learn these kinds of somatic practices, so that you get a chance to practice them in relation. Betty often begins with self-consent practices before moving to a relational consent practice like this. We've included one of these at the end of this section. Please do feel free to try that one as much as you like, before moving to this more relational practice.

## ACTIVITY: THE 3-MINUTE GAME

In pairs, try spending three minutes in each quadrant of the wheel that follows (with your partner taking the opposite quadrant to the one you're in).

In the "take" quadrant, you ask "May I...?" and the person in "allow" can say yes, no, or maybe. In "accept," you ask "Will you...?" and the person in "serve" can say yes, no, or maybe to that. For example, in "take," you could ask "May I tell you about my day?" or "May I hug you?" In "accept," you could ask "Will you give me a shoulder massage?" or "Will you sing me a song?"

Of course, in the allow and serve quadrants, it's vital that you only allow, and do, things that you consent to. So there's a great opportunity in the game to tune into your body and to whether it's responding "yes," "no," or "maybe" to the suggestion the other person makes (if "maybe," we might explore options together until we find something that is a "yes"). It's a good opportunity to practice refusing suggestions that you don't consent to, with strong permission to do so. It's fine to do nothing for three minutes in one or more quadrants if you couldn't find any "yeses."

Figure 6.1: The wheel of consent

Betty Martin also usefully distinguishes between "want to" and "willing to" here. When we're in allow or serve, we may be a "YES!" because we actively want to do the thing that other person asks, or we might be a "willing-to yes," where it's not something we'd particularly have suggested ourselves, but we're very willing to do it if it feels good for the other person. Learning how to distinguish how each of those things feels in the body is really helpful for consensual relating too.

It can be great, in all kinds of relationships, to return to the 3-minute game pretty regularly, to check how easy or challenging it is for you to practice consent together, as this can change over time. It can be helpful to reflect on how you found it each time, and to encourage these practices to inform how you relate the rest of the time.

If these conscious/consensual relationship practices are very unfamiliar to you, it's a great idea to get some support in starting to build them into your life. For example, if you never pause and spend time noticing your bodymind, then meditation, mindfulness, and similar practices can be great—and there are groups where you can practice doing these in supported, trauma-informed ways. There are also great resources, workshops, and regular groups where you can learn practices for emotionally regulating when trauma responses kick in, and for co-regulating with others. Therapists and somatic practitioners can also help with teaching these kinds of things, and also practicing things like rupture and repair, and honest communication, in a safe-enough environment. There's more on all of this in the rest of this chapter and in the further resources. Please don't "go it alone" with any of the practices suggested here if they feel very unfamiliar, or you don't understand how to do them.

When relating with other beings, there can be a lot going on, so—for many of us—it's a great idea to practice consensual relating with ourselves, and objects, to learn what it feels like, so we can then bring that into our relating with other people and non-human animals. If you'd like to do this more relationally—with another person—you could both/all have a go at the practice, and then share how it was for you.

Here's a practice for relating with an object in a self-consensual way. It's based on Betty Martin's Waking Up the Hands practice (see further resources) and similar practices that we're familiar with in Buddhist and somatic communities. If touching things with your hands is challenging for you in any way or not possible at all, feel free to use another part of your body, or to focus on another sensation (sight or smell, for instance), or skip this practice.

1. Find an object you'd like to engage with using touch (e.g. a cushion, a stone, a soft toy or ornament, a piece of fruit).

2. Use your hands to notice all of the details you can about the object (e.g. shape, texture, variation across the surface).

3. Invite your hands to slow down and notice how much you feel as you go slow.

4. Whenever your attention wanders—as it will—gently bring it back to the sensations.

5. Invite your hands to notice which aspects of the object and/or ways of touching it are pleasurable and allow yourself to explore those.

6. Notice any ways in which your body shifts and changes as you touch the object.

7. Notice any ways in which your feelings shift and change as you touch the object.

8. Stay with this process as long as you like.

9. Afterwards, you may like to share the experience with someone else, note how it was in a journal, stretch, and/or try it with a different object.

Then, when you're ready, continue reading...

## 6.2 RELATIONSHIPS IN COMMUNITY

Perhaps the biggest challenge in relating in the conscious, consensual ways that we've explored above, and throughout this book, is that there is so little support to do so. In fact, as we've said, at every level of experience there's actually a strong pull to relate in the exact *opposite* ways (disconnected, unconscious, non-consensual, etc.) (see section 1.3).

This is yet another reason that we need to go very gently and tenderly with ourselves—and others—about our relationship struggles, mistakes, and missteps. It is hugely difficult—if not impossible—to relate in conscious, consensual ways ourselves if:

— the people who we're relating *with* are unfamiliar, or averse, to relating in these ways

— the systems and communities around us do not encourage— or actively discourage—such ways of relating

— the wider culture stigmatizes or ridicules those who attempt to relate in these ways.

Many of the people with whom we relate will struggle to join us in relating in conscious consensual ways. This might be because it's so unfamiliar and challenging at first, and because it often shows us just how non-consensually we were treated growing up, and in other relationships, and how non-consensually we ourselves have treated others. Becoming aware of the places where we have both survived and perpetuated non-consent can be an extremely painful process.

Many of the communities or systems with which we engage also struggle to encourage and enable more conscious, consensual relating. For example, most workplaces under late capitalism—even those with a more radical ethos—struggle to shift to systems and structures where:

— all bodyminds and labor are valued equally

— oppressive behaviors like racism and harassment are fully acknowledged and dealt with on a systemic level

— people are encouraged to be in self-consent, rather than overriding their bodyminds in order to produce certain things in certain ways.

Even communities that are counter-cultural in some ways around relationships—such as radical political communities, spiritual communities, and/or non-monogamous communities—tend to replicate normative ideas, which make conscious, consensual relating difficult (such as hierarchies of different kinds of relationships and/or carceral logics—see next section).

Also, of course, wider dominant culture is—in many ways— invested in maintaining the status quo way of doing relationships, given that it developed in the context of colonialism and capitalism (see Chapter 2). This means that those who try to do things differently are often precarious (in terms of things like legal protections and medical care), and may even be subject to discrimination, hate crimes, media hounding, bullying, and police brutality, depending on the nature of their difference. All this can mean that either we don't feel able to move towards the ways of relating that we believe in—or that might suit us best—or, if we do, we may feel we have to keep it secret, which puts us under different kinds of stress, such as fearing the consequences of being "found out."

So what can we do if we want to cultivate relationships, communities, and cultures that support us in our moves towards more conscious, consensual, caring, connected relationships?

## Co-creating relationship containers

At the relational level, the concept of relationship containers can be helpful. People often think of relationships in terms of connection, but not container. For example, if they feel a connection

264 HOW TO UNDERSTAND YOUR RELATIONSHIPS

with somebody, they pursue a relationship with them, and if they don't, they don't. Their model for what a relationship (partnership, friendship, colleague relationship, etc.) would look like may be pretty much the same for anyone they feel a connection with in that bracket (or have that kind of attraction to).

An alternative to this approach is to ask, with each relationship (old or new):

1. Is there a *connection*? (and what kind it is, whether it's mutual, etc.) and

2. What kind of relationship *container* do we want/need for this relationship? (and where our areas of fit and misfit are on this, how we'll navigate that, etc.)

We may need to prioritize close relationships where people are in agreement that both connection *and* container are important. For example, we've both had experiences where people have suggested that—because we have certain kinds of positive feelings or attractions towards each other—this should be enough to say "yes" to a relationship of a certain kind with them, rather than being up for a careful and ongoing communication about what kind of relationship container we'd need for that.

The kinds of things that we might include in a relationship container—with individuals or groups—include:

— the types of intimacy we would and wouldn't want/need (see section 4.4)

— the pace we'd want/need the relationship to develop at, and it being okay to become closer, or more distant, over time

— how we'd communicate, and how much contact we'd expect

— how we'd describe our relationship to others in our lives, and what support we'd each have around us, and the relationship

– many of the other things we've already considered in the last chapter, and this one, about what we might include in relationship agreements and/or user guides.

One thing we feel is particularly important to think about, in terms of relationship containers, is support systems. In dominant culture, there is an assumption that significant relationships should provide all our needs (and it's a problem if we need anybody else), and that we should keep any difficulties private in our relationships. Both of these assumptions—at best—put our relationships under a lot of pressure, and—at worst—enable us to stay in abusive or toxic relationships. This is because nobody is around to see how bad things have become and all the problems are kept secret and hidden. The people in the relationships may have nobody to check in with about whether the kinds of things that have become normalized between them are okay. Also, they may have nowhere else to go, having lost previous support systems or friends, and potentially not having the financial—or other—resources to extricate themselves. We have both been in situations like this ourselves, which is one of the reasons we are so passionate about relationship transparency and consent (please see further resources for support that *is* available to you if you—or someone you know—are in such a situation).

Where possible, it's great if we can consciously move from closed to more open relational systems, and towards cultivating supportive networks around ourselves and our relationships. This would include—to our minds—cultivating supportive people in our life beyond this particular partnership, friendship, or family, and having at least some trusted people who we agree that we can be completely transparent with about our relationship, maybe even checking in regularly about it. We might also agree who we would bring in to support us if we were navigating a difficult moment or transition (see next section).

**Reflection point: Your relationship support system**

Think about a key relationship in your life. Who would you regard as the support system around that relationship? You might think about the other close people or groups that each of you can go to, to support you in that relationship, the people or groups who know—and support—you together, and the people or groups—including professionals—you could call upon if you were struggling in any way. What about non-human supports? Are there places that you can go—alone or together—which feel supportive, and/or ideas, teachings, or values that are a helpful touchstone for you? If you don't have anyone in one or more of those categories, how might you go about cultivating such support systems and resources over time?

To reiterate, it is sadly still very counter-cultural to even think that a work partnership, romantic relationship, family, or friendship might need this kind of container and/or relational support system. Please don't give yourself a hard time if it's not something you've thought about or developed in the past. It's great even to start considering such things, and hopefully modeling the possibility of thinking in these ways with others in our lives.

## Co-creating supportive communities and micro-cultures of solidarity

Beyond specific relationship support systems, what about communities which might support us in relating in more conscious, consensual ways? Communities can provide a vital buffer between us—and our interpersonal relationships—and the wider culture of relating which can be so traumatized and traumatizing.

There are three main options when it comes to cultivating community:

1. We can *join communities* based around the kinds of relating we'd like to move towards.

2. We can *co-create our own communities* with likeminded people who want to explore these options.

3. We can invite our *existing communities* into support of our relating in these ways—potentially encouraging them to move in similar directions.

Of course, we may well do some combination of all these options. Indeed, that may be an excellent idea, as all of them come with their own potentials and drawbacks.

### Joining communities

Fortunately, these days, there is a lot more scope for finding communities which might be moving towards relating in the kinds of ways that you want to pursue. For example, if you are drawn towards consensual non-monogamy (CNM), there are many online communities, and offline events, around CNM. When we first engaged in CNM, there were only a small number of such communities, mostly around a certain kind of polyamory, and pretty white and middle class. Thankfully, you can now find communities and events that cohere around particular kinds of CNM (e.g. solo polyamory, or more spiritual or political forms), and there are groups and events exclusively for people of color (POC) and/or which are POC organized and center POC experience.

There are also now offline and online groups for many kinds of neurodivergence, and for the crossover between these and other intersections. These include groups for those who want to focus on discussions or mutual support, as well as for those who just want to hang out, play games, or go to the pub with people who share a neurodivergence.

Other relevant groups would include men's groups, women's groups, queer groups, trans groups, etc., which focus on how people relate with themselves and others. Also there are therapeutic groups of various kinds for those who want support accepting and/or shifting their patterns (including support groups for particular mental health conditions, recovery/12-step programs, mindfulness groups, process groups, etc.). Many faith and spiritual communities include group support and events where people hear teachings and engage in practices towards more compassionate, caring relationships with themselves and others. We hope this gives you a taster of just some of the kinds of groups and communities you could explore to support you in your relating.

In our last book *How to Understand Your Sexuality*, we included a section, in the final chapter, about what finding a community can open up and close down. Finding community can help us to feel less isolated, meet likeminded people, find ways of making sense of our experiences, and get support. However, communities can also have their own normativities and pressurizing/alienating unwritten rules, and people in communities can engage in bullying, scapegoating, "us and them" thinking, and even cult-like behaviors.

As with individual relationships, it's worth being careful that we aren't searching for the "one true community" that will meet all our needs, or hoping for a group where we'll find all the safety, dignity, and belonging that we lacked—or lost—as a child. It can be a good idea to shop around to find communities that feel a good fit, check that the communities also have systems of support and transparency, and perhaps engage in multiple communities rather than putting all your eggs in one basket! More about the warning signs to look out for in communities in the next section.

### Co-creating communities

An alternative to joining existing communities is to co-create your own communities, bottom up. This could be anything from a group of friends co-creating a reading group to meet regularly to work through a book about relationships together (great idea!)

to a co-op house share based on a particular intersection or way of doing relationships, and everything in between.

Such groups can be anything from closed to a group of people who have already cultivated trusting relationships over time, to open to anybody who wants to join—maybe on social media. They could be set up for a brief period of time (like the lifespan of a shared project—e.g. making a collaborative zine) all the way through to being completely open-ended. They could be highly structured (like a sharing circle) all the way through to unstructured. The purpose could be very specifically about practicing certain ways of relating, through to nothing to do with that, but just that the people concerned share a certain identity or way of doing things (such as a walking or writing group where everyone is queer or non-monogamous).

We've both found co-creating groups and communities—either within or separate to larger existing communities—to be very helpful. They have given us opportunities to:

- consciously practice certain ways of relating in a safe-enough group setting

- get support from others—who we're not in significant relationships with—about how hard this all is

- learn from others' ways of doing things

- get support through particularly challenging times and retreat away from the rest of our lives.

However, it's worth being mindful of all the risks of groups and communities we mentioned above. Also, it's important co-creating, and revisiting over time, the relationship container for the group/community. We've found that—just like other relationships—people can have very different expectations and assumptions, and be looking for very different things from the group. In MJ's ongoing work support group it has been fascinating to have group sharings about everyone's history with groups, as well as—over time—around how we want to share food, navigate time together, and what we want to use the group for.

If you are co-creating groups or communities, there are plenty of materials in the further resources which offer support around creating groups of micro-solidarity, mutual aid, and accountability, for example.

### Shaping existing communities

The final alternative is to stick with the communities we already have in our lives, but to invite them to support our ways of relating, or even encourage them to shift in those directions alongside us.

This might include, for example, coming out in some way about our ways of relating to our friends and family, and letting them know how we'd like them to support us (e.g. in being polyamorous, self-partnered, or aromantic). Or it might go further in inviting all those in our close circles to engage with check-ins, user guides, or relationship agreements with us, not just those in romantic partnerships.

It might be about asking our political, faith, spiritual, work, or other communities to shift their systems and structures in ways that would encompass or accommodate our ways of relating. For example, we might ask our workplace to change their systems so that they ask about relationships in a different way to "Are you married/single?" or "Do you have a partner?" We might ask our faith community to provide rooms for throuples—not just couples—at their events. We might ask our political party to fight for easier processes for renting/buying multiple-occupancy residences for house shares and/or extended families.

Again—like us—you will likely have mixed experiences with this. The person we're staying with to write this book, Hannah, is a great model of somebody who invites the people in her life into more conscious ways of relating. For example, we love that she sends a pretty regular update about where she's at, and support that would be helpful, to all her close people, and invites them to do the same. Some people reciprocate, others just respond, and some just acknowledge it.

Of course, it's for you to determine whether—and how much—you need the people in your life to accept/embrace your way of relating and/or to shift *their* way of relating in order to experience these as supportive communities, and the boundaries you might place around this. For example, many of us who aim for more conscious, consensual ways of relating have experiences with family members who struggle—or refuse—to engage with consent practices, boundaries, or accessing family therapy. Again, we'll all likely come to different places in terms of how much we accept the differences there, what distance we need those relationships to be at, and whether this changes over time, or not.

## Multiple experiences: Different kinds of supportive community

"For me, Buddhism is all about developing more conscious, compassionate ways of relating with myself and others. There's an idea in Buddhism that we need three refuges in this work: the teachings, the practices (like meditation), and the community. I was really put off going towards community for a long time because of all the #metoo moments I was aware of around various Buddhist teachers. Eventually, I decided to try out all the different sanghas in my local city. I eventually committed to a group and teacher that felt most aligned with my understanding of Buddhism, and I still drop in on events at other retreat centers and locally."

"A group of us created a regular meet-up for people who wanted to discuss relating differently from a political perspective. We really struggled to co-create a group agreement which felt free enough and safe enough for everyone in the group (with all their different traumas, positions, etc.). Over time, we also realized we needed to actually do relational practices in the group—to help people ground, communicate consensually, etc.—as well as just talking about them. It was a very challenging experience at times, but I'm glad we persevered."

"I've been in a co-op where we tried so hard to do conscious, consensual, trauma-informed, access-intimate relating. While it worked well for a time, it was incredibly hard to keep it going, when all of us in the house had our own different challenges going on. It was really disappointing to me at first that we ended up being more of a house share than a caring community, but it is what it is. I look for that kind of supportive community elsewhere these days, and I'm open that things may change again as people move in and out of the house."

"People can surprise you. When I came out as ace and aro, I expected my queer community to be supportive and my family to be terrible. Actually, the one who got it most was my nan! Turns out she'd felt similarly her whole life, and it meant so much to her to see that her grandkid got to actually live that way, when she wasn't able to. Some of my queer friends were weird and pressuring. It really shifted my sense of who my supportive community is."

"Many of my supportive communities are fictional, and non-human. I see models of how I want to relate in TV shows like *Torchwood*, *Sense8*, or *Stranger Things*. I get support when I go out in nature and see how the trees grow separately and together, or read about fungi. I've found post-human ideas by writers like Báyò Akómoláfé and Sophie Strand really helpful for taking the pressure off individual 'me' and considering everything as complex interconnected systems."

The next section explores further the support and holding that we might access from our networks and communities around ruptures, conflict, and consent violations. It also looks deeper at some of the problems that can happen in communities, particularly around these areas.

## 6.3 SUPPORT AND ACCOUNTABILITY

Communities, as we've discussed, can be wonderful places of support. However, when hard things happen within communities, they can also be devastating and heartbreaking. As we said in the previous chapter when talking about interpersonal relationships, most of us don't have healthy models of community repair, loving accountability, and restorative justice. Rather, we're brought up within a system ruled by carceral logic, which promotes shame, isolation, and punishment. The dominant cultures where we live, albeit different, are both ruled by white supremacy. This means that perfectionism and purity culture both play a big role when it comes to ruptures, conflicts, and boundary violations within a community.

### The desire to isolate and expunge "evil" from our communities

You might have witnessed yourselves, either in your local communities or online, either/or thinking that divides people into perpetrators/abusers and victims. While we don't deny that abuse happens—and, in fact, as survivors we do believe that we need to have some mechanism to be able to name it when it does—we've also noticed the strong desire, mostly in Anglo white communities, to separate people into "good" and "bad." We believe that when we do this, we dehumanize ourselves and each other. None of us can be entirely good or bad. All of us have the ability to perpetuate harm, intentionally or unintentionally.

When we distance ourselves from the possibility of doing harm, we can also become more dangerous because we're not aware of those situations within which we wield power and agency and can indeed hurt others. Believing that we can be entirely good, at all times, is a symptom of two characteristics of white supremacy culture we mentioned earlier: perfectionism and purity culture. Perfectionism demands of us that we never make mistakes, and purity culture wants us to be, as it says in the term, "pure"—that is, "good" at all times.

On a community level, this can manifest as a desire to identify, isolate, and exterminate all "bad" actors—that is, perpetrators and abusers. If you've ever watched *Doctor Who*, the Daleks are, in a way, the personification of this desire. They're robots, albeit melded with an organic being, that go around saying "exterminate, exterminate" whenever they see the "enemy," which is usually humans. In the same multiverse, the Cybermen are another personification of the desire for purity, although rather than exterminating humans, they turn them into Cybermen by eliminating all emotions.

Much of *Doctor Who*, we believe, is about what it's like to be messy humans, even though they are a Time Lord (although it's a little more complex than that even). It's about having to make decisions in integrity with your values, even when these decisions have far-reaching consequences. Above all, it's about what it means to love humanity deeply, flaws and all. We believe we cannot eliminate harm by expunging "bad" people from communities, and many activists and scholars—especially Black, Brown, and Indigenous ones—have addressed this much better than we could.

When we engage in this desire to expunge "evil" from our communities, not only are we reproducing white supremacist, colonial, carceral logic, but we can also unleash consequences far beyond what we imagined. For example, if we identify someone as a perpetrator, and let all our communities know that this is who they are, and that anyone who associates with them or any of the people connected to them is evil, we might be impacting communities we're not even part of. When this happens, we move away from a relational framework and into an absolutist, highly individualized framework.

Don't get us wrong: we believe there is a place for both calling out and calling in abuse and poor behaviors; we just think it's a complex dance within larger systems of power, privilege, and oppression. We also recognize that identifying, isolating, and expunging people can, at times, provide us with a communal sense of control and the illusion of absolute safety. This can be soothing, especially within marginalized communities, where many of us have experienced not just interpersonal but also historical, cultural, and social trauma.

Second-wave feminism is a vivid example of this, in our opinion, since some of it was founded on naming people with penises as the only possible perpetrators of violence at all times. This meant, to many people, that eliminating them from the community would eliminate the evil of the patriarchy. We've seen how some of that morphed into increasingly aggressive transphobia, especially trans misogyny, by a small faction of people, and also how it has enabled some cisgender (mostly white) women to enact harm without any accountability, because they cannot possibly conceive of themselves as a perpetrator.

There is so much more to say on this and, as we said, other activists and community-based scholars, such as adrienne maree brown and Sonya Renee Taylor, have indeed written whole books and articles and created resources around this issue (see further resources). For now, we just want to refer back to positioning theory, introduced in Chapter 3, and name that we've been in different locations in relation to this. That is, we:

— have been called out

— have been called in

— have called out

— have called in

— have been cast as impure and "bad"

— have been supported when we've been called out and cast as impure and bad

— have felt isolated and abandoned when we've been called out and cast as impure and bad

— have supported others who have been called out and cast out

of communities in ways that have led to them losing their
lives by completing suicide or coming close to that

— have supported people who have been suicidal and/or hospi-
talized because of the impact of abusive leadership patterns

— have had accountability conversations

— have supported accountability conversations

— have witnessed people and communities be hurt by the ripple
effects of revenge vs. the relational process of accountability

— have struggled with how to even talk about this without
sounding like abuse apologists

— have struggled with our own desire for revenge and visibility
as survivors vs. relational accountability and community care.

It's even scary to write about this right now, but we don't want to
bypass this important topic. When abuse happens within a community, it's devastating, no matter what the dynamics at play. We do
think that an intentional community approach in those moments is
more conducive to our collective healing and liberation. However,
we also don't judge people who have been hurt and feel a deep desire
for a more carceral type of punishment and justice, especially when
those who have perpetrated the abuse have done so unabashedly
again and again, and hold power on a systemic level.

We also don't believe that there is any one perfect tool to
address those moments because anything can be weaponized.
For example, we have witnessed the characteristics of the white
supremacy culture document (see the resources at the end of the
chapter) be weaponized, as well as non-violent communication
being used very violently, and the idea of accountability being
abused rather than used. With regard to the latter, we want to
recognize Tada Hozumi, an activist and teacher, as someone
who clearly distinguished between accountability abuse and

accountability processes, although their work has moved towards a more nondualistic approach since.

So, if we're messy humans that cannot be neatly sorted between good and bad ones, and if any model or tool can be weaponized, how can we even be in community with one another and remain accountable to each other?

## Remaining accountable to ourselves

It might be unsurprising to learn that we think that engaging in deep awareness of our trauma and relational patterns is a good way to start. After all, we've dedicated much of this book to talking about this! We cannot be accountable to ourselves and one another if we don't understand how we've been hurt and how we've hurt others (and yes, to some degree, we believe that we've all hurt someone, but the degree certainly does vary greatly). It can be easy, initially, to collapse into shame, especially if we were brought up within Anglo white culture. After all, if we acknowledge that we've hurt people, we have "failed" to uphold the values of purity, perfectionism, and binary thinking! Shame usually acts as trauma in the body, and if we're in one of the 4F reactions—fight, flight, freeze, fawn—we cannot truly be present with the process of accountability. This is a relational process holding us responsible for the reality of interdependence within our beloved community.

We keep saying that we cannot move outside of culture and that awareness of the norms we're deeply embedded in is essential. Along with this, the knowledge of how we've been shaped by those patterns and scripts, as well as by our familial experiences and relational trauma, is important as well. How can we be supported in this process of excavating and understanding all of this within our own internal systems, though? While books like this one can be helpful, it can feel scary and isolating to do this work alone. We encourage you to nurture community relationships where you can do this work with others. Sometimes, however, we also need to do our own individual work, and we can seek support from a number of sources, depending on many factors, including economic capacity and availability of resources. Some sources of support can be:

- therapy (individual or systemic—i.e. family and/or group therapy)
- healing practices/communities
- spiritual practices/communities
- peer counseling and peer support (either individually or in groups)
- recovery communities
- intentional communities
- friends, partners, families.

We encourage you to have more than one source of support in your life whenever possible, so that you don't end up isolated if a specific relationship, or type of support, doesn't work out or falls apart for any reason. You might also want to bear in mind some principles when looking for support, since it can be hard for many of us to do. We can also be vulnerable to people taking advantage of our trauma and relational patterns, whether intentionally or unintentionally. Some of these principles are:

- *Not being afraid to ask as many questions as you need.* If any one person, group, or community does not tolerate questions, take time to consider why that might be. On the other hand, be aware that sometimes our questions can be driven by an entitlement to comfort (see characteristics of white supremacy culture again in the further resources), so take care to discern where your questions are coming from, but don't be afraid to ask questions!

— *Not walking on eggshells or being afraid of provoking a big reaction.* If you're finding yourself walking on eggshells with a therapist, friend, or within a community, once more, ask yourselves where this is coming from. Have there been volatile reactions within the current relationship, or is the fear coming from past experiences, or both? Have the big reactions been understandable or out of the blue? Was there an apology and/or awareness afterwards? Is it a pattern or a one-off?

— *Looking for systems that are open rather than closed.* This can be tricky because, for example, therapy is a closed system by nature. However, you can ask questions of a potential therapist to find out whether they're part of a consult group, or whether they're active within their professional communities. Poor behaviors and boundary crossings in therapy are more likely to happen when the therapist acts in isolation from others in their field. If you're considering peer support of some kind, is the system open to newcomers or is it more "cult-like"? See further resources for the characteristics of cults to distinguish cult-like groups from relational groups and communities, and for another document highlighting what to watch out for in group dynamics.

— *Considering whether consent is ever mentioned and/or practiced by that person or group.* While we understand that consent is complicated, given sociocultural power dynamics, we also believe it's essential. Consent within a group centers not just individuals but also collective wellbeing. For example, in this ongoing pandemic, a group might ask for people to mask, because they're centering immunocompromised disabled people who are most impacted by the current lack of community care in relation to masking. Some people might see this as "imposing" masking and not being consensual, whereas we view this as a form of mutual community care within the framework of disability justice principles (see Chapter 2).

- *Feeling that your needs are met and your boundaries respected.* This might seem simple but it's essential. Remember here that boundaries are about your own needs and not about controlling someone else's behaviors. It's worth mentioning it here because so few of us have had healthy boundaries modeled to us growing up. We want to make sure that we, as well as others, don't weaponize boundaries as a form of controlling others to soothe our own anxieties.

- *Looking for people and groups that are open to feedback and have ways of providing feedback that are not just direct.* For example, if you have a therapist, you should know which body to complain to if you don't want to give feedback directly to them about a boundary crossing. If you're part of a group, is there a mechanism to provide feedback to someone who is not part of the leadership team, if there is one? This is also connected to the idea of open vs. closed systems that we mentioned earlier.

As always, none of these principles are absolute or uncomplicated. It's almost as if the two of us had written a book called *Life Isn't Binary* (sarcasm)! Much as we wish there were simple answers to these issues, we don't believe there are, unless we want to fall back onto dualistic thinking. We do believe, though, that:

- we can keep asking questions, first of all to ourselves

- we can get to know ourselves and one another better

- we can choose to deepen into healthy interdependence within the communities we choose to engage with.

Given that we've gotten a bit "heady" in this section, below are some practical examples of people who have sought out different types of support to better engage with others within their communities.

## Multiple experiences: Different types of support

"I used to be really angry and reactive. A lot of it was covered up under social justice outrage, but as I went through more therapy, especially somatic therapy that invited me to be more embodied, I realized there was a lot of self-hatred from trauma underneath the righteous anger surface. I still get angry, but I can connect with others more now, which I really wanted before but didn't know how to do. I'm also more able to hear others if I make mistakes. Before, I would need to prove I was right. Now I can consider that I may be wrong, sometimes."

"My coven has given me a lot of support around healing from child-hood sexual abuse. I had done other things, like therapy, but having a consistent coven that has met for years, where a small group of people know me, and I know them, did something for my trust that no other type of support had done before."

"Getting sober wasn't easy but it was essential. I couldn't have done it without the recovery community. My NA group is almost like a spiritual practice for me. I was also surprised to find fellowship in a women's group as a trans woman. I was so nervous about rejection at first since it was all cis women... I have found an even deeper level of healing there than I could have ever imagined. They also supported me in being accountable to some past behaviors I had engaged in when using. They had similar struggles and stories, and that helped so much. They didn't see my past mistakes as 'male socialization' but rather as struggles with intimacy, trauma, and addiction, just like theirs. I can hardly put into words what that meant to me."

"Peer counseling is the constant support in my life. So much has changed over the past decade for me, but peer counseling has been the steady anchor through it all. I have tried therapy, but it didn't really work for me. There is something about the mutuality of this process that fits better with my values and who I am. I feel like I can give and not just receive, and that's so important for me."

"There is nothing that I cannot take to the floor in my authentic movement practice. Whether I am a mover or a witness, I get something out of it every time. No matter what happens within me, or around me, I can come to the floor, be still, and let my movement rise from deep within me, or witness and observe what arises within me. It's not just a beautiful practice; it has kept me alive and helped me move from daily suicidal ideation to much less frequent and less intense levels of suicidality."

We hope that you can see, from the composite multiple experiences above, how important support is to increase our capacity for accountability within ourselves and with one another. We've found that when we're depleted, we tend to disconnect, or collapse quickly into shame if someone says anything negative about, or to, us. This is not helpful to building community and nurturing mutual networks of care, something we're both committed to.

However, we also recognize that we cannot just be accountable to ourselves. We also need to be accountable to one another, in whichever community we are. Even if we choose not to be in any community, we're part of an ecosystem, and we believe we need to also keep ourselves accountable to our non-human kin such as greenbloods, animal companions, bodies of water we rely on, the lands that sustain us, and to our ancestors and potential descendants (not just of blood but also of activism, healing, and spirit).

What does it mean to be accountable, though? In our understanding, the word comes from the Latin *computare*—that is, to provide a count of what is left in someone's care, usually understood as money or property. We like to think of community accountability as providing "a count" to each other of how we're caring for ourselves, the ecosystems we're part of, and each other. If we're truly interdependent, as the disability justice movement has been teaching us for decades, and as Indigenous communities have always known, we're also in each other's stewardship. That is, we're responsible for managing ourselves, the ecosystems we're part of, and our relationships.

This is what we mean by accountability: being available and present to be counted as someone willing to care for themselves, the environment we're part of, and the web of relationships we're born into, and those that we choose as we grow older. This type of accountability cannot be about punishment and carceral logic, if we're trying to nurture beloved communities. Therefore, we turn to models of restorative and healing justice next to explore how these can be helpful in nurturing communities that want to move towards interdependence and away from colonial, white supremacist models.

## Restorative and healing justice possibilities

You might have been brought up within a culture or community that practices restorative and/or healing justice, but chances are that this is more unlikely than likely. Let's take a moment to talk about these models so you can see whether they're something you're interested in finding out more about as ways of relating within communities. We want to be clear that this is not a guide on how to do these processes, as that would be far beyond the scope of this book. There are also much more competent people than us who have written about these topics, as you can see in the further resources section at the end of this chapter.

We've picked these two frameworks because they're relational rather than individualized frameworks, and given that we're writing a book about relationships, they seemed to be the most congruent to discuss when talking interdependence and community building/ nurturing. They're also congruent with our values as abolitionists who straddle working within current systems while aspiring to dismantle them.

Within a *restorative justice* framework, the term "justice" is used not to mean retribution but rather repair within a community that has been harmed by whatever act has been perpetrated. This means that restorative justice is inherently relational, since its goal is to restore relationships within the community, which can happen in a number of ways.

Even though this approach has become increasingly visible in dominant Anglo cultures over the past few decades, many have argued, and we would agree with them, that restorative practices are rooted in Indigenous values and practices. Within this framework, there is no simple formula of "breaking this law equals this punishment" since the process, in a way, is what eventually leads to an outcome that cannot be predicted at the start. This is a truly relational, unfolding process, guided by a set of principles rather than a strict protocol.

We cannot tell you in this book how to do restorative justice, not just because it would mean writing far too much, but also because you cannot do restorative justice alone. This framework can only be applied when a whole community has agreed to it. It's a relational framework that happens within people and not to them. If you're interested in learning more about this process, which can actually vary quite a lot depending on who is implementing it and where it's implemented, we encourage you to check out the further resources section. This approach is also congruent with a healing justice framework.

*Healing justice* can mean a number of things and be applied in a range of contexts. For example, we can talk about healing justice with regard to the judicial, prison-industrial complex, or the medical-industrial complex, or mental health. However, there are some underlying principles that can be applied to this framework, no matter the context:

- *Systemic.* We need both individual and collective healing. One of the goals is collective, not just individual, wellness.

- *Interdependent.* We cannot do this work alone. We need one another, and the reality is that we're interdependent beings who are part of ecosystems larger than ourselves. Within these ecosystems, we exist in relationships and webs of interdependence.

- *Mutual.* This one goes with the two principles above. We need mutuality for interdependence to work in harmony, or we run into imbalances and systemic "sickness" within ourselves and our communities.

- *Dynamic.* It's not something we can achieve once and for all and then rest. Healing justice is a process and, as such, needs to be tended to.

- *Connected.* The struggle for social justice is not separate from our individual wellbeing or the wellbeing of our families and communities.

- *Rooted in solidarity.* Our oppression and our liberation, which includes our healing, are connected. Solidarity is essential if we're striving for the liberation of our whole communities.

- *Accessible.* If some people in our communities cannot access our care, our work is not yet done. Healing justice can only be understood in relation to disability justice principles (see Chapter 2). We are all worthy of care.

- *Transformative.* Within this framework, we're seeking to heal not just ourselves but also our lineages, to disrupt patterns of intergenerational, historical, cultural, and social violence.

- *Liberatory.* We cannot have healing justice without disrupting systems of power, privilege, and oppression, or without dismantling capitalism and truly decolonizing ourselves, communities, and the lands we're on.

- *Abolitionist.* The same systems that oppress us cannot heal us.

They can be helpful at times, but ultimately they will need to be dismantled if we're not to perpetuate colonialist, racist, anti-Black, patriarchal, and cisgenderist normative systems of control.

We cannot tell you if these frameworks and models are for you or not, but we do invite you to check them out if you haven't considered them before. Transformative and healing justice approaches go beyond resolving conflicts or restoring relationships after harm has occurred. They aim to transform the whole system within which conflict or harm occurs and/or to heal the trauma that it is rooted in. This means that it can be hard to envision what these frameworks might look like in practice, especially within our own lives. Below are a couple of team MJ's attempts to engage in processes—personally and professionally—with transformative and healing *aims*, to give you a flavor of the kinds of things we're talking about. Please check out the resources shared at the end of the chapter if you want to engage in such learnings or processes yourself. There are many ways to understand and implement these frameworks in different situations and systems.

## TEAM MJ WRITES:

Sadly we've been through—and around—far too many relationship rifts, group conflicts, and communities where ongoing abuse was recognized, where no transformative or healing justice processes were available. This often meant harm on top of harm as people—including ourselves—engaged from their trauma patterns. It's one of the reasons we love Báyò Akómoláfé's warning to not let our response to a crisis become part of the crisis.

We can think of three examples where we engaged in a more healing/transformative process. Professionally, we supported some people running a queer organization for a while, when they found their different relationship patterns showing up between them. We spent time with one, then the other, then both of them, over some months: listening to how it was for each of them, helping them listen to each other, and coming up with plans about how they might engage with the fits and misfits between them in ways that helped their relationships, their business, and the wider community.

Personally, one time following a consent violation between two friends, we were able to hear each of them from both the self in us who would be capable of such a violation (from his desperate/needy feelings) and the self in us who has survived such violations from others. Then we sat with them together and helped mediate a conversation where they heard each other. It showed us how our vivid plurality could help us in these times to empathize with all concerned, while holding the realities of power imbalances and harm having occurred. Another time, when trauma patterns ruptured a relationship we were in, a group we were part of managed to hold us both so we could remain in that group together. While they were clear that there weren't the resources to have any more of an explicit process around the rupture, it was still valuable indeed to be witnessed through such a time, and to be able to remain in relationship as both of us worked through our trauma around it.

Now that you've read these examples, we'd like to invite you to reflect on what healing and justice mean to you at this moment in time. Then we'll explore the idea of leaving a relationship legacy in the next section.

### Reflection point: What do justice and healing mean to you?

As always, please only engage in this reflection point if you think it might be helpful to you and if it's within your current capacity. Please use whichever method feels best to you at this point in time to process and record your reflections on the questions below.

What do the words "justice" and "healing" mean to you, both separately and together? If you were to give your own definition of justice and your own definition of healing, what would they be? How would you articulate them out loud or in writing to another person? What are your experiences in relation to the ideas, realities, and practices of justice and healing? What do these experiences bring up for you? Within the dominant discourse where you live, what do justice and healing mean? Are your definitions of healing and justice congruent with those in dominant discourse where you live? If so, in what way? If not, why not, and how do they differ? What is your current relationship with each of these ideas—healing and justice? Are you comfortable with your current relationship with the ideas of healing and justice or would you like to shift this in any way?

## 6.4 CHANGING OUR RELATIONSHIP LEGACY (OR AT LEAST STRIVING TO)

One of the things that motivated us, not only to write this book but also to engage in this work of intentionally relating for well over two decades, is our desire to shift our relationship legacy in a number of contexts. Alex remembers being a teenager who didn't believe in current geopolitical borders, and who was often teased, if not mocked, for that belief. They were called young, idealistic, and earnest at the time, and told these beliefs would change as they grew older. Being well past 50, they're no longer told they're young, but they're at times still called idealistic, and they're often called earnest both because of their neurodivergence and because their beliefs about the abolition of geopolitical borders have not changed. They actually have grown, if anything, to include abolitionist beliefs about almost every current system of power. We both share these beliefs because we think it's not possible to dismantle the current systems of power, privilege, and oppression without abolishing the systems and practices that hold them up.

Striving to change our relationship legacy with the ecosystems we're part of, within ourselves, and with one another is not a particularly comfortable or easy process. We've longed for clear answers, probably just like some of you are doing right now as this book winds down to its ending. We've been frustrated and tired, probably just like some of you are feeling right now after reading this book. We've tried a number of strategies, some similar and some different from one another. We had hoped that the path would appear clearly in front of us at some point rather than asking us again and again to just move forward, one breath at a time, often without being able to see further than the end of our nose. We've wanted relief and distraction from the pain that it is to relate intentionally with one another in a world that just wants us to buy more, go faster, abuse our bodyminds as commodities, and use each other as a means to an end. We struggle with everything we've written in this book every day, still, and we often feel like failures and imposters.

## What if I don't want to do this work? Why me?

We have also witnessed people asking themselves, "Why me? Why should I care about a world that has already been given to me abused, raped, and out of balance? Why should I do the hard work of healing from intergenerational family trauma, when I was hurt by those who were supposed to love and protect me? Why should I be responsible for the actions of my colonizer ancestors? Why should I care? Why should I work at this? Why me?" A question we would simply ask back is "Why not you, or me, or all of us?" Why would we not be the ones who need to do this work? In a way, some of these questions usually come from a place of privilege and comfort. They are questions, not exclusively but most often, asked by folks brought up within Anglo white contexts, rooted in protestant ethics.

If you're asking yourself some of these questions, take a moment to slow down and notice where they come from, with as much curiosity, gentleness, and non-judgment as you're able to, at this moment. Also, if you don't want to do this work, you don't have to. We're not here to tell you what is right or wrong, good or bad, or what you *should* do. That would be rather hypocritical of us after telling you again and again that every activity is an invitation, and that there are few to no absolutes! If you're noticing self-judgment, or any judgment really, we hope you can slow down, get curious, breathe, and search for some understanding and wisdom there, right there in whatever feeling you're having right now.

Whatever you choose to do, one thing we would ask is that you not weaponize this book. Please don't use any of this content to beat yourselves or anyone else up, be it morally, emotionally, verbally, or even physically! What this means is that we don't want this book, or, all deities forbid, us, to be put on a pedestal as giving some sort of answer on "how to do relationships right." While we hope this book might offer you some helpful questions for reflections, tools, and insights to better understand yourselves and your relationships, we don't want this book to be an "expert guide." That would be counter to pretty much most things we've written we are for in this very book. Even writing a book about this is, in some ways, a colonial, capitalist way to share knowledge, and we want to recognize this explicitly. However, this is also what we do under capitalism to survive. We write, we hope to sell books, we speak at events, we hold and facilitate space in a number of ways. We're aware of our choices, and all we're trying to do here is offer our knowledge, both personal and professional, and our experiences to you. What you do with them, or this book, is up to you.

## But how do we change that relationship legacy after all?

We honestly don't know. We're part of, or at least we like to imagine that we're part of, a larger movement of people grappling with all these questions. People like adrienne maree brown, Sonya Renee Taylor, Dr. Kim TallBear, Layla Saad, and others before them like Sibilla Aleramo, and so many others, who have grappled with ideas of community, relating, being accountable, being honest with ourselves, and going against normative messages from dominant culture. Colonialism and white supremacy want us to have neatly packaged answers, but we truly don't, although we hope the questions and ideas we offered here have some use for you.

We're inviting you to find your own way to join us in these efforts. We've definitely tried so many things! Even during the past few years of dreaming, incubating, and discussing this book, we've lived very different lives from one another. MJ has been cultivating their relationships within, whereas Alex has been immersed in external relationships at home and work. MJ has written many versions of their relationship user guides, whereas Alex has started and abandoned many versions of theirs, never sharing one with any people in their lives. We've both come to understand ourselves through the lens of neurodivergence but from the perspectives of different neurotypes—autism and being plural for MJ, autism and ADHD for Alex.

We don't know where our relationship will take us next. Currently, this is the last book we've committed to as a team, even though new writing visions might be emerging, taking us in somewhat different, yet connected, directions both separately and together. We're not asking you to do what we've done, because our experiences are different even from one another. We're inviting you to deepen into your own life, your own values and beliefs, your own understanding, your own relationship with land, water, yourselves, and those around you, your own experiences and desire to change whatever legacy you want to dedicate yourself to changing. Maybe some of the tools in this book will help you with this process, maybe not. Either way, our hope is that this wasn't a waste of your time.

Layla Saad is leading the "good ancestor movement," and one of our beloved kin, Donald Engstrom-Reese, has also asked many people who have trained spiritually over the years to explore what kind of ancestor they want to become. One of Alex's beloved friends and coven mates, Colleen Cook, who is now an ancestor, said in a podcast interview with Dr. Pavini Moray, while preparing to die consciously in the spring of 2019, at 51 years old: "I want to be an ancestor who makes mistakes." So, we're asking you to engage in one last activity as we close this book and to consider, if you haven't done so before, what kind of ancestor you want to become when it comes to your relational legacy, mistakes and all.

## ACTIVITY: LEAVING A RELATIONAL LEGACY AS AN ANCESTOR

For this activity, we invite you to consider not just what kind of ancestor you want to become once you're dead but, specifically, what kind of relational legacy you want to leave behind as an ancestor. If you have not engaged in this kind of exercise before it might seem strange, overwhelming, hard, scary, [insert emotional adjective of your choice here...], and that's okay. As with every other activity in this book, please only engage with it if it feels right for you at this moment.

You can explore what kind of relational legacy you want to leave as an ancestor in a number of ways. You might want to write some reflections, for example, or compose a song, make a collage, draw something, take a picture, dance it out, or talk it over with someone you trust, or even in a voice memo, if you're a verbal processor. You might even want to make an altar to your future ancestor self. Making an altar can be as simple as placing a piece of cloth on a surface, maybe with a candle and a photo of yourself. You could sit at your altar to your future, relational ancestral self to do this activity, or do whatever you feel drawn to do, if anything at all.

If you want to, we encourage you to share the results of this activity with the people close to you. You might even want to invite them to do this activity alongside you, and then share with one another. After all, what could our world be like if we all spent some time reflecting on what kind of ancestors we want to become, once we're dead, and what relationship legacy (with the earth, ourselves, and one another) we want to leave behind?

> **REMEMBER...** As we were writing this book, we kept joking that it could be summarized in two words: "Relationships. Hard." We still think so. If anything, maybe now we would use three words: "Relationships. Really. Hard." Please remember that it's okay to go slow, to breathe, to take what's helpful and leave the rest, to make mistakes, to learn, to grow, to change your mind, to begin relationships, to end them, to transform them, and be transformed by them. Whoever you are, whatever you do, whichever kind of relationships you might be in, may you and your relationships be blessed with intentionality and care.

## Further resources

There's a great paper about why we need shame-sensitive, as well as trauma-informed, practice here:

- Dolezal, L. and Gibson, M. (2022). "Beyond a trauma-informed approach and towards shame-sensitive practice." *Humanities and Social Sciences Communications 9*, 1, 1–10.

You can find the Year Compass here:

- https://yearcompass.com

T-MAPs can be found here:

- https://tmapscommunity.net

One approach to sharing circles is described in this book:

- Baldwin, C. and Linnea, A. (2010). *The Circle Way: A Leader in Every Chair*. Oakland, CA: Berrett-Koehler Publishers.

There are links to several resources on consent at the end of the previous chapter. The whole book about the wheel of consent is:

- Martin, B. (2021). *The Art of Receiving and Giving: The Wheel of Consent*. Eugene, OR: Luminare Press.

The link for the instructions for the 3 Minute Game are here:

- https://bettymartin.org/download-wheel

See here for Betty Martin's "Waking Up the Hands" practice:

- https://bettymartin.org/hands

You can find MJ's blog posts about slow relating here:

- www.rewriting-the-rules.com/self/slow-relating

- www.rewriting-the-rules.com/love-commitment/working-dunbars-number-and-other-adventures-in-slow-relating

There are lots of useful resources around developing solidarity groups here:

- www.microsolidarity.cc

Sophie K. Rosa's book, listed at the end of Chapter 2, includes lots of useful information about mutual aid and co-creating communities.

Here's an introductory post on mutual aid:

- www.globalgiving.org/learn/what-is-mutual-aid

There's a useful guide on Mutual Aid 101 here:

- https://gdoc.pub/doc/e/2PACX-1vRMxV09kdojzMdyOfapJU OB6Ko2_1iAfIm8ELeIgma21wIt5HoTqP1QXadF01eZc0ySr PW6VtU_veyp?

Here is how you can get started on creating your own mutual aid network:

- https://afsc.org/news/how-create-mutual-aid-network

There is material on accountability, trauma, and queer community here:

- https://xtramagazine.com/love-sex/why-are-queer-people-so-mean-to-each-other-160978

If you want to read more about accountability and "cancel culture," we suggest:

- Brown, A.M. (2020). *We Will Not Cancel Us: And Other Dreams of Transformative Justice*. Chico, CA: AK Press.

Sonya Renee Taylor talks on moving towards accountability here:

- www.youtube.com/watch?v=3vCKwoee27c

The white supremacy culture website is here:

- www.whitesupremacyculture.info/characteristics.html

For a helpful reflection on the problems of purity culture, check out:

- Shotwell, A. (2016). *Against Purity: Living Ethically in Compromised Times*. Minneapolis: University of Minnesota Press.

Báyò Akómoláfé's writing on challenging urgency is here:

- www.bayoakomolafe.net/post/a-slower-urgency

There is a checklist of cult characteristics here:

- https://cultrecovery101.com/cult-recovery-readings/checklist-of-cult-characteristics

There's useful information about consent, power, and abuse here:

- www.artofconsent.co.uk/_files/ugd/e73e7e_967347525b294269 8c56c8ef24603566.pdf

The original 10 principles of disability justice:

- www.sinsinvalid.org/blog/10-principles-of-disability-justice

For more on healing and restorative justice frameworks, check out these books:

- Thom, K.C. (2019). *I Hope We Choose Love. A Trans Girl's Notes from the End of the World*. Vancouver, BC: Arsenal Pulp Press.
- Page, C. and Woodland, E. (2023). *Healing Justice Lineages: Dreaming at the Crossroads of Liberation, Collective Care, and Safety*. Berkeley, CA: North Atlantic Books.
- Raffo, S. (2022). *Liberated to the Bone: Histories. Bodies. Futures*. Chico, CA: AK Press.
- Kuhn, R. (2024). *Somacultural Liberation: An Indigenous, Two-Spirit Somatic Guide to Integrating Cultural Experiences Towards Freedom*. Berkeley, CA: North Atlantic Books.

There's material on restorative justice in the prison system here:

- https://restorativejustice.org

There is a useful literature review on restorative justice here:

- https://ojjdp.ojp.gov/sites/g/files/xyckuh176/files/media/document/restorative_justice.pdf

The Healing Histories Project is here:

- https://healinghistoriesproject.com

Colleen Cook's interview with Dr. Pavini Moray for Bespoken Bones Podcast is here:

- https://bespokenbones.libsyn.com/episode-55-i-want-to-be-an-ancestor-who-makes-mistakes-on-dying-consciously-fierce-activism-and-tender-learning-to-the-end

If you are in an abusive relationship, you can find a list of support resources here…

If you live in the US:

- https://ncadv.org/RESOURCES

If you live in the UK:

- www.gov.uk/guidance/domestic-abuse-how-to-get-help

If you live in Canada:

- www.canada.ca/en/public-health/services/health-promotion/stop-family-violence/services.html

If you live in Australia:

- www.respect.gov.au/support-services

If you live in New Zealand:

- www.areyouok.org.nz

# AFTERWORD: UNCOVERING AND REMEMBERING OUR INTERCONNECTEDNESS

Whenever we write a book together, our editorial process involves reading what we've written out loud to each other. It's always so lovely to hear each other's words, and how they weave together, in that way.

This time, when we finished reading the final chapter, we were both left with some painful emotions. It was hard to put our finger on exactly what these were, but there was a sense of lack and loss in there, as well as deep grief and intense vulnerability. We wanted to write these final words in case you, dear reader, are left with similar feelings.

In the last chapter, we offered you a sense of what conscious, consensual relationships might look like, as well as providing visions of nourishing communities. We also touched on the kinds of transformative, healing processes that might take place when our various trauma patterns inevitably do play out in relationships and communities in ways that perpetuate harm.

Some of our tender feelings, on finishing this chapter, are in recognition that what we—and, we suspect, many people—have in our lives is in painfully stark contrast with such visions.

- Rather than having mutually nourishing abundant webs of relationships, many of us are very isolated and/or find that most of our relationships are profoundly limited by traumatized and traumatizing dynamics.

- Instead of feeling resourced and resilient in our networks of support, many of us fear what would happen if anything else difficult were to hit, because we already feel so burned out, or at the edge of our capacity, so much of the time. Many of us are also significantly disabled, struggling with mental health difficulties, and/or caring for others. Dealing with anything else on top of that can feel utterly overwhelming.

- While we long for supportive community, mutual aid, and collective care, we may well have found that the global COVID-19 pandemic—and all the other recent connected crises and revelations of deep injustice—have left those around us turned inwards rather than out. We may be painfully aware of the ways in which others in our communities are tending to respond to any new crisis out of their trauma patterns, and of the lack of resources that they have to offer to us in our struggles.

- Instead of being held in loving support when conflicts, harms, and abuses occur, we may have felt very alone as others default to old binary modes of taking sides, or disengage from anything that might be difficult or complicated.

- We may be haunted by all the painful ruptures and rifts that have occurred in our webs of relating, without the collective awareness to understand the systemic and personal traumas involved, or the resources necessary to transform those systems and heal those traumas.

When we notice these kinds of gaps between our current experience and the kind of relationships, communities, justice, and care that we yearn for, we can be left with a sense of being even more dis-connected, alienated, and alone. This can easily spark the shameful sense that there is something wrong with us, which we've explored throughout this book, as well as a fear of engaging with others—and the world—at all, or a rage that our relationships and communities are not better.

We want you to know that we've had all those emotions our-selves. Paradoxically, one of the things that deeply connects us is precisely these painful feelings of disconnection.

It feels important, here, to honestly acknowledge the reality of the pain and trauma that so many of us are experiencing at every level from how we treat ourselves, through our relationships, to our communities and wider cultures. At the same time, might we hold the reality that we *are* inevitably, intrinsically interconnected at every level of being, whether we're aware of that or not?

Our bodies are all made up of materials that were once part of the bodies of other beings and will be again. Our self is not solid but permeable, deeply shaped by all the experiences we've had in relationships. Other beings around us can provoke us into con-tracting into feeling small and incapable, and they can also nurture us into expansion; into capacities and potentials we never thought possible. This can come from something as small as a smile from a stranger on the street, to being witnessed over time in an abiding, loving friendship, in all of our flaws and vulnerabilities.

Holding this bothness—of the painful realities of our lives *and* our deep interconnectedness—is something like holding the con-ditional within the unconditional (see section 2.4). In this kind of understanding, we can maybe let go of all of the huge—sometimes seemingly impossible—goals. Big, idealistic goals like:

— being capable of entirely conscious, consensual relationships

— finally finding a community where we completely belong, with no tensions or conflict

- being able to respond to every conflict and crisis in a totally present, intentional, helpful, transformative, healing way

- feeling we should be "saving the world" in every place that it's currently struggling.

Instead, perhaps, we can make a small, simple everyday goal, of recognizing interconnectedness wherever we find it. This doesn't mean giving up on larger goals, such as our collective liberation and intentional relating. It means recognizing that it's often in our everyday struggles and choices that we build and nurture a new world into existence. Big, bold gestures and changes are sometimes necessary, but, more often than not, change happens in small, incremental, everyday ways.

Here we return to that nested model of understanding relationships that we introduced in section 1.3.

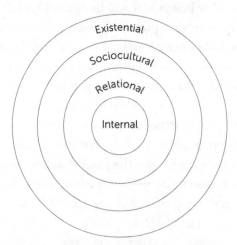

Figure A.1: Multiple levels of understanding relationships

Whether we feel it or not, we *are* interconnected at each of these levels:

- At the *internal* level, each system of our bodymind is interconnected with all the others, as well as with the other beings—microbes and the like—who live within our gut and other organs, enabling much of what we do.

- At the *relational* level, we're interconnected with all the other beings around us, from the pigeon who wakes us up tapping on the window, through the assistant who serves us in the store, to all of the beings who live with—or around—us in our homes.

- At the *sociocultural* level, we're interconnected with all beings around the world, from those involved in the processes that co-create our morning coffee to those whose actions and energies shape the weather we experience today.

- At the *existential*—or spiritual—level, we're interconnected with land, sea, sun, air, and—depending on your worldview—with ancestors and descendants, with deities and spirits, and/or with a meaning greater than ourselves.

We've noticed that different people have different *ways in* to this sense of interconnectedness. For example, we've written in this book about how MJ's way in, currently, is about connecting with their different selves on a daily basis, while Alex's way in is, currently, more about connections with other people and beings. It's just about finding one way in—that works for us at this time. We might make a little space for it every day, in order to gradually expand and deepen our feelings of interconnectedness. You can find some of these ways in, in one of our other books *Hell Yeah Self-Care! A Trauma-Informed Workbook*, but here are some brief examples of ways in, for each of those levels:

- *Internal:* Uncovering our interconnectedness on this level might focus on connecting with the body through somatic practices, self-touch, moving to music, sports, and so on. It might focus on connecting with our feelings through meditation, therapy, creativity, or other means. It might focus on connecting with different parts—or selves—within us through journaling, self-talk, or other explorations.

- *Relational:* Uncovering our interconnectedness on this level might focus on deepening our existing relationships through the kinds of intentional and sharing practices we've described in this book. It might focus on connecting with others' experiences through reading or watching biographies, fiction, or news stories. It might involve attending groups where people share their experiences (like recovery groups, support groups, or spiritual groups), or doing voluntary work which involves listening to—or caring for—others (e.g. crisis phone lines, hospice work, animal rescue, or prison pen pal schemes). It might involve connecting with the redbloods or greenbloods (animals or plants) in our everyday life, by working a shared allotment, for example, or by litter picking, or walking a friend's dog.

- *Sociocultural:* Uncovering our interconnectedness on this level might focus on developing micro-solidarity groups or joining communities in the ways we suggested in the last chapter. It might focus on learning—through reading, watching, or listening—more about the interwoven forces of oppression that shape our lives, or about the way that climate works, and what people have done in the past—and are doing now—to address these things. It might focus on feeling our connectedness with all other beings, through our own meditation practices, or through attending group events where there are shared collective feelings (anything from a grief-tending workshop to a music festival).

- *Existential:* Uncovering our interconnectedness on this level might focus on deepening our existing faith or spirituality through engaging with teachings, practices, and/or community. It might involve connecting with land or water by going for a regular slow wander in local nature, or noticing the ways in which plants and water move through our urban landscapes, or regularly looking up at the sky and noticing which phase the moon is in or how the clouds move. It could include engaging with our creativity—individually or collectively—to make something that feels meaningful and/or connects with others.

There are many other examples at all these levels, of course. Crucially, just deciding to bring our attention to our interconnectedness in one of these ways, little bit by little bit, every day, can start a profound shift to feeling that interconnectedness more on *all* of these levels. We might feel alone, but we're never truly alone. Connection is always available to us because we're part of an ecosystem. However, we might not always be open to experiencing that connection because of all the reasons explored in this book, and more.

Even just remembering—every time we feel disconnected—that right at this moment, all around the world, there are people who are feeling the same way can be an achingly beautiful, sad reminder of our interconnectedness.

We wish you so much love and solidarity on your continued journeys of interconnectedness, as we continue on our own—alone and, inevitably, together.

# Index

Sub-headings in *italics* indicate figures.

# HOW TO UNDERSTAND YOUR GENDER

## A Practical Guide for Exploring Who You Are

### *Alex Iantaffi and Meg-John Barker*

*Foreword by S. Bear Bergman*
*Illustrated by Jules Scheele*

£16.99 | $21.95 | PB | 288PP
ISBN 978 1 78592 746 1
eISBN 978 1 78450 517 2

**Have you ever questioned your gender identity? Do you know somebody who is transgender or who identifies as non-binary? Do you ever feel confused when people talk about gender diversity?**

This down-to-earth guide is for anybody who wants to know more about gender, from its biology, history, and sociology to the role it plays in our relationships and interactions with family, friends, partners, and strangers. Activities throughout the book will engage people of all genders in a thoughtful, practical way, and help you understand people whose gender might be different from your own.

# HOW TO UNDERSTAND YOUR SEXUALITY

## A Practical Guide for Exploring Who You Are

### *Meg-John Barker and Alex Iantaffi*

*Foreword by Erika Moen*
*Illustrated by Jules Scheele*

£16.99 | $21.95 | PB | 352PP
ISBN 978 1 78775 618 2
eISBN 978 1 78775 619 9

**Gay, straight, queer, pansexual, demisexual, ace...? Sexuality is complex and diverse, but it doesn't have to be confusing.**

This down-to-earth guide is the ultimate companion for understanding, accepting, and celebrating your sexuality. Written by two internationally renowned authors, the book explains how sexuality works in terms of our identities, attractions, desires, and practices, and explores how it intersects with our personal experiences and the world around us. With activities and reflection points throughout, this book offers space to tune into yourself and think deeply about your own sexuality, and will be your guide every step of the way.